Edwin Percy Whipple

Outlooks on society, literature and politics

Edwin Percy Whipple

Outlooks on society, literature and politics

ISBN/EAN: 9783743463660

Manufactured in Europe, USA, Canada, Australia, Japa

Cover: Foto ©Suzi / pixelio.de

Manufactured and distributed by brebook publishing software (www.brebook.com)

Edwin Percy Whipple

Outlooks on society, literature and politics

OUTLOOKS

ON

SOCIETY, LITERATURE

AND POLITICS

BY

EDWIN PERCY WHIPPLE

BOSTON
TICKNOR AND COMPANY
211 Tremont Street
1888

CONTENTS.

	PAGE
PANICS AND INVESTMENTS	1
A GRAND BUSINESS MAN OF THE NEW SCHOOL	25
MR. HARDHACK ON THE DERIVATION OF MAN FROM THE MONKEY	47
MR. HARDHACK ON THE SENSATIONAL IN LITERATURE AND LIFE	63
THE SWEARING HABIT	75
DOMESTIC SERVICE	99
RELIGION AND SCIENTIFIC THEORIES	117
AMERICAN PRINCIPLES	127
SLAVERY, IN ITS PRINCIPLES, DEVELOPMENT, AND EXPEDIENTS	150
THE NEW OPPOSITION PARTY	186
THE CAUSES OF FOREIGN ENMITY TO THE UNITED STATES	196
RECONSTRUCTION AND NEGRO SUFFRAGE	207
THE JOHNSON PARTY	231
THE PRESIDENT AND HIS ACCOMPLICES	249
THE CONSPIRACY AT WASHINGTON	273
MORAL SIGNIFICANCE OF THE REPUBLICAN TRIUMPH	287
"LORD" BACON	300
LOWELL AS A PROSE WRITER	306
IN DICKENS-LAND	314

OUTLOOKS

ON

SOCIETY, LITERATURE,

AND POLITICS.

————•————

PANICS AND INVESTMENTS.

THE financial storm which of late swept so piti-
lessly over the commercial world has, like all other
calamities, produced reflection in producing ruin.
Amidst the wreck of their property men began to
meditate upon the laws of trade, and if they could
not pay their creditors, they were at least singularly
fruitful in reasons why such payment was impossible.
A note of hand falling due at a certain day was the
occasion, not of the disbursement of money, but of
profound speculations on the complications of the
Currency Question and the fluctuations of values.
Merchants became political economists, not when
their obligations were incurred, but when they matured; and the connection between debtor and creditor assumed the character of an edifying interchange
of philosophic thought, in which they were mutually
improved, instead of being a cold and harsh relation

1

of profit and loss. As nearly all creditors were likewise debtors, and as nearly all debtors were likewise creditors, the transition from mercenary to medi-
tative relations between men of business was effected
without that profuse expenditure of profane language
which in ordinary times vulgarizes the passage from
facts to ideas. It was seen that to take legal means to
enforce the payment of debts would be simply to transfer the property that remained — if such a thing as
property really existed — into the hands of lawyers, and
as law is made by mutual assent, it was by mutual
assent suspended. Meanwhile all the ethical and
theological maxims relating to the evanescent nature
of worldly goods were hunted out from the innermost
recesses of memory, brightened into epigrams, and
tossed about as good jokes from the banker who could
not pay his bills to the merchant who could not pay
his banker. "Base is the slave who pays!" was no
longer a rhetorical flourish of Ancient Pistol, but a
settled principle of modern finance. Property, deified
but a short time before, was now a broken and prostrate idol. From being the one solid and permanent
thing in the universe, it became the most visionary
and elusive of all objects of contemplation. It was
ten thousand millions of dollars a month ago, — riant,
exulting, glorying in its strength, — and now it hid its
face in shame before the abhorred spectacle of debt.
The feeling of poverty shivered in every heart; and
no person, in the scepticism provoked by the tum-
bling of values, had the impudence to call himself rich.

Wealth, indeed, was an obsolete idea. Men eyed
their debts with a comical horror, and the shrivelled
assets for which the debts were incurred, with a comical contempt. The real sufferers and grumblers
were those capitalists who had lent but had not bor-
rowed; and it was but natural that disappointed greed
should prevent them from viewing the matter in its
wider relations and higher philosophical aspects. The
fabric of our splendid prosperity rested, in a great
degree, on credit. This, argued the debtor class,
ought to have been known by those who supplied the
credit. But credit, as Mirabeau says, is "Suspicion
asleep." One fine autumnal day the fiend woke up;
confidence fled at his first withering glance; each
man believed at once in universal depravity, with but
one honorable exception — himself; and persons re-
puted wise and cautious but a day before, forthwith
acted in the spirit of those Hibernian thinkers on
currency who, in their rage against a Dublin banker,
could hit upon no more felicitous method of wreaking
their wrath than by burning all his bills they could
find in circulation. If the crisis was produced by
recklessness, it was met by timidity and folly. Indeed, one of the most mortifying characteristics of a
panic is the feebleness of thought and nervelessness
of will it reveals in those respectable mediocrities who
occupy the summit of financial society, and who convert the storm into a hurricane by refusing to face it
resolutely from the first.

In regard to the causes of what in after years will

be known as The Great Panic, it seems to us that
those which have been explored by the economist are
merely subsidiary to those which force themselves
upon the attention of the moralist.   The laws of
trade were doubtless violated; but the violation of the
laws of trade was preceded by a violation of the laws
of mind and a violation of the laws of conscience.
Political economy, in its appeals to the industrial and
commercial classes, proceeds on the ground that selfishness may be intelligent, and avarice judicious ; but
selfishness and avarice have an instinctive antipathy
to the general principles which promote self-interest
by cooling the fever of its desires, by bringing its
wishes into some harmony with its capacities, and by
showing the limitations which reason imposes on its
greed.   The month which witnessed the anarchy and
chaos of our industrial system found us plentifully
gifted with selfishness and avarice, but found us deficient in the power of intelligent action.   The characteristic of real intelligence is the capacity to discern
objective facts and laws ; but intelligence must feel
the pressure of some moral impulse, in order to escape from the self-delusions which obstruct the clear
view of objects which are independent of self.   "Poetry," says Lord Bacon, "accommodates the shows of
things to the desires of the mind ;" and certainly in
this sense we could have boasted many poets among
our men of industrial enterprise, had the "desires"
been as poetical as the "accommodation" of facts was
complete.

Some thinkers on the subject find consolation in the thought that there has been no absolute destruction of wealth by the panic, but only a downfall of values. The injury to individuals, however, has been the same as if wealth, and not values, had been destroyed. A government which should violently take the property of some portions of the community and transfer it to other portions, would not destroy any of the wealth of that community, though such an act of monstrous wrong would justify a revolution. The practical result of our commercial revulsion has been a wholesale confiscation of property, which, had it been done by the Government, would have led to civil war; for it is not so much the characteristic of a good government that it protects the property of a nation, as that it protects the property of a nation by protecting its individual possessors. It is frightful to think of the number of individuals who have seen the hard earnings of a life of labor melt and mysteriously disappear in a single day, under the operation of merciless laws which avenged on the whole community the disregard of their monitions and menaces by the improvident, ignorant, and knavish portion of it. The average honesty and intelligence of the country is also satirized in the indifference with which this individual spoliation is commonly regarded. In situations of financial responsibility, incompetency is a moral offence, and its good intentions are proverbially the pavement of hell: the wrong man in the right place is the plague and curse of modern society; but when recklessness and greed are united with incompetency, the wholesome wrath of all good men should be roused against the monstrous combination. Yet every panic in the money market is a revelation of presumptuous folly wielding and wasting the fortunes of credulous and trusting prudence. Wholesale robberies, which no professional thief would ever have the opportunities of perpetrating, are ranked among the necessary incidents and risks of capital invested in corporations. Haydon, the painter, tells us that in one of his many Micawber-like financial entanglements he applied to Coutts, the rich banker, for a loan of four hundred pounds. The banker, though he seems to have apprehended that the investment would be a permanent one, gratified the martyr of debt and " high art " by graciously assenting to his request. As the painter was leaving the house, he noticed the footman spurning from the door a pauper who came to beg for bread. The supplicant for four hundred pounds was received as a distinguished visitor by the master of the house, in the gilded parlor ; the supplicant for a penny was hooted by the master's flunky from the door-step into the street. This is the type of the American mode of dealing with big and little thieves.

There are some persons who think that the rascalities and follies of our business are referable to our paper currency, — especially to bank-bills of low denominations. In answer to this it might be said that in Hamburg, where they have a specie currency, in

England, where they have no bank-bills under five pounds, some of the worst abuses of the credit system have been developed. The most superficial examination of our own credit system will prove that bank-bills form but a small portion of it. We have lately seen a careful estimate of the losses by the failures in the United States since the month of September, and the amount is considerably larger than the whole paper currency of the country. It is, indeed, but natural that men and corporations should issue bills payable on demand with more caution than bills payable in six or nine months. We doubt if excessive credits are produced by a paper currency, or could be prevented by a gold currency. We doubt if any law could be framed which would meet the evils and abuses of the credit system. As long as capitalists think they can make their capital remunerative and reproductive by giving credits, as long as borrowers think they can use capital profitably, so long will credits be given and received. The moment that capital becomes redundant new enterprises start up, more than sufficient to absorb it, and the brilliancy of their pretensions blinds avarice to their folly.

A person once asked Horne Tooke, the celebrated writer of political libels, how far a man could libel the Government and escape being hanged. "I have passed my life," replied Tooke, "in trying to find that out." So each man of business, in our country, seems to learn political economy, not through Adam Smith

and Mill, but through experience of protested notes
and ruinous speculations; and economic principles
of the most elementary character are frequently purchased at the expense of whole fortunes. It costs
some men a hundred thousand dollars to learn the
relations which subsist between supply and demand.
Indeed, principles level to trade are clearly perceived
only by minds which survey them from a higher level.
Pure selfishness never generalizes. Its guiding idea
is best expressed in the imperfect English of the
French coxcomb, " Every man for myself."

We therefore are reluctantly compelled to believe
that the notorious abuses of our credit system, the
frightful commercial revulsions they occasion, and the
agrarian laws they practically inaugurate, will continue to afflict the country as long as so much absurd
and mischievous importance is attached to the idea of
wealth, and as long as it is pursued with such ravenous intensity. The desire of wealth is the dominant
desire of the larger portion of our population, — a desire not so much to *create* wealth by industrial genius
as to *get* it by speculative ingenuity. The morbid
phenomena presented in our world of business only
embody in palpable facts qualities of our national character. The intellect of the country is under the dominion of a low order of motives, which prevent it from
exercising the higher functions of intellect. Smart
men push themselves into the places of able men; and
their only notion of progress is speed which trusts in
luck, with no discernment of paths, and no foresight

of the goal. Now, business cannot be honestly and intelligently conducted when it is conducted under the simple impulse of getting money at any rate. That honesty is the best policy is a principle too large and general to influence the bargain or speculation of the hour; and so flashy and superficial is much of the mind engaged in trade, that it lacks thought sharply to discriminate between acuteness and knavery, a wise reticence and direct falsehood. Half of the light and airy swindlers whose schemes of business rapine end in failure are unconscious of the true nature of their misdeeds, and are really surprised at the hard names sputtered out by the gruff honesty of the old fogies of commerce when their equivocal modes of obtaining money are brought to light. At the worst, they probably conceived their creditors would indulge in language no harsher than that in which little Isaac, in "The Duenna," chuckles over his sharp practice : "Roguish, perhaps, but keen — devilish keen !"

And if wealth and poverty are respectively the heaven and hell of our concrete religion, why wonder that men will do anything to obtain the one and escape from the other? "Worth makes the man," says a character in one of Bulwer's plays ; "and the more a man is worth the worthier he is." Sydney Smith once declared that in England "poverty is infamous;" and in the United States, where man was supposed to have achieved some victory "over his accidents," the accident of property domineers in the public mind over the substance of mind and virtue. To be poor is to be a " poor devil." It is pathetic to observe the moral prostration of our free and independent citizens before some·affluent boor or well-invested booby; or to watch the complacent simper that comes over the face of scornful beauty as she listens to the imbecilities chattered by some weak stripling of fortune who presents to the eye of science nothing but " a watery smile and educated whisker." These follies proceed from no respect for what the rich are, but from a worship of what they possess. Indeed, the worship of the wealth is often combined with a secret contempt, hatred, or envy, of the possessor. Property makes a distinction between man and man as arbitrary and artificial as aristocratic privilege; and our people feel that the doctrine of equality — the doctrine that one man is as good as another — can only be realized by striving to make one man as rich as another. For one person who pursues wealth as an end, from the impulse of avarice, there are hundreds who pursue it as a means, from the impulses of vanity, sensuality, egotism, and the desire to make a good appearance. If the capitalist asserts himself socially as an aristocrat, the democrat trades recklessly on what he borrows from the capitalist in order to be as good an aristocrat as he. A few affluent families, composed miscellaneously of millionnaires vulgar and millionnaires refined, of millionnaires intelligent and millionnaires stupid, combine together, and impudently attempt to confine the meaning of " good society " to the possession of a splendid establishment in a fashionable street, with a large income to support it; and it is curious to see with what ludicrous simplicity their pretensions are admitted, and with what wear and tear of brain and conscience, with what sacrifices of health, comfort, and honor, thousands aim to qualify themselves for entrance into that terrestrial paradise. Under this system the style of living quickly becomes of more importance than the pleasure of living or the object of living. Life means the appearances of life. It means houses, equipages, dress, dinners, a crowd of servants, reception into the awful company of fops and belles, — everything but human souls. A higher life — slightly changed from the definition of the idealist — means a life exalted from West Broadway to the Fifth Avenue. Without ten thousand a year it is impossible to be and know ladies and gentlemen. Existence is fretted away in desperate attempts to make it splendid, conspicuous, and uncomfortable; and after the object is reached, it is found to be a stupendous imposture. As regards any satisfaction in life, it is much better to adopt the theory of that unsophisticated mechanic who asserted that he was as rich as the richest man in town, and supported his assertion by this train of argument. The rich man, he said, had only what he wanted, and he had the same. In regard to luxuries, he doubted if the rich man could claim any superiority; "for at his house they had doughnuts for dinner every day, whether they had company or not." The ideal of good living may not have been high, but there was something sublime in the content.

Now one great result of such a panic as we have lately witnessed is, that it disenchants the mind of the illusions created by the hope of wealth, and the vanities created by the ambition for social position. People, at least sensible people, learn what substances they are and what "shadows they pursue." Events preach to them truths which the most persuasive preachers would fail to convey. And among these truths there is none more important, or more fertile of sobering reflections, than the truth that what a man invests in trade and industry, in railroads and manufactures, is not merely his labor, or talent, or money, but himself; and that property, resting as it does on a deceitful basis of fluctuating values, is among the least solid and permanent of all the things in which a man can invest himself. This proposition would have been scouted as transcendental a year ago; but within a few months the most practical of men have been compelled to admit that wealth, with all its bullying solidity of appearance, has proved the most visionary, elusive, and transcendental of abstractions. The idealists have convicted the materialists of mistaking the shifting sand for the immovable rock, and it is now their turn to dogmatize from the throne of common sense. Facts have demonstrated two of their propositions, which are most repugnant to selfishness and evident to reason: first, that the commercial world being a unit, shocks in one quarter are felt

in all quarters, and that the whole body is made to
suffer for the stupidities and rascalities of any of its
individual members ; second, that the good of all is
bound up in the real good of each ; and now, after
thus indicating the identity of individual interests
with the general interest, and placed political economy
on its true foundation in the Christian religion, the
idealists can further show the perfect practical sagacity of their great principle, that material possessions lack all the elements of permanency, certainty,
and satisfying content which inhere in spiritual
possessions.

We think the most rapid and superficial survey of
the things in which men invest, and in which they are
invested, will prove the proposition. In regard to the
darling object to which American energy and intelligence are directed, the obtaining of property and social
station, we have already shown its transitory and visionary character. All of us have seen men go up
and down with Erie and Michigan Southern, with
Cumberland Coal and Cotton, until the doubt insinu-
ated itself whether they were not mere phantasms to
which stocks and stones gave all the appearance
of reality they possessed. Soul, manhood, vitality,
dropped out of them as Erie fell twenty per cent, or
Cotton tumbled from its proud eminence of price and
place. This fact shows that while these men were
cunningly investing in Erie and Cotton, Erie and
Cotton were far more cunningly investing in them.
To say that they became bankrupt is not to express

the whole tragedy of their lives. In the pursuit of material objects they were insensibly building up their characters, and becoming what they pursued. Mentally and morally they were " breeding in and in " with the transactions of their business. When they failed, their bankruptcy was not merely a bankruptcy of the purse but a bankruptcy of nature. Their souls were insolvent. They consented to be nothing in themselves in order to be everything by the grace of the objects in which they dealt ; and when these last proved deceptions they literally had nothing they could call their own. Wall Street bowed before them for the wealth which was in them. When the wealth vanished, neither civility nor servility could detect anything in what was left to repay the trouble of a nod or a cringe. Fifth Avenue made them members of its society for their establishments. When these came under the auctioneer's hammer, no social qualities were left which " good company," even by the aid of a microscope, could recognize. The universe, it is true, was still full of objects which wealth could neither purchase nor take away; but in them our ruined millionnaires had never thought of investing any portion of their souls. We might have pardoned their venturing their whole fortunes in two or three securities; but it is difficult to tolerate their venturing also in them their whole natures, with a like oversight of the prudence which keeps on the safe side of the world's chances by a wise distribution of its resources. When we contrast the attitude of resolute scorn which

these men formerly assumed toward the highest objects of human concern with their present forlorn
aspect, we can but murmur pathetically, " O Bottom!
how art thou invested ! "

But investments of the kind we are now considering,
namely, investments of human nature, are not merely
made in property : they are also made in politics and
party ; and when made in politics and party, they rest
on a foundation as insecure, and are liable to end in
bankruptcies as fatal, as when made in business. Investment of the soul in politics is often investment in
the changing caprice of the hour, — in rage, envy, hatred, disappointed ambition, in lies, heartache, hypocrisy, and self-deception. The man is possessed by the
delusions and passions, instead of possessing the realities, of political power. Even if he be so fortunate as
to obtain an office, he finds that he has to undergo a
larger amount of vituperation for a smaller amount
of money than the holder of any other kind of office.
No president of a railroad or manufacturing company
would consent, for ten thousand a year, to be the subject of so much public abuse as is lavished on many a
postmaster whose salary is hardly a thousand a year.
Few voters will take the trouble to perform the necessary business of a political organization, but they are
all willing to indulge in more or less contempt for
those who do, — for those who do the " dirty work,"
as they are too fond of calling the work which is done
for their profit and success. There is enough sympathy for broken-down merchants, but who has any

sympathy for a broken-down politician? The orange is thoroughly squeezed; who heeds the peel that is cast into the street?

It may also be doubted if the investment of the brain in partisan catchwords and declamation is a judicious investment of the mental powers. No more efficacious mode of dissipating the mind from a force into a vaporous phantom has ever been devised than the mode of cramming the minds of the young with political phrases, and then irritating their sensibilities to that pitch of enthusiasm which urges them to "utter all themselves into the air." The tendency of such speechifying is to make the mind incapable of observing a fact, analyzing a combination, grasping a principle, or thinking closely, accurately, and con-secutively upon any subject. The vagabond thoughts and shreds of thought, decked out in faded finery selected from the " old clo' " of eloquence, reel from the orator's lips in jubilant defiance of order and se-quence. Or, to change the figure, the brain is inflated to that extent which justifies the hope that the defects of a logic of wind will be overlooked in a rhetoric of whirlwind, and that the absence of ideas will hardly be noted in the terrific clatter of words. Such are the characteristics of many of those astonishing dis-plays of juvenile political eloquence, which should be witnessed, not by citizens desirous of obtaining some facts and principles to guide them in voting sensibly and honestly, but by an audience composed of ladies whose lips are engaged in dissolving the organized perfume of peppermints, and gentlemen whose teeth are busy in penetrating into those appetizing "Aids to Reflection" which lie hid in the shell of the peanut. It is next to impossible ever to reclaim a young man who has once accustomed his mind to think vagrantly in order that he may spout "eloquently." But we still may be permitted to hope that every young person who has made a foolish speech, and been applauded therefor by his party, will consent, for his own good, to abandon his intention of being President of the United States. That his qualifications for the office are undoubted, the peculiar style of his eloquence abundantly proves; but we would respectfully suggest to him the remote chance that some three or four millions of his countrymen may *not* be sufficiently familiar with his claims to select him for the post.

In regard to all the lower forms of politics, we much doubt the wisdom of the man who invests his nature in their perilous chances and changes. But politics have their higher ambitions and more splendid rewards, — those which inflame the passions and stimulate the intellect of the statesman. Even here it is dangerous to invest in anything lower than patriotism; for patriotism affords the only real compensations for that " laborious, invidious, closely-watched slavery which is mocked with the name of Power." It is the misfortune of the United States that few of our eminent statesmen can be content to serve their country and gain an honorable fame in those situations which, though really of the first, are seemingly of secondary

importance. As Representatives and Senators, the
clear perception of their duties is disturbed by a bea-
tific vision of the Presidential Chair. This magnifi-
cent delusion, created by a visionary hope, is too often
the bauble in which they invest their hearts and souls.
Disappointed in that, they are stripped of all that
makes life worth living. Now, for the real purposes
of ambition and patriotism, the office of Senator is a
nobler one than the office of President; and a Senator
is certain to be an honester, wiser, and braver man,
more likely to prove himself qualified for the Presi-
dency, provided the hope of being President has not
warped his convictions and complicated his patriotism
with intrigue. But rub off the varnish which gives
such a mischievous shine to the White House, and to
the eye of reason the office of President has little in
it to inflame an honorable ambition. Events daily
tend to make the President little more than the Dis-
tributor-General of the spoils of office; and for every
office he gives, he turns ten sycophants into nine
personal enemies and one lukewarm friend. Lord
Brougham, in a passage black with bile, but which
should be deeply meditated by every aspirant for
executive office, has shown what a charming and dignified occupation that is which attempts to feed the
hunger for place. Writing from his own experience
of office-hunters, he says that " no one who has long
been the dispenser of patronage among large bodies
of his fellow-citizens can fail to see infinitely more
numerous instances of sordid, selfish, greedy, ungrate-

PANICS AND INVESTMENTS. 19

ful conduct, than of the virtues to which such hateful
qualities stand opposed. Daily examples come before
him of the most unfeeling acrimony toward competitors, the most far-fetched squeamish jealousy of con-
flicting claims; unblushing falsehood in both its
branches, boasting and detraction; grasping selfishness in both kinds, greedy pursuit of men's own bread
and cold calculating on others' blood; the fury of
disappointment when that has not been done which
it was impossible to do; swift oblivion of all that
has been granted; unreasonable expectation of more
only because much has been given; not seldom fa-
vors repaid with hatred and ill-treatment, as if by this
unnatural course the account might be settled between
gratitude and pride, — such are the secrets of the human heart which power soon discloses to its possessor:
add to these that which, however, deceives no one, —
the never-ending hypocrisy of declaring that whatever is most eagerly sought is only coveted as afford-
ing the means of serving the country, and will only
be taken as a sacrifice of individual interest to the
sense of public duty." Now, as much of Brougham's
patronage as Chancellor was ecclesiastical, we may
charitably suppose that our ex-Presidents could testify,
in language at least as gloomy and bitter, of their experience of unclerical applicants. Is it not amazing
that any sane man, who could pick up a subsistence
in a country court, or even on the highway, should
think it the highest of earthly honors to be engaged
in this business of dispensing patronage?

But investments, truly considered, are made in literature, art, science, and philosophy, as well as in business and politics ; and when made in beauty and truth, in laws, principles, inventions, ideals, they are among the most permanent and essentially real and remunerative of all investments of mind and character — provided always that the motives of the thinker are on a level with the subject-matter of his thought. The Swiss who sell their brains are of no higher rank than the Swiss who sell their swords ; and it is doubtless true that the poet, the artist, the man of science, the philosopher, may be impelled by vanities, envies, jealousies, and hatreds, as ignoble as any which influence the action of the knavish trader in money or the knavish trader in political opinions and interests ; but when the search for truth and beauty is inspired by a genuine love of truth and beauty, everything that is gained is a possession forever. The mind is in harmonious relations with the great objective facts and laws it was created to discern, commune with, and possess ; and whether we say that the mind invests in them or they invest in the mind, the result is equally beneficent. If we contrast a broken merchant or a defeated politician with a man of equal intellect who has invested in art and science, we shall see at once the difference between the property that panics can destroy and the property that panics cannot touch. In regard to the joy, the ecstasy, even the solid, practical satisfaction, which come from the consciousness of intellectual wealth,

who shall have the impudence to compare with them
the delights which any material property can give ?
Who shall say that the chuckle of Rothschild, as he
makes a lucky hit in the three per cents, represents
a tithe of the inward ecstasy of Agassiz, as his conquering intelligence subjugates to his science some
hitherto rebellious province of the animal kingdom ?
We doubt if all the money of the banker could purchase the transport that the naturalist finds even in
his jelly-fishes.

It is undoubtedly true that many amateurs who
have mistaken " aspiration for inspiration," the power
of enjoying beauty for the power of creating beauty,
the faculty of apprehending what science has discovered for scientific genius, may have found that the
attempt to invest their natures in literature, art, and
science has ended in mortification and disappointment, — in mental bankruptcy and impossibility to
pay the debt " which every man owes to his profession." This, however, comes from their own inability
to acquire property in Nature, and not from the inability of Nature to confer property on the genius that
can rightly claim it. They are miserable, not because
they are engaged in the pursuit of truth, but because,
through their vanity, they are pretenders to genius.
They might have profitably invested in taste and
knowledge ; they failed only because they traded beyond their capital, and attempted to introduce into
the kingdoms of mind the worst abuses of that credit
system which is the plague of the world of business.

And this brings us to the consideration of those investments which are not only the most solid and lasting in themselves, but which underlie and guide all others which give durable satisfaction to human nature. These are investments in moral principles. Property in moral principles is "real" property, in a higher sense than any legal sense; but these principles are only truly possessed when they are organized into virtues, and then they are good for both worlds. Let any man invest himself in justice, firmness, simplicity, patience, moderation, truthfulness, disinterestedness, charity, and he will quickly realize the truth of the Chinese proverb, that "Virtues, if they do not give talents, supply their place; while talents neither give virtues nor supply their place." Virtues act on the intelligence primarily by prompting the self-scrutiny which results in self-knowledge. The misery and fret of life proceed from immoderate desires. Appetite, passion, egotism, conceit, run away with the mind, corrupt all its processes of thought, and doom it equally to ignorance of self and ignorance of the real character of the vicious or flimsy externals of life for which, as well as to which, it madly abandons itself. The sublime thought in the parable of the Prodigal Son is compressed in the simple words, "when he came to himself," — when exhaustion of all the pleasures of sensuality, and exhaustion of all its penalties, had brought him back to the awful personality lodged in his breast, from which he had been violently swept in the tumult and

storm of his riot. In the same way men learn from
the revulsions of other forms of self-abandonment —
from commercial panics, from mortified political ambition, from failures in achieving fame in the pursuits
of literature, art, and science, from all forms of de-
bauch, sensual, selfish, or mental — what is intrinsic
and indestructible in themselves. Escaped for a time
from the realities of their being, and investing their
life in delusions, the period inevitably comes when
they are compelled to confront the rebuking spirit
within, and stand convicted of folly as well as sin.
The virtues are then remorsefully recognized as the
only sure possessions. It is seen that these teach
economic principles, and give to business all it has of
permanency by giving to it all it has of honesty. It
is seen that these take selfish ambition out of politics,
and keep States alive by patriotism. It is seen that
these lift the sentiments of the man of letters and the
man of science to the level of the beauty the imagination aims to embody, and the truth the intellect seeks
to discover. It is seen, in short, that the peculiar
combination of virtues which is called integrity is
the source of the peculiar combination of faculties we
call wisdom. And it is this thorough integrity of
nature, which implies integrity in business, integrity
in affairs of state, integrity in sentiment, understanding, reason, and imagination, — it is this which is
especially needed in an age like ours, whose activity
and intelligence run so furiously in the direction of
industrial and commercial occupations that nothing

less than the austerest ethics can overcome the frightful temptations to excess or to fraud by which those
occupations are beset; and we trust that the country
will not be compelled to learn through a series of
regularly recurring panics, that virtues, ideal in their
spiritual essence and power, but tremendously actual
in the consequences which follow their violation, are
in their immense utility the most practical of all
things, though they may draw their vitality from invisible fountains of influence, and refer to motives
of action which self-styled practical men are wont
to deride as too fine and abstract for the conduct
of life.

A GRAND BUSINESS MAN OF THE NEW SCHOOL.[1]

I HAD the rare privilege, when I was a lad of fifteen, to make the acquaintance and to be favored with the confidence of a business man of " the new school." So many precious remarks fell from his lips during the period, extending to thirty years, in which I was honored by his approval or by his enmity, that I feel injustice would be done both to commerce and to him unless I recorded his conduct and experience in fitting words.

Mr. Smith had risen to eminence from the lowest social grade. As a beggar boy, his exceptional talent for begging had roused the enthusiasm of a set of elderly maidens, who were attracted by his peculiar whine of helplessness and his peculiar brag of honesty. They put him to school. He learned there the fundamental principles of arithmetic, and little else ; but his aptitude for trade was developed in a marvellous degree. All the spending-money of the scholars was invariably found, at the end of a vacation, in his pockets. Yet no boy could say that he had been cheated. All the lads felt that their bits

[1] As far as the personal pronoun is concerned, this narrative is purely fictitious.

of small silver coin had mysteriously disappeared in
their various business relations with Smith ; but still
they reluctantly confessed that everything was " fair
and square." He plucked them, it would seem, piti-
lessly ; but he stood by his own contracts, as he compelled them to stand by theirs. No act of positive
dishonesty was ever proved against this plausible,
cautious, deferential, and relentless trader. The boys
declared that he was shrewd, cunning, and hard, but
then he was " so obliging ! " They hated him, and
at the same time accepted his services. Could they
have caught him in any act of juvenile rascality, they
would have pounded him into a jelly ; but he was so
discreet in his early preparation for his future career
that at the age of ten he already gave promise of the
great merchant and banker he eventually became.
He robbed strictly within the rules of boy law. It
has always appeared to me that his innate genius
for traffic was rarely more beautifully exhibited in
his after-career than in his manner of dealing with
his school-fellows, most of whom began by despising
him as a beggar, and all of whom ended in recognizing him as a capitalist.

On leaving school, young Smith found that his
possessions amounted to thirty dollars. Instead of
rushing at once to the elderly maiden ladies who had
been his patrons, and depositing the money in their
laps, he speeded to a wholesale fish-house in the city,
and offered himself as a clerk. The senior partner
was attracted by his evident talent, and especially by

his juvenile cynicism as to the practical application of the Golden Rule. The old man felt his youth renewed in looking at the premature youngster, and magnanimously gave him a place in his counting-room at a salary of fifty dollars a year. The keen youth, seeing at a glance that his employers were pious skinflints, instantly joined their church, and to all appearance became a pious skinflint himself. But in the course of five or six years he astonished the firm by showing that he knew more of the whole fish business than they did, and had made some money by quiet speculations of his own. They offered to double, treble, quadruple his salary. But Smith was inexorable. Nothing would satisfy him but a part-nership in their questionable gains. This they reso-lutely refused. Smith promptly set up for himself on a small capital of money, but a large capital of knowledge and intelligence, sold " short " and " long," cornered his former employers in two or three heavy operations, and put them into the bankruptcy court in twenty-four months after he had left them. His cleverness was never more evident than in the way in which he accomplished this difficult feat of beating his former employers by a skilful use of their own methods.

Dominant now in the article of fish, he in the course of a few years ventured cautiously but surely into other departments of commerce. He became a general merchant in other commodities than mack-erel and halibut. He at last assumed the dignity of shipowner, and his cargoes to and from the East and West were carried in his own vessels. The strategy he had learned at school was strictly observed in his large commercial transactions. He had two grand qualifications for business: his mind was quick and his heart was hard. In all financial panics he enforced what was his due relentlessly, regardless of the woe it might bring upon nobler people than himself; but even though money was at three or four per cent a month, he paid punctually all his own notes as they matured. He would thus crush a debtor to the dust — grind him to death; but still every dollar of his property, and every resource of his credit, were freely devoted to buy money, at any rates of interest, to meet his own obligations. To "fail" was to him the worst ignominy. Mean in all minor matters, he was liberal in any sacrifices demanded by the mutations of trade. Almost everybody detested him, yet everybody knew that he might rely both on the skinflint's word and bond.

Such a merchant, perhaps, should be judged by his own principles. He was essentially a bird of prey, with beak and talons somewhat ostentatiously and insolently displayed. He had no sympathy with the great body of the merchants of the country. Indeed, he laughed at all such sentimentality. "Get the better of 'em," was his motto. It may be said that he believed religiously in the maxim, *Homo homini lupus*, — "Man to man is, and must be, a wolf."

At about the time he was a little wearied with

commerce, and had obtained a fortune of two millions, the moneyed world was first amazed by the
rush into Wall Street of securities (ironically so
called) based on the new-born "enterprise" of the
country. Bonds and stocks renewed in him the
charm which merchandise had lost. He became a
gigantic stock-jobber and banker. On account of his
known opulence and his wide reputation for sagacity
and integrity, he was naturally selected by the rogues
and enthusiasts of the nation as the proper person
to negotiate large loans. Whether these loans were
based on unfinished railroads, or undeveloped mines,
or any other financial castles in the air, he contrived
to obtain big commissions on the doubtful or worthless securities he sold. Those who relied on his
ungenial integrity relied also on his hard sense. Believing him, they took his advice. The result was
that his commissions amounted to hundreds and
thousands of dollars, their losses to many millions.
They could not assert that he had done anything to
forfeit his character for honesty, though some naturally growled over the fact that he had himself bought
few of the bonds he had negotiated.

It was at this point of his triumphant success that
I happened to have the honor of being one of his
clerks, and in a short time his confidential one. The
thing that at first most touched me was the simplicity
of his religion. It consisted in the simple phrase,
"Goddam!" This phrase was so often on his lips
that it took me some time to discriminate between

the persons it was justly or unjustly launched against. I believed at first that this peculiar form of religious faith was fulminated against people who righteously deserved the anathema. It is curious how many persons engaged in trade are thus fitly designated. By slow degrees, however, I at last found that my pious employer used this phrase only to blast everybody and everything interfering with his business designs. As I in my innocence looked at the matter, it seemed that his associates in speculation should be as frequently saluted with the condemnation as his rivals and opponents. Probably the most interesting period in the development of the juvenile mind is the first exercise of the faculty of ethical generalization. The moment that faculty was developed in my immature intelligence I began to doubt the purity, though not the sagacity, of my employer. The readiness with which he called upon the Lord of heaven and earth to curse every person and every scheme that at all obstructed the success of his own objects, insensibly dimmed my perception of the natural piety which I at first supposed dictated his outbreak of profane moral indignation. That the Deity should be on his side in every honest transaction, I could very easily understand ; but that He should consign to the lowest pits of the infernal regions anybody who crossed the purposes of Mr. Smith, puzzled me mightily, especially when Mr. Smith contrived many schemes to catch unwary people in his traps, and then fleece them remorselessly. His favorite formula of faith lost all its pious significance in view of such doubtful transactions. But still I was a youth, and was only beginning to learn the connection between such a business and such a religion.

There is probably no greater shock to the mind of a well-intentioned country lad, who has sucked in honesty from his mother's milk, and is sent to confront the temptations of a city with a mother's prayers hovering over him, than when he finds his employer is a rascal disguised as an honest man. Shall he also become a rascal ? Shall he stoop to scoundrelisms which his inmost soul abhors ? It is a matter of uncertainty whether such a lad is consigned to a long-headed rogue or to a merchant of unquestioned integrity. His behavior under such circumstances is a test of his character ; and how laboriously such character is formed is known only to the fathers and mothers and sisters who have combined all their moral energies to form it. There is no reason why the boy should have more privileges and be protected by more affections than the girl ; but the fact that he is, is too notorious to admit of a doubt. The abnegation of sisters to advance their brothers is one of the tragedies of human life. The reverse *should* be the case, but unfortunately it is not.

But to return to my theme. As soon as, with my awakened intelligence, I had penetrated into the mind of Mr. Smith, I began to look upon him with a certain horror. He had the greatest confidence in my honesty, and even allowed me to sign in his name checks

amounting to many millions a month; but he used
his favorite formula of vital religious faith when I suggested that my services were not remunerated by a
thousand a year, and that fifteen hundred would but
poorly recompense my unceasing work in his journal
and ledger.   He really thought that my devotion to his
interests was something due to his pre-eminent position, though he was aware that I might ruin him in a
single day had I chosen to decamp at the close of business hours with his multitudinous stocks and bonds
in a carpet-bag.   He nominally possessed millions;
but he trusted me with all the evidences of his wealth,
and allowed me the power to draw checks on all his
balances in the banks in which he deposited.   Watching like a wolf — " a gray old wolf and a lean " — to
pounce upon his prey, he was singularly blind to the
fact that I, his poorly paid clerk, who had begun to
hate him mortally, might at any moment rush off to
other lands with the spoils of his rapacity in my pocket.
The honesty of clerks, when they have persons who
are essentially knaves for their employers, is one of
the wonders of modern civilization.   It is curious that
I never had the slightest temptation to use the vast
powers with which Mr. Smith endowed me to his
slightest detriment.   I might easily have become a
millionnaire in some European country had I chosen,
like my employer, to become a rogue in my own.   He
invited me to be a rogue by his ingenuous trust in my
perfect honesty, while I was daily recording transactions illustrating every variety of the arts of chicane.

I witnessed the process of plundering, without any desire to plunder the plunderer. This is, I think, a common experience in the life of clerks.

One occurrence during my connection with this estimable man will never fade from my memory. His wife, a meek woman, whom he swiftly scared into the tomb, left him a daughter. She appeared to me a foolish, giggling, bedizened creature, with large black eyes, a pug nose, and a complexion which was red to the point of inflammation. A younger clerk in the office, on a salary of five hundred a year, declared, much to our amusement, that he was madly in love with her. When the other clerks jeered at her obvious defects of person and mind, he raved about her being " natural." Whether or not he ever felt any love for her it is impossible for me to determine, but at any rate he convinced her of the sincerity of his passion. As it was ridiculous to suppose that the father would consent to such a match, the aspiring clerk and the heiress eloped and were married.

Mr. Smith's facility in calling upon the Deity to condemn everybody who interfered with his own will was marvellously increased by this occurrence. He blasphemed with a savage fluency which was wonderful even in him. His son-in-law, however, was a shallow but bright young fellow, with some rich connections. He had been in the office long enough to detect certain secrets of the business. Accordingly he soon appeared in Wall Street as a speculator on a large scale. He made money, backed as he was by relatives

3

who stood by him with their financial support, — that is, as long as they saw his ventures were likely to be successful. Mr. Smith went deliberately to work to ruin him, but at first he did not succeed. The son-in-law, in an early " corner in Erie," took three hundred thousand dollars out of the pockets of the father-in-law in that neat and beautiful fashion so well understood in the operations of stock gambling. We, the remaining clerks, supposed that this loss would endear the son-in-law to the father-in-law by showing that his daughter was married to a person whose spirit was akin to his own. But we made a sad mistake. Mr. Smith became gloomily implacable when I reported the loss to him. He even indulged in none of his piously profane ejaculations. The frown on his brow alone acknowledged his fixed purpose. I felt that the incident was something which altogether transcended his usual fertility in profanity. He ventured his 'millions without stint in an attempt to " corner" his son-in-law. In his first rage he was reckless, but he afterward became cool, cautious, watching every turn in the market, and intent simply on catching the husband of his daughter in what, in the slang of the street, is called a tight place. He at last succeeded. The poor fellow was reduced not only to beggary, but to dishonesty. After desperate attempts to retrieve his position, the son-in-law ended by blowing out what brains he had left. His wife, a withered woman of twenty-five, again entered her father's mansion, but none of us could say that she was " natural." A more

wretched creature — one more thin, cadaverous, and
woe-begone, one whose original homeliness was rendered more pathetically ugly by her misery — never
re-entered a mansion in Fifth Avenue. She died a
year after, and the only exclamation of the bereaved
father, in following her to the tomb, was his favorite
oath, growled in an undertone. He felt that all the
money he had acquired would descend to strangers,
and he was inwardly wrathful that the wife he had
bullied and the daughter he had killed could not be
by his side when he made his own exit into another
and probably a worse world.

The most curious thing in my experience of the
moods of this grand old business man was his sav-
ageness in treating his clerks after his many bereave-
ments had soured him into hopeless misanthropy.
He swore in such a fashion that I was at last compelled to tell him I should pitch him down the stairs
of his own office unless he was more considerate in
his curses. This intimation made him only all the
more furious ; and I regret to record that I parted
with this grand old merchant when his body was
prostrate at the foot of the stairs on which I leis-
urely descended.

This abrupt termination of my business relations
with Mr. Smith naturally resulted in a resolution on his
part to prosecute me, first for assault and battery, and
secondly for swindling. His judicious friends laughed
him out of the first proposition, which was simply
prompted by his rage, and which he soon felt would

lead to disagreeable communications in open court. The second he urged with great rancor and energy, and employed one of those intelligent, meek-eyed, and sharp-eyed book-keepers of fifty, who never in their progress through life get beyond a moderate salary, but who are invaluable to merchants doing a large business, owing to their talent in unravelling the most complicated accounts, and the beautiful dexterity with which they clearly record the most confused transactions. My employer, able as he was in managing his business, was, like many other employers I have known, deplorably ignorant of the mysteries of book-keeping. My successor, after exhausting all the resources of his art, was compelled to admit that when I left Mr. Smith at the foot of the stairs to which I somewhat impatiently consigned him, Mr. Smith owed me one hundred and twenty-six dollars and thirty-one cents. When this was proved to him, he indulged his favorite anathema with more than his usual religious unction, and lavished it on my successor with redoubled force, — all of which the new book-keeper patiently bore with the meekness befitting his station.

I easily obtained a new clerkship, with a salary which I thought was more in correspondence with my services than that which I had obtained from Mr. Smith. Indeed, my new employers allowed me to go to church on a Sunday morning without feeling the burden of a hundred curses launched at me during the week. While the good clergyman was preaching, however, I felt stirring within me the impulses of what I styled a righteous wrath. I thought I could not be a good Christian until I had been instrumental in depleting Mr. Smith of some of his ill-gotten gains. The faculty of generalization had, I suppose, outgrown my sentiment of piety, and I saw clearly the means of touching the only soul my former employer had; namely, that which resided in his pocket. Brooding over many schemes of unmasking and punishing the old rogue, I thought the occasion was at hand in an approaching business panic, which I scented in the air. In this emergency it was notorious that Mr. Smith was very heavily engaged on the side of a body of capitalists who were rushing up shares far beyond their intrinsic worth, regardless of the ominous signs of a revulsion, which were apparent to those cool heads who understand that an annihilation of capital means a depreciation of all values. That some two or three or four hundred millions of capital were certain to be annihilated in the inevitable collapse of certain railroad schemes was plain to me. This I proved to my employers. I showed them that Mr. Smith was sure to be caught in the trap into which he had designed to lure unwary speculators. They acted on my advice, and made a million of dollars. Mr. Smith lost three millions. When I had the honor to call upon him for the settlement of the claims which our firm had against him, it must be confessed he paid punctually, but I had to bear a storm of oaths which seriously wounded my pride. As soon as I held his checks in my hands,

I vehemently told him that my opposition to him was mortal, and that it would never cease until his scoundrelism had reduced his property to its right dimensions. In fact, I enjoyed the exquisite satisfaction of telling him that it was my knowledge of his methods of doing business which had not only saved my employers from falling into his snares, but had enabled them to add a million of dollars to their already large capital. He became red, almost purple, in the face; but his memory of a sudden descent he once made down the stairs of his own office prevented his wrath from assuming a belligerent aspect.

As a result of these transactions, I became a partner in the firm of which I had previously been a highly salaried clerk. We prospered marvellously; but I knew that we must count on the implacable rancor of my former employer. Indeed, I never drew a bill on London or Liverpool, whether it was for five pounds or five thousand pounds, without feeling assured that he would contrive every means in his power to have it dishonored. But his blind, mad hatred of me put him in my power, for his hatred had become morbid. With his immense wealth, established character for formal integrity in business transactions, and shrewd intelligence, he might have injured my firm greatly had he been content to give sly insinuations, doubtful nods of the head, and the other signs with which men of property indicate their distrust or disapproval of adventurous firms which go beyond their capital, and strive to place themselves on a level with the Rothschilds, Barings, and Hopes. But he was not satisfied with this judicious malice, based on a clear mercantile perception of facts and principles. He was enraged that a person to whom he thought a thousand dollars a year was a fair equivalent for services received, should dare to send out bills of credit, receivable all over the civilized globe, and pretending to be as good as specie in hand. The success of our firm in our legitimate business as bankers did not deceive me as to the intentions of the malignant creature with whom we had to contend. The generality of merchants laughed at his threats; they received our bills without any questioning; but I knew that my original defiance of a duel to the death would be answered. Mr. Smith was worth about fifteen millions; we were worth about five; and I felt that, his wife and daughter being dead, he had no stronger purpose in life than to gratify his malevolence by ruining his old clerk.

The first clash came in 1857. We were victorious; and in protecting our own property in good securities, we necessarily took from our desperate enemy two millions at least. Watchful of him as ever, we successfully withstood his assaults during the anxious years of the Civil War. I was so perpetually conscious of his enmity, that I felt his hatred palpitating in every variation in the stock-market, especially in every fall in the price of the securities of the United States. He detested the Union cause almost as much as he detested me. It was, in his estimation, a " nigger war," a war undertaken by the North without any provocation, a war against the " rights " of the South. The bonds of the United States were not, he said, worth the paper on which they were printed. He bet so desperately against a possible Union success, that it seemed as if he were possessed with a mania. Our firm held the bonds of the United States to the extent of ten millions of dollars. He knew this fact, but he did not know that we had sent them to prominent bankers in London, Paris, and Frankfort, and had obtained a credit on them of five millions to secure our bills of exchange. . With this advantage, we were invulnerable. He thought, when gold went up to 280, that we must be ruined; but the tranquillity with which we continued to draw on European bankers, the ease with which our bills were negotiated, and the promptness of their payment when they fell due, gradually impressed him with the fact that our affairs were conducted on a solid basis of ten millions in gold. By his foolish distrust of the resources of the country, he had lost the opportunity to double his fortune; by his mad assault on the solvency of the United States, he had lost half of the fortune with which he began his crusade against the public credit; and bitterer than all, he discovered that our financial patriotism had added largely to the wealth of the firm. He never recovered from this disappointment. His energies were worn out in his long fight. He grumbled and growled and swore in a minor key. In a few months he retired from his den in Wall

Street to his den in Fifth Avenue. There, tormented with the feeling that he had sunk three quarters of his immense property in an endeavor to gratify his impotent malice, he pined away. The clergymen of the Church to which he nominally belonged were not wanting in attentions and consolations to the old reprobate. They bore his incessant swearing with Christian meekness, having ulterior views on his remaining property, which they justly estimated as still large, and which, they thought, might be advantageously used in the service of the Lord, though every reference of Mr. Smith to the Lord was an explosion of senile profanity shocking to all Christian ears. The blandness with which these smooth clerical gentlemen listened to his oaths indicated that they had much to hope by the bequests of his will. On his death-bed his red eyes, in the malignant glance they cast at the pious circle gathered to witness the departure of such a saint, might have suggested some doubt as to the possibility of the wolf becoming a lamb; but the innocent brethren were satisfied, and Mr. Smith, according to them, made a pious end.

Mr. Smith, in fact, was a remarkable instance of "the merchant of the new school." He rose gradually to the eminent position he enjoyed by industry, frugality, natural sharpness of intellect, and natural hardness of heart. He early learned that honesty was the best policy; that cheating in small things was the greatest mistake an ambitious youth could make; that to keep his word and to pay his obliga-

tions were the conditions of commercial success; that
knavery in such matters did not pay; and accordingly, with such a reputation for formal business
integrity, he eventually rose to be one of the most
accomplished leaders of business banditti that Wall
Street ever saw. Had he frequented gaming-tables,
and been known to lose or gain one or two hundred
dollars a night, his character might have been ruined.
That he frequently lost or gained a million in the
mutations of the stock-market did not affect his reputation as a business man at all, or incapacitate him
from being respected as a " worshipper " in a fashionable church. Had he organized a band of robbers,
and shown eminent skill in petty larceny and bur-
glary, acutely eluding the officers of justice always at
his heels, and betraying his confederates the moment
they rebelled against his leadership, he might have
been a new Jonathan Wild; but he would have been
a thoroughly disreputable man, with no position in
the financial world, no station in society, no pew in
the sanctuary. Besides, he could not have amassed
more than a few hundreds of thousands of dollars in
thus making obvious rascality a trade. He was too
shrewd to be deluded, even when a boy, by the tempt-
ing promises which recognized dishonesty presents
to the youthful imagination. He early perceived that
a reputation for integrity was necessary to be established before any extensive acts of financial rapine
could be successfully perpetrated. Swindling in small
things he early learned to despise, in order that he

might the more surely swindle in large things. The moral element in a transaction never troubled him at all; its possible legal aspect troubled him much. His logic in all these matters showed the enlargement of his intellect. Why, he said, garrote a capitalist in the street as he is returning home at night from his office? The most that could be gained by such an operation would be a watch and a pocket-book, with danger of being arrested by the police, tried in the courts, and sent to prison for a term of years. Better to garrote him under the full noonday sun by a corner in stocks, and thus deprive him of all his property, without any risk of being called to account for the robbery before any of the tribunals of justice. Morally, of course, the proceeding was identical with that of a sharper, with loaded dice, who allures his victims into games of chance, or of a free-booter who lies in wait at the corner of a road to plunder a stage-coach; but it had the immense advantage over these of being legally safe, and of holding out the promise of a hundredfold more booty. Indeed, he held that the difference between a great operator in stocks and an ordinary thief was the difference between a monarch who makes war to steal the territory of a neighbor and an individual murderer who kills the wayfarer he designs only to plunder. This horrible old spider of speculation experienced a certain grim delight in gazing at the flies as they fell successively into his cunningly spun web, and when he darted out upon them, they were devoured with all the savage and ravenous glee with which a cannibal devours the ribs and joints of a missionary.

Not the least noticeable peculiarity in Mr. Smith's character was the absence in him of most of those qualities of avarice which we associate with the idea of a miser. He never seemed to gloat over his wealth, but rather gloated over the power it gave him to prey on his less opulent or intelligent fellow-citizens. He pinched and starved his clerks, not so much because he was too mean to give them adequate salaries, but because he wished to demonstrate to them that they were, as long as they chose or were compelled to stay with him, his abject slaves. After his fortune was made, his avarice was concentrated in making himself a money *power*. As Napoleon only considered one conquest as a step to others, so this creature ruined his competitors in Wall Street to-day, only to form new combinations to ruin fresh competitors to-morrow. He intensely enjoyed, not his wealth, but the means his wealth afforded him of preventing others from acquiring it. Having no heart, his only happiness was in the play of his intellect and the indulgence of his malignant propensities. In studying him, I have been more and more impressed with two things,— first, that human life is mercifully limited to seventy or eighty years; and secondly, that old men, divorced from all family connections, with no grandchildren playing about their knees, and with no memories but those which record the triumphs of their greed of power and gain, are apt to be the deadliest enemies

of the human race. *Their* life has been an enormous
failure, however large may be their property; they
know the fact when they have become old, however
much they have doubted it in their vigorous age; and
such men are the real misanthropes of the business
world, — human wolves which only the decay of the
physical powers prevents from becoming spiritual
devils. Mr. Smith was saved from being a devil
because the Lord did not accord to him the lon-
gevity of Methuselah. He died very respectably, with
a number of godly clergymen and philanthropists
around his bed. In his will he left all his remaining
property to certain rather heretical religious and
benevolent associations, not one of which expected
the old cynic would give it a dollar, because it had
never toadied him. He had a grand burial, — indeed,
a weeping New York followed his hearse to the tomb.
On the next day he was forgotten, except by those he
had cheated. The rage of the sect of Christians to
which he was nominally attached, and whose min-
isters had condoned his offences against Christian
sentiments and principles in the hope that he would
leave his ill-gotten money to its academies and
churches, was secretly but not less bitterly expressed.
The old man, in making his will, probably anticipated
this pious indignation, and chuckled over it with a
kind of senile glee. He doubtless thought, in his
ironical scorn, that those who had been preaching,
for the fifty years he had attended their services,
against the devil, would not condescend to accept the

devil's dollars. Certainly every dollar he had earned belonged to the devil rather than to the Lord. As there was no church here on earth which was formally organized in the name of Satan, he probably felt that the best way he could adopt to reach *his* master was to leave his money to a class of persons he had always abhorred, because they assumed to be reformers, abolitionists, "liberal" Christians, and whom he was taught by his clergyman to consider as little better than atheists on account of defects in their religious creed. He accordingly left his money to them in the hope that they would serve the cause to which he had devoted his life. What would be his rage could he know that the money he had obtained by inflicting suffering was devoted to allaying it, — that the devil's money was strictly expended in advancing the cause of the good Lord? Peace to his ashes! I wish I could add, peace to his soul! But alas! in the whole course of his life he never showed that he had any soul.

MR. HARDHACK ON THE DERIVATION OF MAN FROM THE MONKEY.

I CAN stand it no longer, sir. I have been seething and boiling inwardly for a couple of years at this last and final insult which science has put upon human nature, and now I must speak, or, if you will, explode. And how is it, I want to know, that the duty of hurling imprecations at this infernal absurdity has devolved upon me? Don't we employ a professional class to look after the interests of the race — fellows heavily feed to see to it that gorilla and chimpanzee keep their distance; paid, sir, by me and you to proclaim that men — ay, and women too — are at the top of things in origin, as well as in nature and destiny? Why are these retained attorneys of humanity so confoundedly cool and philosophical, while humanity is thus outraged? What's the use of their asserting, Sunday after Sunday, that man was made a little lower than the angels, when right under their noses are a set of anatomical miscreants who contend that he is only a little higher than the monkeys? And the thing has now gone so far, that I'll be hanged if it is n't becoming a sign of a narrow and prejudiced mind to scout the idea that we are all descended from mindless beasts. You are a fossilized old fogy, in

this day of scientific light, if you repudiate your relationship with any fossilized monstrosity which, from
the glass case of a museum, mocks at you with a
grin a thousand centuries old.   To exalt a man's soul
above his skeleton, is now to be behind the age.   All
questions of philosophy, sir, are fast declining into a
question of bones, — and blasted dry ones they are!
The largest minds are now all absorbed in the ugliest
brutes, and the ape has passed from being the butt of
the menagerie to become the glory of the dissecting-
room.   And let me tell you, sir, that, if you make
any pretensions to be a naturalist, you will find those
of your co-laborers who defend the dominant theory
as great masters of hard words as of big ones ; and if
you have the audacity to deny that man is derived
from the monkey, it is ten chances to one they will
forthwith proceed to treat you *like* one.

Now I go against the whole thing, sir.   When the
public mind first took its bent towards science, I, for
one, foresaw that the devil would soon be to pay
with our cherished ideas.   Under the plea of exercising some of the highest faculties of human nature,
these scientific descendentalists have exclusively devoted themselves to the lowest objects of human concern.   The meaner the creature, the more they think
of it.   You, sir, as a free and enlightened citizen of
this great Republic, doubtless think something of
yourself ; but I can tell you there is n't one of these
origin-of-species Solons who would n't pass you over
as of no account in comparison with any anomalous

rat which you would think it beneath your dignity to
take the trouble of poisoning. There is n't a statesman, or philanthropist, or poet, or hero, or saint in
the land, sir, that they would condescend to look at,
when engaged in exploring the remains of some ignorant ass of the Stone Period. As for your ordinary
Christian, he has no chance whatever. The only man
they think worth the attention of scientific intelligence is pre-historic man, the man nearest the monkey. And this is called progress! This is the result
of founding schools, colleges, and societies for the
advancement of knowledge! No interest now in Homer, Dante, Shakspeare, and Milton, — in Leonidas,
Epaminondas, Tell, and Washington, — in Alexander,
Hannibal, Cæsar, and Napoleon. They, poor devils,
were simply vertebrates ; their structure is so well
known that it is unworthy the attention of our modern prowlers into the earth's crust in search of lower
and obscurer specimens of the same great natural division. What do you think these resurrectionists on
a great scale, these Jerry Crunchers of palæontology,
care for you and me ? Indeed, put Alfred Tennyson
alive into one end of a museum, and one of those horrible monsters whose bones are being continually dug
up into the other, and see which will be rated the
more interesting object of the two by the "great
minds" of the present day.

And now what is the consequence of thus inverting
the proper objects of human concern ? Why, if you
estimate things according to their descent in the scale

4

of dignity, and occupy your faculties exclusively with organized beings below man, you will tend to approach them. Evil communications corrupt good manners. You can't keep company with monkeys without insensibly getting be-monkeyed. Your mind feeds on them until its thoughts take their shape and nature. Into the " veins of your intellectual frame " monkey blood is injected. The monkey thus put into you naturally thinks that monkeydom is belied; and self-esteem, even, is not revolted by the idea of an ape genealogy. In this way the new theory of the origin of man originated. Huxley must have pretty thoroughly assimilated monkey before he recognized his ancestor in one. The poor beast himself may have made no pretensions to the honor, until he was mentally transformed into Huxley, entered into the substance of Huxley's mind, became inflamed with Huxley's arrogance. This is the true explanation, not perhaps of the origin of species, but of the origin of the theory of the origin; and I should like to thunder the great truth into the ears of all the scientific societies now talking monkey with the self-satisfied air of great discoverers. Yes, sir, and I should also be delighted to insinuate that this progress of monkey into man ·was not so great an example of " progressive development " as they seem inclined to suppose, and did n't require the long reaches of prehistoric time they consider necessary to account for the phenomenon. Twenty years would be enough, in all conscience, to effect *that* development.

Thus I tell you, sir, it is n't monkey that rises ana-
tomically into man, but rather man that descends
mentally into monkey. Why, nothing is more common than to apply to us human beings the names of
animals when we display weaknesses analogous to
their habitual characters. But this is metaphor, not
classification; poetry, not science. Thus I, Solomon
Hardhack, was called a donkey the other day by an
intimate friend. Thought it merely a jocose reference
to my obstinacy, and did not knock him down. Called
the same name yesterday by a comparative anatomist.
Thought it an insulting reference to my understanding, and did. But suppose that, in respect both to
obstinacy and understanding, I had established to my
own satisfaction a similarity between myself and that
animal, do you imagine that I would be donkey enough
to take the beast for my progenitor? Do you suppose
that I would go even further, and, having established
with the donkey a relation of descent, be mean enough
to generalize the whole human race into participation
in my calamity? No, sir, I am not sufficiently a man
of science to commit that breach of good manners.
Well, then, my proposition is, that nobody who reasons himself into a development from the monkey has
the right to take mankind with him in his induction.
His argument covers but one individual, — himself.
As for the Hardhacks, they at least beg to be excused
from joining him in that logical excursion, and insist
on striking the monkey altogether out from their
genealogical tree.

And speaking of genealogical trees, do the adherents of this mad theory realize the disgrace they are bringing on the most respectable families? There is not an aristocracy in Europe or America that can stand it one moment, for aristocracy is based on the greatness of forefathers. In America, you know, nobody is aristocratic who cannot count back at least to his great-grandfather, who rode in a carriage, or — drove one. As for the Hardhacks, I may be allowed to say, though I despise family pride as much as any man, that they came in with the Conqueror and went out with the Puritans. But if this horrible Huxleian theory be true, the farther a person is from his origin, the better; antiquity of descent is no longer a title to honor; and a man must pride himself in looking forward to his descendants rather than back to his ancestors. And what comfort is this to me, an unmarried man? With a monkey in the background, how can even a Hapsburg or a Guelf put on airs of superiority? How must he hide his face in shame to think, that, as his line lengthens into an obscure antiquity, the foreheads of his house slope, and their jaws project; that he has literally been all his life aping aristocracy, instead of being the real thing; and that, when he has reached his true beginning, his only consolation must be found in the fact that his great skulking, hulking, gibbering baboon of an ancestor rejoices, like himself, in the possession of "the third lobe," "the posterior cornu of the lateral ventricle," and "the hippocampus minor." Talk about radical-

ism, indeed! Why, I, who am considered an offence
to my radical party for the extremes to which I run,
cannot think of this swamping of all the families in
the world without a thrill of horror and amazement!
It makes my blood run cold to imagine this infernal
Huxley pertly holding up the frontispiece of his book
in the faces of the haughty nobility and gentry of his
country, and saying, " Here, my friends, are drawings
of the skeletons of gibbon, orang, chimpanzee, gorilla;
select your ancestors; you pays your money and has
your choice." I don't pretend to know anything
about the temper of the present nobility and gentry
of England; but if the fellow should do this thing
to me, I would blow out of his skull everything in it
which allied him with the apes, — taking a specially
grim vengeance on " the posterior cornu of the lateral
ventricle," — as sure as my name's Hardhack, and as
sure as there's any explosive power in gunpowder.

And in this connection, too, I should like to know
how the champions of this man-monkey scheme get
over a theological objection. Don't start, sir, and
say I am unscientific. I am not going to introduce
Christianity, or monotheism, or polytheism, or fetich-
ism, but a religion which you know was before them
all, and which consisted in the worship of ancestors.
If you are in the custom of visiting in good society,
you will find that that is a form of worship which has
not yet altogether died out, but roots itself in the
most orthodox creeds. Now you must admit that
the people who worshipped their ancestors were the

earliest people of whose religion we have any archæo-
logical record, and therefore a people who enjoyed the
advantage of being nearer the ancestors of the race
than any of the historical savages to whom you can
appeal. I put it to you if this people, catching a
glimpse of the monkey at the end of their line, if the
monkey was really there, would have been such dolts
as to worship it ? A HE worship an IT! Don't you
see, that, if this early people had nothing human but
human conceit, that would alone have prevented them
from doing this thing? Don't you see that they
would have preserved a wise reticence in regard to
such a shocking bar-sinister in their escutcheons?
Worship ancestors, when ancestors are known to
have been baboons! Why, you might as well tell
me our fashionable friend Eglantine would worship
his grandfather if he knew his grandfather was a
hodman. No, sir. That early people worshipped
their ancestors, because they knew their ancestors
were higher and nobler than themselves. To suppose the contrary would be a cruel inputation on the
character of worthy antediluvians, who unfortunately
have left no written account of themselves, and therefore present peculiar claims on the charitable judgment of every candid mind.

You have been a boy, sir, and doubtless had your
full share in that amusement, so congenial to ingenuous youth, of stirring up the monkeys. You remember
what an agreeable feeling of elation, springing from a
conscious sense of superiority to the animals pestered,

accompanied that exhilarating game. But suppose, while you were engaged in it, the suspicion had flashed across your mind that you were worrying your own distant relations ; that it was undeveloped humanity you were poking and deriding ; that the frisking, chattering, snarling creature you were tormenting was trying all the while to say, in his unintelligible speech, " Am I not *to be* a man and a brother ? " Would not such an appeal have dashed your innocent mirth ? Would you afterwards have been so clamorous or beseeching for parental pennies, as soon as the dead walls of your native town flamed with pictorial announcements of the coming menagerie ? No, sir, you couldn't have passed a menagerie without a shudder of loathing or a pang of remorse. How fortunate it was, that, for the full enjoyment of your youthful sports, you were ignorant of the affecting fact that the monkey's head as well as your own possessed the " hippocampus minor " and " the posterior cornu of the lateral ventricle " !

I admit that this last argument is not addressed to your understanding alone. I despise all arguments on this point that are. I, for one, am not to be reasoned out of my humanity, and I won't be diddled into turning baboon through deference for anybody's logic. My opinions may be up for argument, but I myself am not up for argument. In a question affecting human nature itself, all the qualities of that nature should be addressed. Self-respect, respect for your parentage and your race, your moral instincts, and

that force in you which says " I," — all these, having
an interest in such a discussion, should have a voice
in it; and I execrate the flunky who will allow himself to be swindled out of manhood, and swindled into
monkeyhood, by that pitiful little logic-chopper he
calls his understanding. I am not " open to conviction" on this point, thank God! I don't pretend to
know whether a " third lobe" is in my head or not,
but I do know that Solomon Hardhack is there, and
as long as he has possession of the premises, you will
find written on his brow, " No monkeys need apply ! "

Do you tell me that this is a matter exclusively for
anatomists and naturalists to decide? That's the
most impudent pretension of all. Why, it's all the
other way. Have I not a personal interest in the question greater than any possible interest I can have in
the diabolical lingo of scientific terms in which those
fellows state the results of their investigations? Have
I delegated to any College of Surgeons the privilege
of chimpanzeeizing my ancestors? No, sir. Just
look at it. Here are the members of the human race,
going daily about their various avocations, entirely
ignorant that any conspiracy is on foot to trick them
out of their fatherhood in Adam. While they are
thus engaged in getting an honest living, a baker's
dozen of unauthorized miscreants assemble in a dis-
secting-room, manipulate a lot of skulls, and decide
that the whole batch of us did not descend from a
human being. I tell you the whole thing is an atro-
cious violation of the rights of man. It's uncon-

stitutional, sir! Talk about the glorious principle of " No taxation without representation " ! That is simply a principle which affects our pockets, and we fought, bled, and died for it. Shall we not do a thousand times more for our souls ? Shall we let our souls be voted away by a congress of dissectors, not chosen by our votes, — persons who not only don't represent, but infamously misrepresent us ? Why, it's carrying the tactics of a New York Common Council from politics into metaphysics ! And don't allow yourself to be humbugged by these assassins of your nature. I know the way they have of election-eering. It is, " My dear Mr. Hardhack, a man of your intelligence can't look at this ascending scale of skulls without seeing that the difference between Homo and Pithecus is of small account," — " A man of your candid mind, Mr. Hardhack, must admit that no absolutely structural line of demarcation, wider than that between the animals which immediately succeed us in the scale, can be drawn between the animal world and ourselves." And while I don't comprehend a word of this cursed gibberish, I am expected to bow, and look wise, and say, " Certainly," and " Just so," and " It's plain to the meanest capacity," and be soft-sawdered out of my humanity, and infamously acknowledge myself babooned. But they can't try it on me, sir. When a man talks to me in that fashion, I measure with *my* eyes " the structural line of demarcation " between *his*, and with my whole force plant there my fist.

Do you complain that I am speaking in a passion? It seems to me it's about time for all of us to be in a passion. Perhaps, if we show these men of science that there is in us a little righteous wrath, they may be considerate enough to stop with the monkey, — make the monkey "a finality," sir, and not go lower down in the scale of creation to find an ancestor for us. It is our meek submission to the monkey which is now urging them to attempt more desperate outrages still. What if Darwin had been treated as he deserved when he published the original edition of his villanous book? If I had been Chief Justice of England when that high priest of "natural selection" first tried to oust me out of the fee-simple of my species, I would have given him an illustration of "the struggle for existence" he wouldn't have relished. I would have hanged him on the highest gallows ever erected on this planet since the good old days of Haman. What has been the result of a mistaken clemency in his case? Why, he has just published a fourth edition of his treatise, and what do you think he now puts forward as our "probable" forefather? "It is probable," he says, "from what we know of the embryos of mammals, birds, fishes, and reptiles, that all the members in these four great classes are the modified descendants of one ancient progenitor, which was furnished in its adult state with branchiæ, had a swim-bladder, four simple limbs, and a long tail fitted for an aquatic life." Probable, indeed! Why, it is also probable, I suppose, that this accounts for the latent tendency in the blood of our best-educated collegians to turn watermen, and abandon themselves with a kind of sacred fury to the fierce delight of rowing-matches. The "long tail fitted for an aquatic life" will also "probably" come in course of time. Student-mammals of Harvard and Yale, what think you of your "one ancient progenitor"? Inheritors of his nature, are you sure you have yet succeeded in cutting off the entail of the estate?

We have been brought up, sir, in the delusive belief that "revolutions never go backwards." It's a lie, I tell you; for this new revolution in science does nothing else. It is going backwards and backwards and backwards, and it won't stop until it involves the whole of us in that nebulous mist of which, it seems, all things are but the "modified" development. Well, in for a penny, in for a pound. Let us not pause at that "long tail fitted for an aquatic life" which made our one ancient progenitor such an ornament of fluvial society, but boldly strike out into space, and clutch with our thoughts that primitive tail which flares behind the peacock of the heavens, — the comet. There's nebulous matter for your profound contemplation. That is the flimsy material out of which stars, earth, water, plants, jelly-fish, ancient progenitor, monkey, man, were all equally evolved. That is the grand original of all origins. We are such stuff as comets' tails are made of, — "third lobe," "hippocampus minor," "posterior cornu of the lateral ventricle," and all the rest. "Children of the Mist," we are made by this "sublime speculation" at home in the universe. Nebuchadnezzar, when he went to grass, only visited a distant connection. The stars over our heads have for thousands of years been winking their relationship with us, and we have never intelligently returned the jocose salutation, until science taught us the use of our eyes. We are now able to detect the giggle, as of feminine cousins, in the grain whose risibilities are touched by the wind. We can now cheer even the dull stone which we kick from our path with a comforting "Hail fellow, well met!" We must not be aristocrats and put on airs. We must hob and nob with all the orders of creation, saying alike to radiates, articulates, and mollusks, "Go ahead, my hearties! don't be shamefaced; you're as good as vertebrates, and only want, like some of our human political lights, a little backbone to have your claims admitted. You are all on your glorious course manward, *via* the ancient progenitor and the chimpanzee. It seems a confounded long journey; for Nature is a slow coach, and thinks nothing of a million of years to effect a little transformation. But one of these days our science may find means to expedite that old sluggard, and hurry you through the intermediate grades in a way to astonish the venerable lady. Liberty, equality, and fraternity, — those are the words which will open the gates of your organized Bastiles, and send your souls on a career of swifter development. Trust in Darwin, and let creation ring with your song of "A good time coming, Invertebrates!"

Well, sir, you want logic, and there you have it with a vengeance! I have pitched you back into nebula, where these fellows tell me you belong, and I trust you're satisfied. Now what is my comfort, sir, after making my brain dizzy with this sublime speculation of theirs? Why, it's found in the fact that, by their own concession, the thing will not work, but must end in the biggest "catastrophe" ever heard of. The whole infernal humbug is to explode, sir, and by no exercise of their "hippocampus minor" can they prevent it. This fiery mist, which has hardened and rounded into our sun and planets, and developed into the monkey's "third lobe" and ours, does not lose the memory or the conceit of *its* origin, but is determined to get back into its first condition as quickly as circumstances will admit. It considers itself somehow to have been swindled in every step of the long process it has gone through in arriving at our brains. It does n't think the speculation pays; prefers its lounging, vagabond, *dolce far niente* existence, loafing through the whole space between the sun and Neptune, to any satisfaction it finds in being concentrated in your thoughts or mine; and accordingly it meditates a *coup d'état* by which the planets are to fall into the sun at such a pace as to knock the whole system into eternal smash, and reduce it to its original condition of nebulous mist, sir. Do you like the prospect? I tell you there is no way of escaping from conclusions, if you are such a greenhorn as to admit premises. I have been over the whole chain of the logic, and find its only weak link is the monkey one. Knock that out, and you save the solar system as well as your own dignity as a man, sir; retain it, and some thousands of generations hence the brains of your descendants will be blown into a texture as gauzy as a comet's tail, and it will be millions of ages before, in the process of a new freak of development in the unquiet nebula, they can hope to arrive again at the honor of possessing that inestimable boon, dear equally to baboons and to men, "the posterior cornu of the lateral ventricle"!

MR. HARDHACK ON THE SENSATIONAL IN LITERATURE AND LIFE.

HAVE I read Miss Braddon's last? Ay, and her first too. Why, during the last three or four months I have been through a whole course of sensational novels, and, in imagination, have married more wives than Brigham Young, and committed more homicides than Captain Kidd; and I flatter myself I have got at the whole secret of the thing. It's whiskey for the mind, sir, — the regular raw, rot-brain fluid of the Devil's own distilling. What do you suppose is to become of the intellects and hearts of a generation which takes to such a terrible tipple? They are all at it, — men and women, boys and girls, imbibing the stinging, burning, corroding beverage as though it were as innocent as milk. "Drink, pretty creature, drink," — that is the song of the Circes and the Comuses of the new school of depravity, as they hold their yellow cups to the lips of sweet fifteen: "This, my dear, has a delicious flavor of theft; this of arson; this of bigamy; this of murder. Drink, and Newgate and the Old Bailey will be more familiar to you than the school-house and the church! Drink, and you will draw the charming convicts out of their cells, and

have them all nicely housed in your own imagination!
Drink, drink, drink!"

But, you retort, do not the greatest writers deal
with the greatest crimes? Is Shakspeare himself an
economist of the dagger and the bowl? Why object
to contemporary romancers for taking criminals for
heroes, when criminality enters so largely into the
heroes of all dramas and romances? You think you
have me, do you? Well, others before you have been
infatuated with the idea that they could get Solomon
Hardhack into a corner, but he always found a road
out of it as wide as the Appian Way. I admit at once
that I have no objection to murders when they are
perpetrated by Shakspeare or Scott. The more the
better, say I. When the old woman told her doctor
that she feared her health was failing, because during
the past week she had not, in reading the newspaper,
"enjoyed her murders," she caught a glimpse of the
great principle of all art, sir. When I read Macbeth,
when I see it performed by actors of imagination, I
enjoy the murders. When I read or see a coarse melo-
drama, I don't enjoy the murders. What's the reason? Why, my artistic sense is satisfied by the first,
and shocked by the second. The tragedy lifts your
whole nature — sentiment, conscience, reflection, imagination, whatever there is in you — altogether above
actual life into the ideal world of art. You become
conscious of a new, strange, and vivid play of all your
faculties; and there is delight in that, even though
you may now and then shudder or blubber. It is an

escape out of all the conditions of your daily life, and you feel ten times the man you were before the fine sting of the dramatist's genius sent its delicious torment into your soul. Now, how is it with the melo drama? Why, you are in the mud and dust of the earth all the time you listen; everything is intensely commonplace, not excepting the rant and the crimes; when a character is stabbed, or has his brains blown out, or, what is better, blows out his brains with his own hand, it is simple murder or suicide you witness, and there's no enjoyment in witnessing either, except perhaps the enjoyment you feel in thinking that the wretched spectacle has come to an end.

And here we have the whole philosophy of the sensational in fiction. You are, let me suppose, a commonplace and common-sense man, sir. If I were a person without an atom of genius, and yet were compelled by circumstances, like many of my unfortunate fellow-creatures, to gain my living by writing novels, I should have you in my eye while I wrote. I should so manage my story as to galvanize a small part of your mediocrity out of all its relations to the other parts. You would still be the commonplace fellow you were before, *plus* " a sensation." My book would be as artistically worthless as a police report, but to you it would be a specimen of literature; and I should have the inexpressible satisfaction of transferring money from your pocket into mine, without going through the extremely tedious process of attempting to get a fine sentiment into your heart or a new idea into your head.

Indeed, sir, you will find that it is your ordinary, matter-of-fact, bread-and-butter, practical people, rather than your romantic and poetic ones, who are swindled by sensations. The sensational is a revolt against humdrum, through the means of a vulgar wonder. Let me tell you an illustrative story. Once upon a time a vagabond pedler appeared in a secluded village, and called the people round him by ringing a big bell. When his audience had become sufficiently large, he stopped ringing in order to make this announcement: "All you young women here with small mouths will have a husband!" The spinsters present pursed and puckered up their lips, and murmured, "Dear me! what a pretty little man!" Then he rung his bell again, with still more startling emphasis, and said in his deepest and loudest tones: "And all you young women here with large mouths will have two!" Instantly the lips were stretched to their utmost width, and from them all came the wondering exclamation, "Law!" Now don't tell me that Miss Braddon had n't heard of this story when she wrote "Aurora Floyd," for it was exactly this open-mouthed wonder that she desired to produce when she made the interest of her plot centre in bigamy. You know, sir, how quickly you, and the rest of people like you, exclaimed, "Law!"

The great defect, then, to my notion, of the romancers of rascality is, that there's no romance in them. They treat you to hard, ugly, "slangy," prosaic fact, and throw in some wild nonsense, or brutal

ruffianism, or cynical villany, just to give it a coarse
zest. Neither sentiment nor imagination is addressed.
The heroes commit just such crimes, and encounter
just such penalties, as you find printed in the newspaper records of the criminal courts. Take Miss
Braddon's "Birds of Prey," which is one of her latest
attempts at a sensation, and notice how bare and bleak
is the atmosphere of the story, and how commonplace
as well as bad is the company she drags you into.
But this photographing of poisoners and swindlers is
not characterization; this power to interest you in
society where you fear your pocket will be picked is
not art.

So much for the novels that please a practical man
like you, sir. Now, what kind of author do you support when it enters your brain that your moral nature
needs to be braced? Tupper, of course; for you and
your set have sent that " Proverbial Philosophy " of
his through a hundred editions. He has just the combination of truism and vagueness, do-me-good reflection and windy vastness, to fill your idea of the moral
sublime. And then what a poet he is in his ethics!
Your idea of the beautiful is of course identical with
your notion of the big; and he goes over the whole
universe to gather images of bigness for your delec-
tation, doing a larger business in mountains, earth-
quakes, and firmaments than any other metaphor-
monger of the day. Did it ever occur to you that,
even in moral significance, one of Burns's daisies
outvalues all of Tupper's empyreans?

You must be a patron of art, too ; that is, you are
one of those men of dollars who are engaged in corrupting all the promising painters of the land by urging them to the production of panoramic pictures, in
which there shall be an almost photographic representation of some strange or big thing in nature, but
in which all the life and spirit of nature shall be left
out. You value things in art just in proportion as
they recede from the artistic. Here is a little picture,
representing a bit of grass, a cow, and a cottage.
How you turn up your nose ! There's nothing in it
to create a sensation, I admit ; but there is something
in it to touch a sentiment, if sentiment you had to
touch. The landscape is thoroughly humanized, sir,
and if you had ever seen a simple landscape in nature, — you've stared, no doubt, at thousands, — you
would feel the fact. But that stupendous picture of
mountains you can, of course, appreciate. You never
even stared at such a phenomenon as that, and it
stirs your languid consciousness with a new sensation. But still the painted bit of grass is greater, as
a work of art, than the painted chain of mountains,
and would be worth more in money if purses in our
day had not unfortunately lost their artistic perception. Did you ever read Hawthorne's essay on the
town-pump of Salem ? Well, the town-pump of Salem
is n't so important a matter as the battle of Waterloo ; but then, Hawthorne's description of the pump
has infinitely more significance to the intellect than
Alison's description of the battle. Now, in estimating

pictures you make the mistake of judging by the subject painted, and not by the genius that paints. And so far you are a fool, sir. Don't redden! The fools in art are the most sensible men in business, and at any rate are in the majority.

A man like you must have a religion, too, and as you pride yourself on being a very sensible and practical man, you probably have a false and bad one, sir. I don't care where you go to church ; I know that, if you must have sensations in literature and art, you must have them also in religion. Ten to one you are a reader of Dr. Cumming, and are charmed with the grandiloquent way he transfixes Napoleon II. on one horn of the dilemma of the Beast, and the certainty he expresses every year that the world is to be destroyed in the next. No ? Why, you certainly cannot be a Mormon, though the novels you read might tempt you, if you lived in Utah, to look with favor on that over-connubial faith. I see how it is, — you 're a Spiritualist. You believe in no miracles that don't pass under your own eyes and into your own ears. You need to have your religion rapped into you. You cannot perceive the spiritual unless you have a sensation of it. Now, mind, I don't doubt there are many fine natures interested in the phenomena of what is called Spiritualism, and expect to draw something out of it to satisfy their spiritual curiosity or aspiration. But they are not the sensation-mongers of the creed ; they are not the persons who exhibit the spirits of the departed to an intelligent public at so much a head. You, however, as I repeatedly have had the honor of reminding you, are an eminently practical man, and of course easily humbugged on all matters where real spiritual discernment comes into play. Your notion of spiritual communion with the dead is a gossip with ghosts. And such ghosts! Why, your next world, sir, is filled with nothing but bores and dunces, and existence there would be passed by any reasonable man in one long, everlasting yawn! You never read Bacon, or Milton, or Channing; yet I admit you have succeeded in making Bacon and Milton and Channing talk to you — true table-talk! But then, Bacon, freed from all limitations of the flesh, talks like Tupper, and Milton like Robert Montgomery, and Channing like Mrs. Trimmer. You have got a spiritual world, I concede, but it is one into which poets pass only to be deprived of their imagination, philosophers of their wisdom, saints of their sanctity, and all persons of their brains. The "revelations" may be very creditable for tables to make, for tables are of wood, and " wooden " is English for *bête;* but considered as coming from disembodied souls, they cast discredit on the human mind itself. And then, sir, what follies you practical men slip into! 'T is a pity that with all your boasted sense you have n't some sense of humor to see the ludicrous element in your faith. The mediums who allow you to have a chat with the denizens of the spiritual world, — how inexpressibly moderate they are in their charges! You know perfectly well that the mysteries of your religion are presided over, in many cases, by persons who communicate with the dead simply for the purpose of getting a living; by showmen turned priests and sempstresses ambitious to be sibyls, — priests who are content to exchange a revelation for a shilling, and sibyls who "charge a pistareen a spasm"!

Well, it might at least be hoped that we should have none of these sensations in science. Never was a greater mistake, sir. In the process of being popularized, science is becoming melodramatic; and such melodramas! I don't know how it is with the real investigators, the plodding, conscientious fellows who are engaged in adding to our knowledge of facts and laws. It is, however, to be supposed that they are leading lives more or less obscure, arriving at limited results by hard labor and patient thought, loving truth more than notoriety, and untroubled by any ambition to excogitate a theory of the universe out of the depths of their own consciousness. Poor devils! Do they suppose that a public, craving new sensations and desirous of having a slap-dash statement of the origin and development of all things and all beings, cares for the little they can tell about the works and ways of nature? Probably if questioned as to some of the novel and splendid scientific theories now in vogue, they would profess complete ignorance of such deep matters. They would answer the querist somewhat as Mr. Prime Minister Pitt answered the lady who asked him for the latest news.

He had n't, he said, read the papers, to which, doubtless, she instantly referred, and found more information there about Mr. Pitt's acts and intentions than
Mr. Pitt himself could have given her. The fact is,
the question we now put to every man of science is
practically this: " What is your pet method of allowing God Almighty to build the universe ? " This, of
course, compels every pushing, self-glorifying, sensational *savant* to bring out his plan of creation for
our amusement and edification. We put the various
schemes to vote, and the one which has the noisiest
and most theatrical accompaniments commonly carries it. Now, I call all this creating God after man's
image, and the universe after man's crotchets, for I
find that every plan is the measure of the mind which
gets it up, and is ridiculous considered as a measure
of Infinite intelligence. Even if you leave the Deity
altogether out of your scheme, as an " hypothesis
which has now ceased to have any practical interest,"
you create, not a world, but merely a sensation. It is
to be presumed that God can get along better without you than you can without him, and certainly his
existence is not one of those questions which can be
determined by popular suffrage. If the vote were unfavorable, I am not without a suspicion that he would
still contrive to keep his place at the heart of things,
and assert his reality in ways emphatic enough. In
fact, the whole business of building up universes, as
now conducted, is decidedly overdone, sir. You get
nothing out of it but words, and what, as an old theo-

logian says, are words "against Him who spoke worlds,
— who worded heaven and earth out of nothing, and
can when he pleases word them into nothing again " ?

But you may say that in all I assert about the
sensational in religion and science, I am talking of
matters about which I know nothing. There you are
right, sir. But how is it with business? Here is
something which a man of plain understanding and
ordinary conscience may speak of without incurring
the charge of presumption. Now what is one of the
most frightful characteristics of our present mode of
doing business? Is it not the building up of great
fortunes out of colossal robberies? And the thing
is done by a series of sensational addresses to the
cupidity of the cheated. High interest notoriously
goes with low security; but we have, sir, in this
country, a class of rogues who may be called the
aristocracy of rascaldom, and who get rich by dazzling
and astonishing others into the hope of getting rich.
They are the contrivers of enterprises which propose
to develop the wealth of the country, but which commonly turn out to be little more than schemes to
transfer wealth already realized from the pockets of
the honest into those of the knavish. They are the
financial footpads who lure simple people into stock
" corners," and then proceed to plunder them. They
make money so rapidly, so easily, and in such a splendid sensational way, that they corrupt more persons
by their example than they ruin by their knaveries.
As compared with common rogues, they appear like

Alexander or Cæsar as compared with common thieves
and cutthroats. As their wealth increases, our moral
indignation at their method of acquiring it diminishes,
and at last they steal so much that we come to look
on their fortunes as conquests rather than burglaries.
Indeed, their operations on 'Change vie with those of
military commanders in the field, and are recorded
with similar admiring minuteness of detail. They
are the great sensations of the world of trade, and
have, therefore, more influence on the imaginations of
young men just starting in business than the dull
chronicles of the great movements of legitimate commerce. Now, sir, take the universal American desire
to get rich, and combine it with the rapid, rascally
way of getting rich now in vogue, and you will find
you are breeding up a race of trading sharks and
wolves, which will eventually devour us all. Honesty
will go altogether out of fashion, and respectability
be associated with defect of intellect. Why, the old
robber barons of the Middle Ages, who plundered
sword in hand and lance in rest, were more honest
than this new aristocracy of swindling millionnaires.
Do you object that I am getting into a passion?
Why, sir, I have purchased dearly enough the right
to rail. Did n't I put my modest competence into
copper? And to recover my losses in copper, did n't
I go madly into petroleum? And did n't the small sum
which petroleum was considerate enough to leave me
disappear in that last little " turn " in Erie ?

THE SWEARING HABIT.

A CURIOUS volume has recently been published in London, entitled "A Cursory History of Swearing," by Julian Sharman. The author has lightly sketched the annals of swearing, whether legal or irreverent, from the dawn of civilization to the present day. He has traced back many English oaths that by natives are commonly thought to be original contributions to the English vocabulary of imprecation and malediction, to French, Roman, and even Greek sources. We are so defective in our scholarship, as far as it relates to the art and practice of profanity in all nations and all times, that we hardly dare to question some of the results of his investigations, because the " comparative method," however successful it may be in its applications to various forms of religion, has not yet succeeded in giving to blasphemy the precision and sureness of a science.

It would seem that the habit of using oaths adapts itself to almost all classes of character, from the lowest nearly to the highest. The profane use of sacred words slides naturally into the expression of mere animal rage, but it also sometimes bursts out in the utterance of righteous wrath at fraud, oppression, and wrong. The most repulsive phase of profanity, however, is that which is most common. A man of refinement cannot walk the streets of any city, or the lanes of any country village, without having his sense of decency shocked by senseless oaths and imprecations, whether coming from the lips of a hack-driver cursing his horses, or a farm laborer cursing his oxen. Any impediment, no matter how inevitable, is the occasion for bestowing upon it a torrent of the dirtiest and most sacrilegious terms that the language contains. In some cases this profanity among uneducated men is the result of a very limited command of words to express their feelings of impatience, anger, jealousy, spite, and hatred; in others, mere levity of mental and moral constitution leads them to adopt the common and accredited forms of blasphemy, without any thought of their import; but in too many cases the words express the real passions of coarse, hard, dull, envious, and malignant natures, indifferent to religious or moral restraints, finding a certain delight in outraging ordinary notions of decorum, flattering themselves with the conceit that in ribaldry and blasphemy they have some compensation for the miseries brought upon them by poverty or vice, and indulging in outward curses as a verbal relief to their inward " cussedness " of disposition and character.

From the houses of all these classes issue a crowd of children that have breathed an atmosphere of blasphemy from their birth, who are proficient in the language of execration and malediction learned at the parental hearth or den, whose every third word is an oath, who are educating themselves in that form of "self-culture" which may eventually lead them to the penitentiary or the gallows, and who, in the energetic words of an old divine, "seem not so much born as damned into the world." It does not require any deep sense of religion in the man that threads his way through a group of these infantile tramps, these childish ruffians, — spawned on the sidewalk before their wretched habitations, — to feel a thrill of horror as he hears the oaths that spontaneously leap forth in their little shrill voices. Well, they have been born and brought up in households in which the "wet damnation" of bad whiskey in the stomach has found its appropriate expression in the hot damnation of execrations rushing to the lips. But then the "pity of it," the horror of it, when you think of the desecration of childhood. Everybody imbued with the least tincture of literature is aware of a certain sacredness that ideal minds, especially minds of a poetic cast, attribute to children born in happy circumstances! There is a feeling that the child, in its innocence, is nearer to its Maker than the grown-up man, brought into direct contact and conflict with the practical facts of life. If we disregard Wordsworth's sublime ode, "Intimations of Immortality, from Recollections of Early Childhood," we still must have some respect for the emotion that uplifts the imagination and affections of such an apparent worldling as Thomas Moore, in his exquisite representation of the child in "Paradise and the Peri." What a picture is that of the

hardened ruffian, as he gazes on the innocent boy
playing among the roses of the vale of Baalbec!
Then, as he hears it, —

". . . the vesper call to prayer,
  As slow the orb of daylight sets,
Is rising sweetly on the air,
  From Syria's thousand minarets.
The boy has started from the bed
  Of flowers, where he had laid his head,
And down upon the fragrant sod
  Kneels with his forehead to the South,
Lisping the eternal name of God,
  From Purity's own cherub mouth."

Now contrast this with the way " the eternal name
of God " is bandied about by the reckless urchins and
the unsexed girls that line the streets to every railroad station in every city in the United States. The
merely respectable man shudders as he passes by
these outcasts, and congratulates himself, perhaps,
that he has hidden his offspring in some country
nook, where such words are unheard. But he is mistaken. The disease of profanity is infectious. It
spreads like the measles, the scarlet fever, and diph-
theria; and ten miles of space cannot preserve his
own little innocents from the contagion. The great
mystery of life, if considered in the light of what is
called God's Providence, is the solidarity, the essential union, of mankind, so that every wickedness and
corruption in the low and degraded populations mount
up into the higher and more educated ranks, just in
proportion as the higher in rank, wealth, and cultiva-

tion neglect the lower sunk in poverty, ignorance, and
vice. ·There is no apparent reason why their offspring
should have a share in the contamination of the little
outcasts they shrink from in the streets. The Sunday-
school, the genial home, the academy, the college, the
exclusive social position they enjoy, — these will keep
them from the dismal fate of the wretched "lowest
classes" they pity but make only ineffectual attempts
to raise. What is the result? It is seen almost daily
in funerals, where pious fathers and mothers, who
have worked and prayed to shield their children from
the talk of the profane and the practice of the vicious,
have vainly striven, in scrutinizing the features of
their dead and dishonored sons, to call back in
memory "the smile of cradled innocence on the lips
of the coffined reprobate." The tragedy of life and
death is there. You should have known that you
cannot preserve your own protected children from
contamination, unless you labor to protect the neglected children of improvidence, carelessness, and
vice from what seems to be their inevitable doom.
Self-protection, dissociated from mutual protection, is
the imminent danger that our present civilization is
called upon to meet.

So far the practice of swearing has been condemned
on what the reader might call religious or sentimental
objections. Still, even those who ignore or deny the
existence of God, or have only a faint traditional
sense of religious obligation, are impelled by their
common sense and regard for common decency to

stigmatize profanity as at least vulgar. The conventional gentleman, though fifty or eighty years ago he might consider an oath as an occasional or frequent adornment of his conversation in all societies, now reserves it for " gentlemen " alone, and is inclined to deem it slightly improper in the society of ladies. The improvement has been gradual, but it is still growing, and in ordinary society blasphemy is banished from the polite tattle and prattle of good company, on the ground that it indicates a coarse nature, or a very limited command of the resources of the English language to express sterility of mind and vacuity of heart.

But there is a coarse fibre in the physical and moral constitution of the English race, which was early indicated by its habit of profane swearing. Curses were accepted as the signs of manliness. The author whom we have taken as our guide makes a desperate attempt to defend his countrymen in this respect. He shows that a profane use of sacred words is common to all races and nations, barbaric as well as half civilized. This fact must be admitted; but in regard to modern times one must think that the English have excelled all other nations in the meaning and emphasis they have put into their words. The Latin races swear more constantly and more volubly than their Teutonic brethren, but their execrations are trivial in comparison with the deep-mouthed and fierce-hearted oaths of the Anglo-Saxon people. The imprecations of the Italian, especially, seem to be mere outbursts of physical irritation, without any solid purpose in them; but in the ordinary English soldier and sailor profanity expresses character. It is needless to go farther back than the invasion of France in the fifteenth century. The English were called by the French peasants, who did not understand their language, "the Goddams." The heroes of Agincourt were thus named, after their favorite oath. When, afterward, the last step to make France an English province, or to make England a province of France, was thwarted by the genius and faith of Joan of Arc, it is curious that this wonderful peasant-girl was accustomed to name the English, as distinguished from the French, "the Goddams." This is the more to be noticed because she had an utter horror of profanity. When she took command of the six thousand soldiers that, under her lead, threw themselves into Orleans, she first required that the profane and dissolute French men-at-arms who marched under her sacred banner should entirely banish from their minds, as well as from their lips, their copious stores of ribaldry and blasphemy. La Hire, one of the bravest and coarsest of her captains, growlingly consented to talk like a decent human being. Yet she always spoke of the English by the name they had doubtless acquired by the profusion with which they lavished their national imprecation on their enemies. Her knowledge of the English language was probably confined to this single phrase. When she was preparing her assault on one of the

strongest forts that the English had erected against
Orleans, she was asked by a French soldier to partake
of a breakfast of fish before she set out on her haz
ardous expedition. " In the name of God," she exclaimed, "it shall not be eaten till supper, by which
time we shall return by way of the bridge, and I will
bring you back a Goddam to eat it with." And in
her lonely dungeon, after she had been captured and
imprisoned, she proudly said to the earls of Warwick
and Stafford, " You think when you have slain me
you will conquer France; but that you will never do.
No! although there were one hundred thousand more
Goddams in this land than there are now."

English culture, as we have said, may have banished from polite society the favorite oath of the
English race; but the rough, stout soldiers, sailors,
and pioneers of the race have carried the name that
Joan of Arc bestowed upon them in the fifteenth
century, to every savage and civilized clime in which
they have appeared. It is four hundred years since
their distinguishing imprecation was heard by Joan
on the walls of Orleans; yet it is uttered now with
equal emphasis on our own Western plains, by those
pioneers that use, or rather misuse, the English tongue.
After New Mexico was organized as a Territory of the
United States, a gentleman of our acquaintance was
sent there to occupy an official position. When he
arrived at the point from which the wagon-train of
oxen and mules was to set forth for the place of his
future residence, he noticed that recent rains had

made the miserable roads seemingly impassable. He asked a wretched-looking Indian savage, lounging about the station, if he thought the train would get through. " The ye-hoes may," he answered, " but I don't believe the Goddams will." These terms he considered the English names of the animals he pointed out; for he had never heard their drivers mention them as oxen and mules, but he so understood their exclamations and execrations as to discriminate between the designation given to the patient and forbearing ox, and that plentifully bestowed upon the obstinate and resisting mule. In fact, he had only taken his first lesson in the English language, as taught by our boasted pioneers of civilization.

Mr. Sharman (if that be his real name) attempts to trace the oath to a French source. He declares that at the time of Joan of Arc, " dame Dieu! " was common on the lips of Frenchmen, that the word *Dieu* could not be pronounced by the rough Englishmen, and " that they were accordingly forced to anglicize it to fit it to the remainder of the oath ; " but this derivation fails, because it is easy to prove that the English never were driven to borrow such sulphurous expletives from any nation they invaded. Their " morning drum-beat " does not more certainly circle the earth daily with their martial airs than with their martial blasphemies. The French wits and satirists have never wearied of fastening anew on the Englishman the name by which he was called four centuries ago. Voltaire, in his mock-heroic poem of " La Pu-

celle," makes Talbot die, after a hard struggle, with an
intense utterance of the favorite English malediction
foaming from his lips. Beaumarchais, in the "Mariage
de Figaro," laughingly extols the beauty and compact-
ness of the English language; you only need, he says,
one expression (quoting that we have so often mentioned), and it will go a great ways. There are other
words, he adds, used occasionally by the English in
conversation, but the substance and depth of the language is in that magical oath. In 1770, Lord Hailes
gives it as his experience, that in Holland, when the
children saw any English people they exclaimed,
" There come the —— —— ;" and that the Portu-
guese, when they see an English sailor, accost him
with, "How do you do, Jack, dash you?" Captain
Hall, many years ago, told us that when a Sandwich
Islander wished to propitiate a British crew, he exhibited his knowledge of the language they spoke by
exclaiming, "Very glad see you! Dash your eyes!
me like English very much. Devilish hot, sir! ——
——." We have a faint remembrance of a French
comedy, written about a century and a half ago, in
which a French imitator of English manners has contrived to express his Anglican tendencies by swearing, " Dieu-moi-dam." In 1789 a farce was played in
Paris, in which one Williams enters a cabaret, with
the oath that betrayed his nationality. The person
addressed repeats the curse, and instantly adds,
" Monsieur est Anglais apparemment." Indeed, this
vice of profanity is so common in the English race

that historians of manners, all playwrights and novelists, have emphasized it. From the time of Henry
VIII. to the time of George IV. it raged with the
virulence of an epidemic. As the English race and
language seem bound to possess the greater part of
the earth, it is a pity that British soldiers and sailors
should have heretofore preceded its missionaries in
the conquest of savage or what are called pagan nations. It is said that there are certain barbarians in
whose limited dialects every word is associated with
some obscene or profane idea, and that the missionary
is utterly unable to convey to them a spiritual truth
or dogma, because the Bible, translated into their
language, becomes a support to their degeneration,
rather than affords an impulse to their regeneration.
It is probable that the civilized people that first meet
with them for the purpose of conquest or trade, only
add new words to their restricted resources of expression in native obscenity and profanity. It is to
be regretted that the great colonizing enterprises of
Britain, if we except the persecuted nonconformists
that settled New England, carried English coarseness
and brutality and profanity to the same shores to
which they introduced British civilization. How
could the followers of Drake, Raleigh, and Cavendish
regard blasphemy as a serious offence, when they
must have known that their maiden queen, the hot-
tempered, despotic Elizabeth, swore as lustily as they
did? Even grave historians tell us of a bishop who,
when he muttered some reluctance to obey, in one

instance, her imperative command, was stunned by
her passionate answer: "Do it, or, by ——, I will
unfrock you!"

In noting the connection of British profanity with
British colonization, the disastrous attempt of the
Scotch to colonize the Isthmus of Darien must not
be overlooked. The expedition carried a goodly company of clergymen to convert the heathen natives,
and Christianity was intended to consecrate commerce. The colony failed as miserably in its theological as in its commercial aim; and the historian
tells us that " the colonists left behind them no mark
that baptized men had set foot on Darien, except a
few Anglo-Saxon curses, which, having been uttered
more frequently and with greater energy than any
other words in our language, had caught the ear and
been retained in the memory of the native population
of the Isthmus."

But to return. Through the reigns of James I. and
Charles I., the habit of swearing continued in the
higher as well as the lower classes. It was checked
somewhat in the despotic domination of the Puritan
Commonwealth, but broke out again, at the restoration of Charles II., with a fury that nothing could
withstand. Macaulay tells us that in the reaction
from the austerity of the Commonwealth the generation that succeeded delighted in doing and saying
whatever would most shock their defeated enemies.
As the Puritan " never opened his mouth except
in Scriptural phrase, the new breed of wits and fine

gentlemen never opened their mouths without utter-
ing ribaldry of which a porter would now be ashamed,
and without calling on their Maker to curse them,
sink them, confound them, blast them, and damn
them."

" The Glorious Revolution of 1688," whatever it did
for constitutional liberty, did not do much to make
profanity unfashionable. Lawrence Hyde, Earl of
Rochester, did not swear in his cups more lustily
than Sir Robert Walpole, the astute Whig Premier,
in his orgies at his country seat. Pelham, and his
brother, the Duke of Newcastle, afterward the heads
of the great Whig connection, were not famous for
profanity, neither was Chatham ; but the plays of the
period, and the novels of Fielding and Smollett, prove
that profanity was quite an ordinary exercise of the
English lungs. To " swear like a lord " became, with
the rustic as well as the city populace, as much an
object of admiring wonder, as " to get as drunk as a
lord." Even women of rank did not hesitate to imi-
tate — of course, at a respectful distance, befitting their
inferior sex — the more masculine profanity of the
acknowledged lords of creation. It is difficult to say
how long they availed themselves of their precious
privilege. Sarah, Duchess of Marlborough, who did
not die — much to the regret of her relatives — until
1744, once called at the house of an eminent judge
on business. Learning from the footman that he was
not at home, the old harridan departed, in one of her
furious fits of irritation, without condescending to

mention her august title. The servant, when questioned by the judge on his return to the house as to the name of his visitor, could only answer that she had not mentioned her name, but that " she swore like a lady of quality."

There is, unhappily, a class of men who, in different degrees of depravity, seem possessed by the devil. They experience a strange delight in exalting their own wills above all moral law. They are sufficient to themselves. They despise what they call the poor weaklings of superstition, who are ruled by such abject sentiments as wonder, reverence, and awe. They disbelieve in them because they have never felt them. They are under the delusion of a moral and mental color-blindness, and have no vision of spiritual facts that are plain to humbler mortals. It is difficult to assert that they have souls, either to be saved or to be exposed to the other alternative; but if beneath the thick scum of evil experience that has settled on their minds and characters there remains a faint, unextinguished spark of immortal fire, their souls are of a kind that " rot half a grain a day," and promise to go on rotting until they reach the appointed term of their earthly lives. These creatures find a strange pleasure in showing their superiority to common folk, by disgusting all decent people whose ears unfortunately come within reach of their tongues, by their ribaldry, and shocking by their blasphemy all devout people that are placed in the same predicament. The world has been sufficiently sermonized on the sin of

self-righteousness; but neither preacher nor satirist
seems to have emphasized the opposite vice, namely,
self-unrighteousness, though it is but too common.
The self-righteous man is ever self-complacent when
he views the multitude of trembling sinners that have
not, as he has, a through ticket to pass from the tomb
to the Celestial Kingdom, signed by the proper authority; the self-unrighteous man, scorning all consideration of the possible life beyond the grave, laughs
at the fears of those whose cry is, "What shall I do
to be saved?" and by his conduct and conversation
seems to be eager to mock the supplication of penitent hearts by defiantly substituting for it that other
question, "What shall I do to be damned?"

It is curious how many men of eminent ability, or
eminent frivolity, have asserted their self-unrighteousness in this fashion. The frivolous do it to astonish
their fellow-coxcombs by a display of what they call
courage, with probably little deeper feeling than that
of the good boy, brought up to reverence holy things
on the mechanical method adopted by his self-righteous parents, who accordingly hated in his heart all
the uncomprehended words they had lodged, by a ma-
chine process, in his memory, and who sulkingly con
fided his secret scepticism to a companion of his own
age and degree of theological culture, as they returned
one Sunday from church, in the words that he "didn't
care for God, nor Christ, nor any of 'em!" But this
desecration of what is essentially sacred is connected,
even in the most frivolous natures, with a certain per-

versity, which Edgar Poe thought, or said he thought, inherent in the constitution of human beings. It certainly seemed in him to be inherent; it doubtless in many cases comes, like the gout or any other transmitted physical disease, by inheritance; but as to the mass of human beings perversity is generally the perversion of qualities originally intended for good. When it appears in shallow minds and hearts, this perversity is expressed in the fundamental dogma of profligacy, that vice and profanity confer distinction. Consequently, a rivalry springs up among the professors of this school of licentiousness and blasphemy, and lies are told by these aspirants for an infamous reputation, not for the purpose of denying the crimes against society that they have actually committed, but for the purpose of circulating monstrous rumors of their success in blasting the reputations of virtuous wives whom they know only by name, and of unspotted maidens they may have chanced to meet in a drawing-room. So great a poet as Byron stooped to this ignoble ambition. The published " Memoirs " that relate to the social manners and ethics of both France and England during the last and the first quarter of the present century, are full of details respecting this detestable race of shallow-hearted, feather-brained, and thoroughly depraved coxcombs. The creatures still survive, often in the highest circles of fashionable society. To do them justice, it must be admitted that they are commonly physically brave. The English Guards, at the battle of Waterloo, maintained their reputation for valor better than the Imperial Guard that "dies but never surrenders;" and their gallantry forced from Wellington the curt remark, "The puppies fight well." In the Crimean War the "dandy" officers exhibited the same English pluck, with, we trust, a higher regard for morality.

It may be said that those who have contracted the habit of using oaths to give force, emphasis, or audacity to their conversation, are roughly divisible into two classes, — the reclaimable and the irreclaimable. The first class is composed of men who swear from the surface and not from the substance of their minds; who, provided they have a sufficiently strong motive, can cure themselves of the habit, as they can cure themselves of the habit of smoking or drinking, by means of reflection and volition. It is difficult, however, to rouse careless and heedless natures to a sense of the folly and indecorum, not to say the wickedness, of their flippant blasphemies. Charles Lamb, when once asked why he did not give up the practice of smoking, humorously replied, "Because I cannot find an equivalent vice." It is in some such light way that practitioners in swearing are apt to evade the remonstrances of friends whose sense of decency their easy and voluble stream of profanity disgusts or shocks. Still, these men are reclaimable, though after conquering the habit they may occasionally show that they once allowed themselves to be conquered by it. Thus, we knew a man of talent and energy who had cultivated the art of swearing from his youth upward, but who, in mature age, had married, had become a father, and had to some degree " experienced " religion. Still, in moments of high emotion, when he was off his guard, an oath would slip into the beginning of a sentence that ended in something like a prayer. Thus, on one occasion, when he was dilating to us on the theme of his happiness in his new life, he rapturously exclaimed, " By ——! my friend, when I look at that child of mine, and think of what he may become to me, I feel thankful to God that he has vouchsafed to me such a blessing!"

The second class of swearers we have called the irreclaimable, for the reason that profanity has become a part of their organism. About thirty years ago an Englishman, who had been lessee and manager of Drury Lane Theatre, and in that capacity had had an altercation with Macready which resulted in a prosecution against the actor for a personal assault, came to the United States for the purpose of lecturing on the stage. His memory was full of recollections of distinguished actors, and his power of mimicking their great " points " was remarkable. His imitations of the elder Kean were specially notable, in respect both to voice and gesture. But his seemingly unconscious profanity astonished even those whose oaths were about one in ten or fifteen of the words they used in familiar conversation. He swore as instinctively as he breathed. At a dinner to which he had been invited, the present writer sat on the right side of him and a clergyman on the left. The latter was introduced to him as

Doctor C. Mr. B. began to talk fluently of his experience with actors and of the drama, sprinkling his
sprightly narratives with so many unnecessary expletives that his right-hand neighbor had to whisper to
him that Doctor C. was not a doctor of medicine, but
a doctor of divinity. The scene that ensued was supremely ludicrous. Mr. B. turned, with extreme earnestness and politeness, to the clergyman, professed his
great regard for "the cloth," dashed his eyes, body,
and soul to everlasting perdition, declared if he had
known the profession of his auditor he would not have
used such words as might be offensive to his sacer-
dotal ears, and in three minutes contrived to condense
into his apology more blasphemies than he poured
forth in the original offence. Everybody present must
have been impressed with the fact that in him, as in
many similar swearers, profanity was a secretion in
the throat.

We have only space to devote a little consideration to what may be called executive swearing.
Though this may be more or less effective as a means
of menace and intimidation, as it comes from the
mouths of resolute, aggressive, strong-minded, coarse-
grained men, who are habitual swearers, it has still
the greatest power when occasionally employed by the
strict economists of the language of profanity. The
rarity of an oath increases its force. General Lee
felt the truth of this when Washington, at the battle
of Monmouth, discharged upon him a series of maledictions for his misconduct, which owed their smiting

force to the fact that he had been selected from all the
subordinate generals of the Revolutionary army to call
forth such unaccustomed words from the lips of the
general-in-chief. " Beware," says the poet, " beware
the anger of a patient man." Fortitude and self-command are not virtues of cold natures, but are really
powers fused into intrepid character by an inward fire,
the external expression of which is sternly repressed ;
but there are occasions in war — though General
Grant seems never under any circumstances to have
been provoked into profanity — when folly, stupidity,
disobedience to orders, or treachery, is so plain that
the hidden heat in the heart of the commander rends,
for a time, all obstructions to its seemingly profane
utterance, and blazes out in words that strike the person at whom they are aimed with the effect of blows.
In the lives of most eminent men, specially distinguished for their fortitude, we notice these infrequent
escapes of moral wrath, though the terms in which
they are clothed may be such as disgust us in the
language of a pot-house belcher of oaths. Shakspeare, who has touched almost every phase of human
character, has not overlooked these occasional outbursts of passion in men that are noted for coolness,
self-possession, and self-command. Take this passage
from the third act of " Othello " : —

"*Iago.* Is my lord angry ?
   Emilia. He went hence but now,
And certainly in strange unquietness.
   Iago. Can he be angry ? I have seen the cannon,
When it hath blown his ranks into the air,

And, like the devil, from his very arm
Puffed his own brother : and can he be angry ?
Something of moment then ; I will go meet him ;
There's matter in 't indeed, if he be angry."

This parsimony in the use of profane expressions is
specially noticeable in men of business, when the merchant or banker is a man of integrity and of high business capacity. There is, of course, a large number
of traders whose natures are irritable, petulant, and
passionate, who seize every opportunity to exercise
their proficiency in profanity ; who swear jocosely
when they have made a good bargain, and fiercely
when they have made a bad one ; who pester the ears
of their clerks and shopmen from morning to night
with their resounding execrations, and impartially
curse their Maker whether they have failed or succeeded in cheating others. Such shops and counting-
houses are kindergartens for the practical teaching of
blasphemy. But able men of business rarely indulge
in this license of the tongue. A number of years ago
we knew intimately a Boston banker of exceptional
capacity, who in all conditions of the money-market,
especially in periods of financial panic, was ever im-
perturbably calm. It happened that on one occasion
he had joined in a moderately successful speculation
with an outside operator, and his partner for the time
was to come at ten o'clock in the forenoon to claim
his share of the profits. At nine o'clock the banker
had placed in his hands proofs that the other party
had played false in the whole transaction. The would-

be swindler entered the office of him whom he considered his dupe, in an easy, confident manner. The banker looked not so much at as through him, subjected him to a few stern, searching questions, and the scamp's confused and hesitating answers confirmed his guilt. Then came out the hoarded wrath of the banker, in terms that seemed to force their way into the very soul of the detected trickster. His fit reply would have been, in the words of an old English dramatist,—

> "I have endured you with an ear of fire ;
> Your tongue has struck hot irons on my face ! "

But failing in these forcible expressions, which so well indicated the appearance of his ears and cheeks, he stumbled down the office stairs with the gait of a man consciously bound for the place to which he was wrathfully consigned. We do not remember having heard the banker swear either before or after this supreme occasion.

Some arbitrary rulers have a tendency to assume a certain grandiloquence in their oaths. William the Conqueror swore by "the Splendor of God;" Henry II., by "God's Eyes;" and Charles the Bold, by "the hundred thousand devils of hell,"—in this phrase indicating how accurate a census he had taken of those inmates of pandemonium who most had possession of himself. Other rulers, gifted with a strong sense of religious duty, have denounced terrible punishments against the profane. Saint Louis of France ordered that the tongue of the utterer of oaths should be branded with a red-hot iron; and his gay courtiers were driven to ingenious contrivances of verbal arrangement, by which they might express the substance of swearing without using the words. At the period of the English Commonwealth the soldier was compelled to abstain from profanity by fear of the penalties attached to its use. In 1649 a quartermaster was tried by a council of war for the offence, declared guilty, and sentenced, not only to have his sword broken over his head, and to be dismissed from the service, but to have his tongue bored with a red-hot iron. In the old drama of " The Witch of Edmonton," the author cautions, through the mouth of the devil himself, the passionate blasphemer against what may be the result of his callings on the devil : —

> " Thou never art so distant
> From an evil spirit, but that thy oaths,
> Curses, and blasphemies pull him to thine elbow."

Indeed, in hearing some men swear, the hearer is almost converted to the old doctrine of demoniac possession. What most impresses us, is the utter senselessness, the pure insanity, of his curses and maledictions. For it is the Almighty that this " aspiring lump of animated dirt " blasphemes. The folly of it can only be fitly described in that energetic and vivid passage in which Dr. South draws the contrast between the power of the offender and the divine object of his puny wrath. " A man so behaving himself," he says,

7

" is nothing else but weakness and nakedness setting itself in battle array against Omnipotence; a handful of dust and ashes sending a challenge to all the host of heaven. For what else are words and talk against thunderbolts, and the weak, empty noise of a querulous rage against him who can speak worlds, — who could word heaven and earth out of nothing, and can when he pleases word them into nothing again? "

DOMESTIC SERVICE.

WE live under a republican form of government, where the rights of the citizen are supposed to be jealously guarded by law. Leaving out some limitations on the right of voting, which will readily occur to every reader, the statement is correct. The political rights of the individual are on the whole well secured and maintained; but these are not sufficient to confer social happiness. Political rights enable a man to have a voice in deciding what persons shall rule over him, and make and execute the laws of the country. But his political well-being may be relatively perfect while his social well-being is constantly vexed and tormented by certain peculiarities in the organization, or rather disorganization, of his household. He votes at certain times and at certain places once, twice, or thrice a year, and the annual expenditure of time in exercising this august privilege of the freeman is hardly an hour; but—taking man and wife as one—as soon as he proudly leaves the polls and enters his own house, he is no longer an independent citizen of a "great and glorious country," but an abject serf, utterly dependent on the caprices of his domestics, or, as they are ironically named, his "help." He finds his wife the victim of an intolerable tyranny, which presses on her every day and almost every hour, exerting her energies in often vain attempts to put down an insurrection in the kitchen, or to conciliate the insurgents. He may have been during the day threatened by a strike of the laborers in his workshop, and have used all the resources of his patience, intelligence, and character in so adjusting matters that his men, being reasonable beings, agree to a compromise between labor and capital which does justice to both. When he arrives at his house he encounters a conflict in which sullen stupidity, or vociferous stupidity, each insensible to reason, is engaged in battle with the "lady of the house." This last conflict is too much for him; he commonly succumbs with the meekness of a galley slave, and with a rueful countenance tries to eat his half-done potatoes and over-done beefsteak with the solemn composure of a martyr at the stake.

It is important here to note that this is not a question of equality. The nominal master and mistress of the house may be just and humane, considerate of the rights of others, and sensitive not to wound their feelings; but they have to submit to the mortifying fact that the object of their help is to render them helpless; that a despotism is established in their house; and that their tyrants are their hired servants. There is more or less resistance going on for a time, but the autocracy of the kitchen is firmly established in the end. Frequent changes of help do little good. One spirit seems to animate the whole class. The

new-comers announce, in true monarchial fashion:
"The Queen is dead. Long live the Queen!" Those
who are dismissed find comfort, as they depart, in
hearing this triumphant strain from the lips of their
successors. They glow with the thought that the
household from which they are expelled will still be
taught to know that domestic life is indeed a "fitful
fever;" that the art of "slaughtering a giant with
pins" is not yet extinct in the world; and that the
process of converting homes into hells is as well
understood by the incoming as by the outgoing denizens of the house.

There is a story going the round of the newspapers
to this effect, that a wife, after reading the report of
Queen Victoria's speech, told her husband she was
now a convert to woman suffrage, as the queen had
made as good a speech as a king. Her husband
objected on the ground that Victoria, like the rest
of her sex, when she says anything always makes a
mess of it. "Look," he continued, "at the Irish —"
"Yes," she retorted, "look at the Irish. If she had
half the trouble with her Bridgets that I have, who
blames her —" "But that is a matter of statesmanship, and not of domestic affairs," was his response.
Her reply was crushing: "My dear, it requires statesmanship to run domestic affairs. You just try it."
Probably this excellent stateswoman, with her power
of managing refractory tempers and enforcing necessary rules, must often have been beaten in her efforts
to maintain her persuasive or belligerent supremacy,

— must have sometimes sighed as she heard what Hood calls that "wooden damn" with which Bridget, after a reproof, slams the door as she descends to the realms she rules, and heard, with a sinking of the heart, the crash of crockery (sworn to be accidental) which occurred soon afterward. In fact, no states-man or stateswoman has yet solved the problem — and it may be that it is a problem impossible to be solved by human skill and intelligence — how to har-monize the relations between those who hire and those who are hired, so that persons of limited in-comes can have a comfortable home. Take the ma-jority of modest householders, who set up house-keeping on fifteen hundred or twenty-five hundred a year, and ask them, after twenty years' experience of the petty miseries attendant on their employment of one or two domestics, the terrible pessimistic ques-tion, "Is life worth living?" and it is to be feared that their answer would be a sorrowful or splenetic or passionate "No!"

More than half a century ago, Colonel Hamilton, one of the officers who won their laurels in Welling-ton's campaigns in Spain and Portugal, published a book which he called "Men and Manners in America." He criticised both our men and manners with a caus-tic severity such as might have been predicted when a bigoted Scotch tory assailed the people and institu-tions of a republic. His work exasperated almost every American who read it, and Edward Everett never wrote a more popular paper than his scorching criticism of it in the "North American Review." The book is now forgotten. Still one sentence in it survives in the memories of antiquarians, and it is this: "In an American dinner party, the first dish served up is the roasted mistress of the house." It is to be supposed that the author only condescended to dine with persons distinguished by their opulence or official position; and it seems to prove that domestic service, fifty or sixty years ago, in the mansions of the rich was as much in a state of anarchy, owing to the incompetence or ill temper of the cook and her assistants, as it is now in humbler dwellings. Indeed, who has not occasionally seen, at ordinary dinner parties where no aristocratic Colonel Hamilton is present, the flaming countenance of the mistress of the house, as she takes her seat at the head of the table, indicating how hard has been her contest with her "help"?

But at the time a Mrs. Schuyler, or a Mrs. Adams, or a Mrs. Quincy may have appeared to the British guest as a victim to the incompetency of her cook, a representative of the great house of Devonshire was subject to a tyranny of another kind. The duke happened to be prejudiced against port wine, which those who were admitted to his great dinner parties preferred to other wines. The duke's butler, knowing his master's taste, provided the best champagne and claret that could be purchased in Europe, but bought the worst port he could find at a low price, and charged the duke at the price which was notoriously demanded by wine dealers for the best. The imposition was successful for years. Nobody who was invited to the dinners of a duke could dare to remonstrate against the liquid logwood they swallowed as port. At last one friend had the courage to tell the duke that his butler was a rascal. The result was an investigation of the facts; the offending servant was ignominiously dismissed, but not until he had amassed a comfortable amount of some two or three thousand pounds as a compensation for his disgrace.

This is a pertinent illustration of the difference between our domestics and those of England. People are never tired of berating ours as barbarians, and contrasting them with those of England, who are thoroughly tamed and trained, and do their work with exemplary skill and propriety. In the great houses of England most of the servants are sycophantic and crafty, bending their knees in prostrate adoration before the "gentry" they serve, but at the same time taking every secure opportunity to pick their pockets. An English servant of an English noble is apt to be the most ignoble of men.

But the female English domestic is the ideal of many American women who can afford to hire one. The history and literature of England show the incorrectness of this assumption. Take the literature of England from the time of Charles the Second, and you will find that a majority of the clear-cited dramatists and novelists represent the servant maids as the obedient accomplices of their mistresses in every questionable act they do but plundering those whom they serve. Even to the present day one can hardly enter a theatre without finding the pert and unscrupulous chambermaid of the comedy to be a lively combination of liar and trickster, an expert in effrontery, malice, and mischief, and destitute equally of the sense of honor and the sense of shame.

In the last century, Fielding condensed the whole class in his Mrs. Slipsop. " My betters ! " she indignantly exclaims, " who is my betters, pray ? " As to the large question of domestic service, Dickens and Thackeray, in our own generation, have shown what people have to endure in the continual hostility between the kitchen and the drawing-room. David Copperfield, when he has won the adorable Dora, his " child wife," is daily tormented by the doings and misdoings of the wretches she employs as servants, and whom the adorable Dora is utterly incapable of converting into " help ; " and in the household of Mr. Dombey, what a picture is presented of the kitchen aristocracy of the mansion in which the great merchant dwells, and in which he has the pretension to believe that he is the lord and master ! How is he looked down upon, when he fails, by the meanest menial whose business it is to scrub the floors of his house ! Indeed, the description of the assembly of Mr. Dombey's domestics, when it is known that the firm of Dombey & Son has fallen into cureless ruin, is one of Dickens's masterpieces. Thackeray, in all his novels, seems to be haunted with the idea

of the utter falsity of English domestics, from the
august butler of the palatial mansion down to the
wench who does the lowest work of the cheap boarding-house. He is never more cynical than when he
records the scandalous and unfavorable judgments
delivered by the tenants of the kitchen on their masters and mistresses. One would hesitate, indeed, to
undertake the forming of a household in England, if
he were dolorously impressed by Thackeray's monitions as to the essential antagonism between those
who dwelt below the drawing-room and those who
dwelt in the room itself. The two, being separated
by distinction of caste, can rarely have with each
other cordial human relations. There may be formal subordination and obedience on the part of the
servants; but hate, envy, uncharitableness, rankle
beneath the mask of sycophancy they wear.

Much has been written about realistic fiction as
distinguished from fiction which is eminently unreal-
istic; and English novelists who belong to the latter
class are still prone to push upon the attention of
their readers a revival of the old feudal relation
between mistress and maid. It seems from these
novels that they are bound together by the ties of
mutual affection. The mistress condescends to make
her maid her confidante, confides to her all her
griefs and joys, and is rewarded for her protecting
kindness by awakening in the bosom of her maid
a sentiment of love which is entirely independent of
self-interest. The husband of the lady is ruined by

a trusted friend, who proves to be a villain, or he is
made a bankrupt by some unfortunate speculation,
or he is suspected of a crime which compels him to
fly from his home and country, — at any rate, he dies
forever or disappears for a time. The disconsolate
wife or widow calls the roll of her " pampered min-
ions," pays them their wages up to the day of their
separation, and they depart from the house with an
ill-concealed scorn of their ruined employer. But one
aged domestic remains; she protests that she will
never leave her mistress; she will serve her without wages, — nay, all the money she has saved up for
a series of years shall be forthcoming at this moment of financial distress in the household ; and ends
by flinging herself into the arms of her dejected mistress, and in a flood of tears declares that she will
never desert her beloved mistress — never! never!!
never!!! Three points of admiration hardly do justice to the pathos of the scene. Scores of novels
might be named in which it is rehearsed to the immense satisfaction of sentimental readers, who would
never do anything of the kind themselves. Practical
people are now apt to consider this disinterested, this
sublime self-devotion of the feminine servant to the
feminine employer as something bordering on the un-
real, so far as their experience goes. Perhaps some
of them are malicious enough to remember Mrs.
Micawber's repeated statement to David Copperfield,
when the hot punch was passed around the table,
that, despite the injurious opinions which her dis-

tinguished relations had formed of her husband's capacity to get an honest living for himself and family, she would never desert Mr. Micawber — never, never, never !

Indeed, persons of limited incomes, whether poets, scientists, mechanics, clerks, or philanthropists, are commonly subjected, and always have been subjected to the tyranny of domestics, without regard to their place of residence in one country or another. Neither genius, nor integrity, nor virtue, nor fame, nor saintliness of character, can check a virago's tongue when she condescends to enter a comparatively poor man's home, after she has served an apprenticeship, even as scullion, in the mansion of a millionnaire. Perhaps nothing could better illustrate this fact than to cite an instance from the biography of one of the most prominent poets of the century. Thomas Campbell, after publishing " The Pleasures of Hope," and many immortal lyrics, such as " Hohenlinden," " Ye Mariners of England," and " The Battle of the Baltic," which had thrilled the whole nation, settled down in Sydenham with his wife and child, — poor, but with a great and wide poetical fame. In a letter to another immortal, Walter Scott, he humorously narrates a comic epic which had occurred in his own home. It seems that he hired a cook, recommended to him as faithful and sober, who had been, with her husband, for many years on board of .a man-of-war. In the course of seven weeks, however, she developed her real character, and went from bad to worse. "One fatal day," Campbell says, "she fell upon us in a state of intoxication, venting cries of rage like an insane bacchanalian, and tagged to our names all the opprobrious epithets the English language supplies. An energetic mind, in this state of inflammation, and a face naturally Gorgonian, kindled to the white heat of fury, and venting the dialect of the damned, were objects sufficiently formidable to silence our whole household. The oratrix continued imprecations till I locked up my wife, child, and nurse to be out of her reach, and descending to the kitchen, paid her wages, and thrust her forthwith out of my doors, she howling with absolute rage. During the dispute, she cursed us for hell-fire children of brimstone, whose religion was the religion of cats and dogs. I asked the virago what was her religion, since her practice was so devout. 'Mine,' says she, 'is the religion of the Royal Navy,' at the same time showing a prayer-book. After vainly trying to set the house on fire, this curious devotee set off for London on the top of a stage-coach, cursing as she went."

It seems to us that this is a typical scene. It has been witnessed since by so many small householders, that it is needless to remind them that a certain element of ceremonial religion mixes with the ribaldry and blasphemy of such domestics. "Mine," the drunken brute exclaims, "is the religion of the Royal Navy." All persons who have borne an active part in turning such creatures out of their houses must have noticed that a vague sense of formal piety finds utterance in their wild maledictions; still it is a piety which comforts itself in predicting sure future damnation to the masters or mistresses who call it forth. But perhaps the worst of the matter is, that such domestic hornets develop the habit of swearing in employers who previously had shown no tendency to the vice. Indeed, to many heads of families a course of housekeeping is a school of profanity.

The domestic service of the United States is mostly composed of immigrants who differ from their employers in race, manners, and religion. In one of the most splendid orations of Edward Everett, he happily contrasted the peaceful emigrants who came from Ireland, Germany, and other European countries to settle here, with the descent of the barbarians on the Roman Empire. The former came to increase enormously the wealth and productive power of the nation they peacefully invaded; the warlike mission of the latter was to destroy and devastate what the genius and industry of former centuries had accumulated. The former came to create new capital; the latter to annihilate the capital which had previously been added to the stores of civilization. Indeed, the immense debt which we owe to what is called foreign labor — though laborers from abroad are so swiftly assimilated into the mass of our citizens, that the word foreign hardly applies to them — is practically incalculable. It has been for some time considered that the yearly additions to our population from this source is, in a great degree, an index of our advancing prosperity.

There are evils resulting from this rush of new powers and influences into the rapid stream of our American life, but the evils are overcome in time by counterbalancing good. It certainly is provoking to have a few foreign socialists, escaping perhaps from the prisons of their native countries, or from the fear of being imprisoned in them, coming to this land of liberty and labor, and in corner groceries and lager-beer saloons announcing the doctrine that laborers cannot get their rights, unless they begin their crusade against capital by robbery, arson, and murder ; but it is hard to convince a workman who really works, that he is to become better off by destroying the palpable and permanent monuments of previous generations of laborers, such as houses, mills, railroads and, other evidences of labor capitalized. Indeed, the belligerent socialist is merely a reproduction of Attila and Alboin, acting a part which is foreign to our present civilization.

This is one side of foreign immigration, — its beneficent side. The other side relates to the mothers, daughters, and sisters of the inflowing host, who " go out to service," and who control most of the business. The gradual disappearance of American girls from service in families is a calamity both to themselves and the public, and it is based on an absurd prejudice that they lower their position and forfeit their independence in doing what they call menial work. They

accordingly rather prefer to labor in factories, or
swell the crowd of half-starved sewing-women, than
to gain board, lodging, and good wages in a private
family. The result is that the Irish, German, and
Swedish women, who have had no education qualifying them for the business of cooks and general household work, learn their duties by experimenting on the
meats given them to prepare for the table, and on the
floors and carpets they are to scrub or sweep. This
Kindergarten system results in educating them at last
into domestics, but it is at the expense of a great
breaking of crockery, a series of burnt steaks and
chops which are uneatable, and a trial of the employer's patience, which gradually results in nervous
prostration. The servants undoubtedly follow the
Baconian theory that knowledge is obtained by observation and experiment; but their experiments resem-
ble those of the Irish pilot, who, after remarking to
the captain of the ship that the coast was full of
sunken rocks, casually added as the vessel struck,
"and that is one of 'em!"

It would be a lesson in the study of human nature
to note all the varieties of experience which the mistress of a house passes through when one servant,
who has been educated in this way, departs, and
another, who has also obtained an approximate idea
of what good housekeeping means, applies for the
vacant place. There is no form of "interviewing"
more prolific than this of incidents illustrating the
conflicts and collisions of adverse specimens of

human character. There, for instance, is the interesting invalid, who is bullied and browbeaten by the energetic virago who storms into the house, demands the wages which she thinks her services are worth, obtains them, and then dominates the household, reigning supreme until the master of the establishment is compelled to interfere, and dismisses her with words that savor more of strength than of righteousness. The list might go on to include the fretful, the economical, the bad-tempered, the shrewd, the equitable, the humane female heads of households that require help, but find it difficult to procure from those who offer it. Perhaps it would be well to condense and generalize the whole matter in dispute by citing an example in which the applicant for a situation was confronted by a woman who had a touch of humor in her composition. In all the dignity of second-hand finery, resplendent with Attleboro' diamonds and rubies which must have cost at the least a quarter of a dollar a gem, the towering lady sweeps into the parlor, and demands a sight of the lady of the house. The meek lady of the house appears. " I understand you want a second girl to do the housework." " Yes," is the gentle response. The high contracting parties forthwith proceed to discuss the terms of the treaty by which the claimant for the office of second-girlship will condescend to accept the place, stating her terms, her perquisites, and her right to have two or three evenings of every week at her own disposal, when her engagements will compel her

8

to be absent from the house. The reply is, " It seems
to me, if we comply with your terms, it would be
better for my husband and myself to go out to service
ourselves, for we never have had such privileges as
you claim." " That is nothing to me. I have lived
in the most genteel families of the city, and have
always insisted on my rights in this matter. By the
way, have you any children?" " Yes, I have two."
" Well, I object to children." " If your objections,
madam, are insuperable, the children can easily be
killed." " Oh! you are joking, I see. But I think I
will try you for a week to see how I can get along
with you." The curt response is: " You shall not try
me, but the one minute which elapses between your
speedy descent from those stairs, and your equally
speedy exit from the door." The high contracting
parties being unable, under the circumstances, to for-
mulate a treaty agreeable to both, the applicant for
the vacant place disappears in a fury of rage.

It may be said that this is a caricature of what
actually occurs in such interviews and encounters;
but it has an essential truth underneath its seeming
exaggeration. In almost all the professions and occupations in which men are engaged, the supply is commonly more than equal to the demand. In domestic
service the supply of intelligently trained servants is
notoriously far short of the demand. One must notice
the readiness with which clubs, of late, are formed,
for advancing all imaginable causes which can arrest
the attention of intelligent, patriotic, philanthropic

men. They meet weekly, fortnightly, or monthly, at
some hotels noted for their excellent method of cook-
ing the fish and flesh which are daily on the dinner-
tables of the members, but cooked on a different
method. The Sunday newspapers report the effusions
of eloquence which the Saturday meetings call forth.
The clubs multiply also with a rapidity which puzzles
ordinary observers to account for their popularity.
Perhaps a simple reason may be timidly ventured as
an explanation of this phenomenon. Men who are
classed as prosperous citizens like a good dinner,
which they cannot get at home, and at stated periods
they throng to a hotel, where the Lord sends the
meats, and at the same time prevents the devil from
sending the cooks.

It will be said that this attack on the present disorganization of our domestic service is one-sided. It is.
Doubtless much may be urged in reply, arraigning the
conduct of employers, and defending that of the em-
ployees. Many evils of the present relations between
the two might be averted by a mutual understanding
of each other's motives and aims. Still the previous
education of domestics, not only in the enlightenment
of their minds, but in the regulation of their tempers,
is the pressing need at present. If some charitable
person should start a College for the Education of
Female Domestics, its success in increasing human
happiness would prompt others to follow in his lead.
Such a college might turn out thousands on thousands
of competent servants every three or four months.

The diplomas it would give would command attention at once; and the way now followed, of sending to the girl's "references" and receiving evasive replies, would be discountenanced. It would also give all classes of domestics a great lift in social estimation; the certificates, that they have graduated with honor in such colleges, would be equivalent to the B.A. or A.M. of colleges of another sort, when a young student applies for the position of schoolmaster in a country town or village. At any rate, a vast mass of unnecessary misery in families might be prevented, and a large addition made to the stock of human happiness.

In the various works written by devout, learned,
and "liberal" theologians on the harmony between
religion and science, there appears to be a general
oversight of the "esoteric" doctrine — the inner and
fundamental principle — of much current scientific
theorizing. Theologians are apt to consider the question as if it were simply a question of the credibility
of the Bible. It goes much deeper than that. It
relates to religion itself, — not merely to the Christian
religion, but to all religions. Historically it is admitted, on rationalistic grounds, that what is called
"the spiritual nature of man" demands a religion of
some kind. The philosophic scientists question the
propriety of this appeal to man's spiritual nature.
The theological rationalists are, in fact, quite orthodox in comparison with many of the theorists of
"advanced" and advancing science. And even
among the latter there are degrees of audacity.
Some of them question the possibility of a personal
God, but are willing to compromise with man's
"spiritual nature" by admitting the validity of a
vague Pantheism. Others, shocked at the sentimentality of their speculative brethren, remind them that
Pantheism is as much opposed to positive science as

Deism. The human understanding, according to the
latter class, is simply the result of a development of
the forces of Nature, which dates back to the nebulous mist out of which worlds were formed, and
which arrived at last, through the travail of un-
counted millions of years, to the brain of the monkey,
and has thence been developed into the brain of
Aristotle and Descartes, of Dante and Shakspeare,
of Kepler and Newton. Conceding that God, or gods,
may be ahead in this process of development, it is an
outrage, they insist, on common sense to assert that
either God or gods are back of it. " We know," they
say, " nothing of the matter ; our faculties are too
limited to see any sense in what theological and
metaphysical dogmatists have confidently announced.
But, modest thinkers as we are, we recommend that
men confine themselves within the sphere of positive
knowledge. In positive knowledge no God is apparent. On our theories of positive knowledge, no God
can ever be apparent ; for finite intelligence must
ever be confined within the limits of finite facts and
laws. We can get along very well without your hypothesis of a creative God, — a hypothesis which has
now, in the language of a selfishly sagacious French
bookseller, lost all interest with the public. You say,
quoting one of your antiquated religious books, that
the heavens declare the glory of God ; we say, after
M. Comte, that they rather declare the glory of
Kepler, Newton, and La Place. You say, from the
same authority, that man was created a little lower

than the angels ; we are satisfied in knowing that he
has been developed into a condition which is now,
thanks to " natural selection," a good deal higher
than that of the monkeys. The fundamental point
of difference between you and us is this : " That we
do not admit your right to speak of a living God,
either personal or impersonal. In making the assertion, you simply show your ignorance of the progress
of scientific philosophy, based, as it is, on ascertained
facts and demonstrated laws. At the best, your assumption must be considered premature. All we
know is that we have got far beyond our immediate
ancestor, the monkey. Monkey has become man.
Rest in that consoling fact."

Theologians and metaphysicians, who may be disposed to be perfectly fair to their opponents, answer
these theorists in this way : " Admitting your explanation of what we call the creation of nature and
man, there is still no need to deny a Creator. Your
theory, supported as it is by many facts scientifically
established, but with many other facts entirely un-
explained, may be God's method of creation. We
are willing to admit that He created, according to
your conceited method ; but why deny him ? " The
scientific theorists answer : " We can do without
him." " But where did you get your nebulous matter ? " " That," is the sulky reply, " is something
outside of positive science." " But you, after all, rest
the world, as in the old times, when philosophy was
notoriously un-positive, on an elephant ; and you can't

find anything for the elephant to stand on." "We don't trouble ourselves to find anything for it to stand on. That's a work beyond the capacity of the human faculties." " But, if it be beyond the capacity of the human faculties, it is still shown by experience that it is not beyond the capacity of human nature." "What you call human nature, as distinguished from human intelligence, is a confused mass of stuff, made up of sentiment and imagination, and of no logical bearing on the question." In short, men of this kind indicate, mentally, a disease similar to that which oculists style color-blindness. People afflicted with color-blindness are often gifted with more than ordinary understanding; but it is impossible to argue with them on the difference between red and blue. " They do not see it." They are men of a vigorous intelligence, who, in a similar way, can get no idea of Cause. They are deficient in the power of perceiving it, and think that those who *do* perceive it are under a hallucination. The mental, like the bodily eye, is apt to be blind in some respects when it is uncommonly sharp-sighted in others.

It is obvious that the advanced guard of scientific theorists have, at least, as much *un*-scientific presumption, bigotry, and intolerance as some of their most unreasonable theological opponents. Hypothesis is an admirable aid and guide to investigation; but it is as intolerable when it dogmatizes scientifically as when it dogmatizes theologically. Positive philosophy has no right to go beyond generalized

knowledge, from theories of the universe, and then
enforce them on the intelligence of mankind as indisputable facts, which it is idiotic or superstitious
to deny or to denounce. It violates its own principles
in attempting to explain what it declares to be essentially unexplainable. The heart of the mystery
has notoriously not been yet reached by science. If
we give up the old idea that man was created in
the image of God, let us have manliness enough to
refuse assent to the proposition that he was created
after the image of Huxley, or Darwin, or Spencer.
However much we may honor the force and com-
prehensiveness of such individual minds, they still
are not gods. Holmes in a recent paper humorously
wonders whether the race will hereafter substitute
Anno Darwini for *Anno Domini;* and thinks that,
even in case of such a change, the convenient A. D.
will be retained. This stroke of wit lights up as by
a flash of lightning the absurdity of supposing that
any scientific theory of the present day can control
the science of a thousand years hence.

But, leaving out of view the scientific theories
which are put forward to satisfy man's insatiable
intellectual curiosity, the essential question comes up:
" Will man, centuries hence, be content to substitute
generalized knowledge for religion ? "

It seems to us that the inmost essence of man,
his soul, will more than keep pace with the progress
of his mind in knowledge. God will be as near to his
heart as now, and as distant from his understanding

as now. The Divine nature will never lose its intimate
hold on human nature, and never be comprehended
by the human intellect. God will be everlastingly *in*
the soul of man, and everlastingly *outside* of the grasp
of his thought. As the scientific development proceeds, it will be more and more felt that God leads it
on. His "grace" will be recognized by future New-
tons, as well as by future Wesleys. We were never
more struck by an intense shock of surprise than
when we heard a distinguished naturalist say, at a
dinner-table, that at the critical moment of his investigations, at the time his mind was on the brink of a
discovery — at the time he was, as he thought, penetrating into a jealously guarded secret of Nature — he
involuntarily uttered a prayer to God to guide and
direct him. He felt, he said, the Divine Presence as
soon as he really entered His heretofore concealed
domain. He was impressed with his own individual
nothingness in coming into direct contact with a new
natural truth. He prayed by instinct, not by reflection. Indeed, he would be rejected now from
most churches as imperfect in the faith; but still
he prayed while he was in the spiritual ecstasy of
discovering. He felt the need of divine "help" in
his human work, and he frankly acknowledged it.

We suppose that no thinker is more repugnant to
orthodox divines than Ernest Renan. His defects
are obvious; but he is still true to what may be
called the right side of the fundamental question at
present argued between theologians and such scien-

tists as ignore or deny God.   He accepts the theories
of development and evolution without a question.   In
a remarkable article, contributed some ten years ago
to the "Revue des Deux Mondes," but of which his
admirers equally with his adversaries seem to be
strangely ignorant, he regrets that he had not chosen
science rather than history for his work in life.   But,
he adds, what is science but history in its most comprehensive form ?   Science gives the history of evolution, in the long passage of the nebulous mist into
its final product, the brain of man.   That, says
Renan, is God's method, as far as science now knows
it.   But science shows that, in the slow but sure
operation of natural laws, the solar system must be
destroyed.   Still the catastrophe is far from being
probable, much less certain.   A million of years is a
comparatively short period in the figures of astronomy.   If scientific men have during the past hundred
and fifty years made such enormous advances in the
discovery, control, and application of the forces of
Nature, why should they not, in the course of a million years, contrive to arrest the seeming tendency
of our little solar system to self-destruction ?   In a
century and a half much has been done ; what may
not be done in ten thousand centuries in a " square "
fight of the quick faculties of mind against the slow
operations of matter ?   A hundred thousand of centuries would be a very moderate computation for any
disturbance which would knock our planet to pieces
and dissolve it into the shining dust out of which

systems are made. Our foremost men of science are
mere babes in knowledge, as well as in power, compared to the men who will rise within the next thousand years, if science and invention go on at their
present continually accelerated pace. Why, on this
principle, should not man at the end of a million
years obtain control of the whole solar system ?
Why should he not at that distant period be in the
position of the God of the present popular theology ?
But Renan is careful to add: Man in this supposed
enormous extension of his power over Nature, would
still find the Infinite just as far beyond his thought
as he is now, and just as near his soul as he is now.
No possible increase of his power can decrease the
sense of his dependence. The enlargement of his
knowledge can only give him a larger perception of
the Divine Omniscience ; the increase of his power
can only give him a more vivid feeling of the Divine
Omnipotence. Carry out the principle of human
progress as far as you may, extend it to the time
when man will be almost the master of Nature, and
God will be still as far off as he is now, and the
spiritual nature of man will crave him even more intensely than it did when " stocks and stones " were
worshipped as divinities.

We have referred to Renan because he happens
to be a person who feels the need both of the mind
and the heart. He is a " rationalist" of the extreme
type. He accepts both the facts and the theories of
scientists. But, in his French way, he still softly

exclaims, " Glory be to God ! " Mild, polite, complimentary as he is to the *savants*, he still says to them : " Gentlemen, your idea of ignoring God and the spiritual nature of man is Darwinism reversed. You will conduct us back to the monkeys, rather than aid us to extend the space which separates us from them."

In concluding, we would say that the idea of a personal and infinite God is at the base of all religion, as far as religion has any interest to the "advanced" scientists of the present time. Renan predicts that a million of years hence the scientists will be more inclined to admit this fundamental truth than they now seem disposed to be. It appears ridiculous to declare that God Almighty is still alive, and that our modern theorists have not succeeded in dethroning him. The disciples of Epicurus represented the gods as laughing at the folly and shortcomings of men. Can we not, without irreverence, think of God as, at least, *smiling* at the vagaries of the men that he has endowed with exceptionally vigorous powers of scientific speculation? He is everlastingly safe from all attempts of human beings to deny or ignore him ; but the sceptics are no less his agents than the believers. He uses them as instruments to keep practical piety on a level with doctrinal piety. Every revolt ends in adding to his adherents. That nobody can evade God is just as apparent in the present " enlightened " age as it was in the worst ages of superstition ; and it will be as apparent millions of years hence as it is now. The Devil himself serves Him. Indeed, the Devil is, after all, raised up, now and then, to teach theologians that there is something in their doctrines or in their lives which needs to be corrected.

AMERICAN PRINCIPLES.

I⊤ has been very well said that he has the best
digestion who never is reminded that he has any
digestion at all, and that the model of all stomachs
was that of the eupeptic clodhopper, who devoured
his food without any uncomfortable after-thoughts, or
ever knowing that he had any stomach. The same
principle holds good of the body politic, and it is a
sign that something is out of the way in the social
system whenever it is so restless as to be continually
feeling its pulse or looking at its tongue, and asking
the doctors what can be the matter. Our good Old
America is now somewhat in difficulty of this kind,
and has painful misgivings lest he may have taken
into his capacious mouth some foreign substances that
cannot possibly be assimilated. He is asking himself what is proper food for himself and his children,
somewhat more careful than usual of the distinction
between the true American and the foreign elements.
Sometimes our ambition has been to expatriate ourselves as much as possible, in our manners and habits
at least, if not in our residence. In the parlor or ball-
room we have been fond of being French ; at the con-
cert and opera, Italian ; over the cigar and the choco-
late, Spanish ; after dinner, over the bottle, not a few

have been inclined to be English ; at elections, the
fashion has been somewhat Irish ; in philosophy, German ; while a few inglorious citizens have been disposed to play the Turk, and, under the lead of Joe
Smith, run into abominations that would have made
Mohammed's beard curl with disgust.   Now we are a
little less ashamed of our own birth and breeding, and
our own natal star shines out with new radiance from
the studded heavens.   Some of our people have indeed
discovered new charms in Russia, and their polar star is
in the constellation of the Great Bear.   Not a few there
are who have been ready to doff the Hungarian plume
for the Russian sable, and pledge the nation to the Czar,
as before to the Magyar dictator.   But the most prominent tendency of late has seemed to be toward a more
positive nationality of our own ; and surely the present
position, as well as the intrinsic importance of the subject, justifies an article upon the characteristics of the
true American, as we understand them.

   We start in a very commonplace way, and maintain
that the true American is, first of all, true to his soil,
or to the land of his birth and home.   It is sometimes said, indeed, that it is a sorry kind' of feeling that attaches itself to localities ; that it is the
heart of a cat that stands by the mere place, while the
human heart goes with friends, and finds its home
wherever they are.   For this very reason we should
be true to our own country ; for we look upon it, not
so much as a vast tract of land, as the abode of our
friends, the sphere of our labor, and the inheritance

of our children. The land may be, in fact, called
the homestead of the nation, calling out at once our
toil and our tastes, our energy and our affections to
till and beautify its domain. We may even go further,
and say that the land is the physical framework of
the nation, — the earthly organism through which it
develops its powers. Look at our country in this
way, and instead of seeing so many square miles of
territory, we behold the limbs and features of a gigantic physical constitution. The great lakes and rivers
are our country's heart and arteries ; the mountains
the shoulders and backbone ; the forests the lungs ;
the sea-coast the arms ; the flowing winds and waters,
with all the great currents of trade, are the healthful
tides of circulation that feed and quicken the colossal
brain. Every country has its own peculiar form and
physiognomy, and ours is sufficiently marked to make
it ours. Bounded by twin oceans and their mighty
tributary gulfs and lakes, our America has a unity
from God's own hand ; and what God hath joined, let
not man try to put asunder. The Mississippi, with its
various roots and branches, repeats in every wave the
compact of our national union between North and
South. The twin oceans no longer divide East and
West. God has raised up two providential men to
join the Atlantic to the Pacific shore. Fulton's re-
volving wheel and Franklin's electric wire have made
San Francisco neighbor to New York ; and California
is but one of the pockets of our great seaports.

The American, in being true to his country, will be

9

true alike to its productive utilities and to its adapta
tion to beautiful tastes.   With him the useful and the
beautiful should be but different aspects of the same
bountiful heritage ; and in the march of his comprehensive and far-seeing policy, refinement walks hand
in hand with industry.   The landscape smiles more
sweetly to the eye from the plenty that is garnered
from well-tilled fields, and the trees of the forest
whisper a richer blessing when their murmur joins
with the voices of the children and parents whose
home rises from beneath the friendly shade.   Let the
physical resources of our country be developed by our
largest policy and bravest enterprise.   Let the mill-
wheels of the North cry out to the cotton of the South,
" Come forth, and let us work together, and weave
for our country a nobler tissue than the loom can produce ! "   Let the teeming grain-fields of the West
wave health and greeting to the workshops of the
East, in token of the mighty compact between the
agriculture and the mechanism of the nation.   Let
the gold that is washed by waters from the Rocky
Mountains shout out to the iron and the coal in the
Alleghanies, " Come forth, and let us run such a race
together as the world has never seen ! "   The gold
giving the sinews, and the iron the arms and feet, and
the coal the moving power in a campaign of peaceful
industry that shall make war hide his diminished head.
By a due encouragement of agriculture, by a judicious
protection of our own manufactures, by a wary guar-
dianship of our commerce, let all the industrial inter-

ests of the country be quickened and reconciled, until America shall be the blessing of Americans, without being the foe of any nation under the sun. Let beautiful tastes follow in the wake of wholesome utilities. Let every man who cuts down a tree, where its place is needed for nutritious grain, honor the beauty that falls to the ground, transfer its grace to the waving corn, and not fail to plant another tree wherever its shade is needed. Let the landscape-gardener, the surveyor, the architect, combine their taste with the teachings of Nature, and have an eye to radiant health and artistic beauty, quite as much as to gain and convenience. Let the poet and the orator not spare their gift, nor fail to weave into their verse and eloquence the names that stand for the loveliness and the grandeur of our land. God has given America goodly gifts, yet they have been too little developed. Her treasure, like that to which the divine kingdom was likened, is hidden in a field, and only he who tills the field faithfully can find it. Says that philosopher among geographers, Guyot: " America looks toward the Old World ; all its slopes and its long plains slant toward the Atlantic, toward Europe. It seems to wait with open and eager arms the beneficent influence of the man of the Old World. No barrier opposes his progress ; the Andes and the Rocky Mountains, banished to the other shore of the continent, will place no obstacle in his path." Thus invited by the very inclination of the land, the chosen man came, and began to cultivate his domain. The wilderness became a garden.

Stand at the mouths of one of our great rivers; look upon the forest of masts at our wharves, so freighted or fruited with the products of our soil, to be exchanged for the commodities of every land under the sun; read the returns of our census; then speak not of the great things that America has done, but of the grandeur of her future if her sons are only true to her soil.

Her sons — who are her sons? They, of course, who best embody her spirit and carry out her destiny. They are pre-eminently the sons who have the blood of the sires who made America our mother. We maintain, then, in the next place, that the true American is true to his blood, — the old blood that came hither from Europe in the veins of our wisest and strongest colonists (not last nor least of whom were the pilgrims of the "Mayflower," and the Dutch of Manhattan, our own peculiar ancestors). All history shows the power of blood over circumstances as much as agriculture shows the power of the seeds over the soils. The main strength of the American nation has come from the free people of Northern Europe. — the Teutonic, and especially the Anglo-Teutonic races, who brought liberty and law to the New World. We are not disposed to narrow down our nationality, much less our humanity, by any prejudices of race, and we are ready to allow that there has been a great deal of folly on both sides, in the quarrel between the Celtic and the Anglo-Saxon partisans. The Anglo-Saxon is but one tribe of that great division of the Caucasian family to which our people belong. As known in Europe, the Caucasian family has had three branches, — the Celtic, the Teutonic, the Slavonic. The Celt and the Teuton have had many a bloody quarrel with each other ; but of late much of their blood pulsated to the notes of the same martial music, under the flags of France and England, that waved together their defiance against the Slavonic banner floating on the the walls of Sebastopol. Of the three branches, thus far the most vigorous and fruitful in our modern history has been the Teutonic, and those who have been ingrafted upon its stock. Now it is very clear that the chief portion of the American people came from the Teutonic branch, no matter whether — as in the case of New England, Virginia, and Maryland — the seed went first from ·Northern Europe to England, and thence to America, and so became Anglo-Saxon ; or whether — as in the case of New York, New Jersey, and Pennsylvania — it remained in continental Europe until transplanted hither in the Dutch and Germans. Call the majority of our people Anglo-Teutonic, Anglo-Gothic, Anglo-Germanic, or Anglo-Saxon, as you will. No matter, if we only know what the terms mean, and designate by them the descendants of the Northern Europeans who came to America, and made the English language the voice of their faith and their freedom.

Two great classes of men appear in history : the one class impulsive, impassioned, tending strongly toward a sensuous ritual and a centralized priesthood and empire; more ready to persuade than to reason, to ·venture than to persevere; not a little prone to exaggeration alike in speech and action, yet full of generous enthusiasm, and, by very temperament, electric and eloquent; the other class self-poised, deliberate, jealous of priesthoods and thrones, calculating the end carefully, and very slow to yield an inch of the ground once taken; at the same time cautious and courageous, fond of solid comfort, yet readier far to starve than to beg, and more quick to deeds than words; constitutionally suspicious of large talk and fine sentiment. Of the former class the Celt is the most conspicuous and characteristic specimen, whether full blooded, as in most of Ireland, and in the Scotch Highlands, or modified by other races, as in France, Spain, and Italy. Of the latter class the Anglo-Teuton, or the Anglo-Saxon — if we must retain the common but somewhat incorrect word — is the most characteristic specimen that we can choose from the great Teutonic family to which he belongs. It is he who has given our country most of its character, ideas, and institutions. The Frenchman on our northern frontier with his volatile nature, the Spaniard at the South with his reserved, impassioned zeal, were not to rule; and the destinies of North America were to be decided chiefly by the race that founded Jamestown and Plymouth, and gave language and law to the land. If we are to distinguish at all between these two sets of English colonists, — the cavaliers of Virginia and the Puritans of New England, —

we must rank the latter as of the purer Teutonic type, and having less of the mixture of French blood which the Norman aristocracy received from their abode in France and bequeathed to the new nobility of Norman England. Yet in these the Northman's blood predominated over the Celtic mixture, and it may be said with truth that the main founders of the nation, whether English, or Dutch, or German, brought with them hither the hearts of freemen, and claimed every triumph of popular liberty not as the gift of a strange bounty but as the restoration of an old right. Our blood is free blood, and has been so for ages, during the march of our fathers from their first home in Central Asia to the western coast of Europe and thence to America. We sell our birthright whenever we sell our liberty for any price of gold or honor.

Yet follow out the lessons of our blood, and we find that our hearts are not bound to beat unkindly toward races of different lineage. The civilization of Europe has sprung from the mingling of the three great races of the Caucasian family. Who can spare from our literature the great names given by each branch, who scorn Copernicus because he was Polish and probably Slavonic, who scoff at Dante because Celtic, and who refuse to place them upon the same place of honor as our own Milton, and Shakspeare, and Newton? Surely the New World should not be less generous than the Old World, and we are not to repeat on these great shores the petty feuds that have fallen into disrepute in Europe. There is room for the Celt of every clime, whether from Italy, France, Scotland, or Ireland. Of the latter branch of the Celtic family we have had perhaps a little too much, especially of a certain quality. We have had too much of the dregs of Erin in our political cup, and the tea has been considerably too green for the pure American taste. But why not cure the evil in our own way, instead of borrowing any new tyranny from the British oppressor ? We are for giving the Irishman the same justice that others of similar blood and creed have found, and we are on this very ground in a better way to prevent his doing us the injustice which some of his bad advisers may have been scheming. We believe that there is a providential aspect in the relation of the Irish to America, and in the tendencies, old and new, which balance their influence. They, for the most part, represent the form of worship once supreme in Christendom, and thus hold up for our careful study and practical scrutiny the whole genius and history of ages which now stand embodied in churches and colleges whose crosses are rising on every side among our academic halls and city spires. The young, restless heart of the nation is thus rebuked by the stern rule of Hildebrand, and the new science of Yale and Harvard is now startled as by the spectre of the ancient Iona, roused from her sepulchral sleep in mouldering cells. The Celt brings hither a church that can teach the American many a lesson in personal discipline and spiritual experience ; yet he must have a very defective vision to see any prospect of Romanizing the heart of a nation in its whole history and progress so indomitably Protestant as ours. The old North blood in our veins never beat kindly toward the Pope ; the sons of the sea-kings never had much fancy for the amateur fisherman who professes to sit in Saint Peter's chair ; and the ancient quarrel is not likely to be made up so long as the blood lasts. Yet it should be a part of our freedom and faith to give all creeds liberty of utterance, and we are not in any way to invade the spiritual privileges of the new-comers to our shores because they are taught by a priesthood such as Charles Carroll recognized. Let us be willing to see the worthy elements in all religions, and not play the Pharisee in the name of Him whose gospel came from the Nazareth that the Pharisee scorned. If we fight Rome we must fight with our weapons, which we understand, and not with hers, in which we are no match for her. If we try to beat the Jesuits by secret cabals and conspiracies, they probably understand that game better than we. The better way is to fight darkness with light ; and every morning's sunshine with its expanding radiance teaches the true policy of freedom against spiritual despotism. Remember that the Celt must be Americanized in time, if we only let him be, and that nothing can tend more than personal proscription to arrest the virtually Protestant feeling that is already putting a check upon priestly interference in our financial and political affairs, and claiming for the Roman Catholic people the right to hold and control ecclesiastical property which they purchase. France has put a check upon Romish domination, and her chief prelates have been an honor and strength to the nation. May not American liberty do as much as the French throne, and pastors of the stamp of Fénelon and Cheverus here teach piety to their flocks without teaching servitude, and win souls to God without mortgaging our soil to the virtual subjects of a Roman king? The true course of toleration and caution will help the Celt as much as ourselves, and the sooner he learns in the true school a little of our own self-reliance, the better for all parties.

We must not forget to consider the providential balance between him and his emigrant companion the German, or between the Irishman, the Anglo-Saxon's original neighbor, and the German, so nearly his kinsman by common Teutonic origin. It will be well for us if we are sagacious in playing off the excesses of the two against each other, and offsetting Irish impulsiveness and zeal for the priesthood by the German's more phlegmatic individuality and political radicalism. Far more of a neutralizing power than we usually suppose comes from the constant battle going on between the more ultra German democratic organs and the Irish Catholic presses in this country. So long as one party maintains, as it sometimes does, that every church and all religion is a conspiracy against liberty, and the other maintains, as it sometimes does, that all liberty of opinion is impiety, and that a little burning of Bibles and Bible readers may not always be a bad thing, we are willing that they should use each other up, confessing that we feel somewhat like the backwoodsman's wife, who saw her drunken husband fighting with a bear, and said that for her part she was for fair play, and "did n't much care which licked." Neither, however, is to prevail; and the old blood, with its sober balance between freedom and order, is to carry the day against the new centralization and the new anarchy.

In some respects we may not be unwilling to win advantage from the new-comers to our shores. Perhaps our hereditary stiffness, in joint and manner, may be a little lessened by the contact with Celtic enthusiasm, and our tongues may be loosened by French vivacity as much as our roads are smoothed by Irish spades. Perhaps, too, our excessive proneness to luxury and ostentation may be somewhat corrected by German frugality and taste. We must not forget that Germany is famous for something more than lager bier, *sauerkraut*, and tobacco-pipes, and that the purest art and the deepest scholarship comes to us from countrymen of Luther and Schiller, who are sometimes in danger of starving on our shores for lack of the Yankee tact in catching the nimble dollar as it flies.

If fairly understood and judiciously treated, the foreign element cannot be a very dangerous one. By the last census the foreign-born portion constitutes but eleven per cent of our free population. If we make a rough guess and divide this eleven per cent into two equal parts, one would be nearly all Celtic and the other nearly all Teutonic. Thus, of these two drops of blood transfused into our body politic, the one is more quick with Celtic oxygen, the other more solid with Teutonic nitrogen, and the heart of the nation does not lose its balance by the transfusion. Let that heart beat bravely in the good old way, and it will take the new elements without harm into its circulation. It is indeed true that our patience has been sorely tried in some quarters, and that it demands of a native American no little philosophy to keep cool when he sees the ignorant horde of foreigners crowding our ballot-boxes and clamoring for our land and goods, spending their earnings in good times on beer and whiskey, and criticising our soup in bad times. We have been too long imposed upon by the braggadocio of foreign ruffians, and it is high time to stop their mouths. But while we revise our naturalization laws, and demand perhaps longer residence and proofs of sufficient education before admitting foreigners to citizenship, let us not forget that most of the difficulty has come from the baser sort of our own politicians; and our pot-house demagogues, aided perhaps now and then by a foxy ecclesiastic, have been the wire-pullers of the disgraceful business. The statistics of the last census have thrown daylight into the political arena, and it is the revelation of the weakness of the foreign element among us more than any secret societies that has raised the cry, "America for Americans!" — a cry quite just if we define the term

"Americans" largely enough to cover all loyal citizens of our republic,— lovers of its liberty and laws.

After all that may be said of the new elements, the old blood is the main dependence of the nation, and the coming of the Anglo-European to this hemisphere is the chief event in history since the rise of the Christian religion. With his coming came the union of the two hemispheres, so beautifully delineated by the poet among our geographers. America, lithe and graceful, in form a woman, waiting, guarded by twin oceans, was unconscious of her mighty destiny that was to ally her with Europe so remote and unknown, — Europe, as a continent, square and solid, like the figure of a man. May we not recall Tennyson's exquisite description of the sleeping beauty as we think of America, our fair mother, before startled from her slumber by the coming of her lord ? —

> "Year after year unto her feet,
>   She lying on her couch alone,
> Across the purpled coverlet,
>   The maiden's jet-black hair has grown,
> On either side her trancèd form
>   Forth streaming from a braid of pearl :
> The slumbrous light is rich and warm,
>   And moves not on the rounded curl.
>   .   .   .   .
> "She sleeps ; her breathings are not heard
>   In palace chambers far apart ;
> The fragrant tresses are not stirred
>   That lie upon her charmèd heart."

In God's own time the ocean gates were passed. The bravest of the Europeans won America for his own; the winds of heaven, in their deepest swell and their gentlest whispers, chanted the marriage hymn; and the race that sprang from that union bears the best blood of the Old World and the New in their veins. To that old blood the true American will be true, or he parts with his birthright.

True to his soil and to his blood, he will be true to the institutions founded upon this soil by men of his own blood. Whenever those institutions are in danger, whether on the part of absolutists or anarchists, he will rally under the old banner of liberty and order. The simple story of the rise of our national government is answer enough to both classes of destructives who are trying to undermine its foundations. This nation was the providential organization and growth from the stock of our ancestors out of this new country. They brought with them its seeds, or all the seminal principles of a free government. From their open Bible the free faith of Luther and the free press of Gutenberg held out to them a majestic promise. In the cabin where the Pilgrims signed their simple compact of self-government they put the best rights of the Old World into their signature; and although, perhaps, they did not think of it at the time, Alfred the Great with his jury, and the Barons of Runnymede with their Magna Charta, held for them the pen. Without any common theory, the various colonies, from their own spirit and under the action of circumstances, grew into a nation. To understand our government we must not begin with the central power, and go down to the homes of the people; but we must begin with the households and neighborhoods, and go up to the central power. The scattered colonists wished to follow their business, educate their children, and enjoy their religion in the New World. Hence the laws, schools, and churches of the townships, and in time the Confederacy of States. The republic grew like a living tree, instead of being hewn out like timber, or hammered out like a dead stone. It grew; and the Revolution itself was but one stage of a growth that had already been going on for a century and a half, — little more, indeed, than the dropping of withered blossoms that the fruit which they had covered might come to light. Our laws were not paper manufactures, but the organic expression of the public life; and our Constitution marched because the vitality of the nation was in it. The Dutch Republican, the Virginia Loyalist, the Massachusetts Puritan, the Maryland Catholic, the Pennsylvanian Quaker, all grew into a harmonious people; and never since time was has there been such a national commentary upon the text, "Diversities of gifts, but the same spirit." The aim was to secure individual liberty and social order, to vest in each township power adequate to its responsibility, and to delegate to the central State and National Government no more than the needed authority. Thus wiser than France, so cursed by centralization as to leave the whole nation to the mercy of the army or the mob of Paris; wiser than Switzerland and Ger-

many, so broken into separate dynasties as often to
afford no common front, the United States of America
enjoy a Confederacy without centralization, and state
and town and individual rights without disintegration
or anarchy; at once free and strong, independent,
yet united. We are to look well to it that we keep
this balance true, and are to have a wary eye upon
all disorganizers, whether of home or foreign growth.
Local institutions he leaves to local jurisdiction, and
national rights he defends against local usurpations.
Quite as little is he inclined to listen to destructives
of foreign as of home growth, and he has as little
affection for the black-capped Jesuit who stands ready
to steal away our individual and local rights in the
name of a great centralized absolutism, as for the red-
capped communist who, under the pretence of individual freedom, strikes at sacred rights of person and
property which autocrats have not dared to threaten.
Their black and red are not our own true blue.

It will be well if the recent revival of native American feeling awakens the nation to a careful study of
its own origin, progress, and organic laws. It will be
well if the general disgust at the ravings of the thousands of vagrants who have recently been venting their
ignorance and impudence against our institutions,
leads us to compare the organic principles of our
government with the air-castle that some of their
windy theorists would put in its place. Destroy the
National and State Senate as too aristocratic, bring
the people together to vote directly upon every public

question, and, instead of representatives, have commit-
tees to carry out the popular will at once, — whether
to declare war, or to build a ship, or coin a new cent,
— what a set of Solons we should be, according to
these radicals! Our State and National Governments
would vanish like the dew, and in their place there
would be an everlasting series of town meetings, all
talk and no action, until some old-fashioned American
would move that we return to the old ways of Washington, or some Cromwell or Napoleon drove out the
new nonsense with sword and bayonet. America is
now an organic body, a nation with bones and mus-
cles, compactly joined. Destroy the organism of the
various constituent parts that are harmonized by the
central life, and instead of this compact body with
each limb true to itself and to the whole, we should
have a monstrous mollusk, an animated jelly-bag
without any internal skeleton, like a flabby sunfish
tossed by the waves, or an overgrown oyster, having
no bones but its shell, and waiting to be devoured, at
the breaking of the shell, by the first adventurous
sword.

Stand up stoutly for the doctrine that in this country the individual man, and the local community, and
the minor party are not to be sacrificed to the central
power whether by democratic or aristocratic usurpation, and we honor America in her noblest sphere.
We will not speak with contempt or disparagement
of the decisions of the majority in this country, for
the popular vote has secured to us a degree of liberty

and privilege hitherto unexampled on the globe. Yet
may we not be peculiarly proud of the influence and
honor accorded by our people to the minority and its
leaders? Put upon a marble stone the names of the
leaders who have opposed the opinions of the majority,
whether Hamilton, Jay, the Adamses, Webster, Clay,
and their peers among the dead and living statesmen,
what man of any standing among the majority would
dare to deface that stone, or deny it the place of honor
in the temple of our liberty? Honor to America for
the favor here shown to those who in important points
oppose the popular will. It is something to be proud
of that so much of the ablest thought of this country
has been on the unpopular side, and the people have
welcomed in the Senate hall, the press, and the pulpit,
powerful thinkers, writers, and orators, who have
boldly arraigned the current of popular opinion. Red
Republicanism is prone to cut off the heads of the
opposition. American Republicanism has allowed
the leaders of the opposition to hold their heads as
high as the popular favorites, and when they have
died it has shed tears over their grave, and the nation
has put on mourning for the bereavement. Such is
the proper genius of our institutions, and the true
American will honor the spirit alike in its freedom
and its order as the true growth upon our soil from
the blood which his fathers brought hither from the
Old World. Washington, Franklin, Adams, and their
fellows, not Rousseau, Robespierre, and that ilk, laid
the foundation of our institutions.

Are we to stop here and say nothing of the reaction of America upon Europe, nothing of the hopes of humanity and the world? Much might be said upon each branch of this theme, but we are content here with making a single simple remark, and maintaining that the American is truest to humanity everywhere when he most loyally respects the rights and the duties of men in his own personal, social, and civil relations. We have not done much at inventing philosophies, and we do not claim for our two native American religions, Mormonism and Spirit Rapping, any divine honors; but we may lay claim to a civil order which aims to secure to the individual man the largest measure of privilege enjoyed upon the face of the earth. If we were to send to the Great Exhibition at Paris the best specimen of our products, it would not be a bedquilt or a piano, a militia major or even a Broadway dandy, strong as might be the claims of the latter alike as a natural and an artificial curiosity; but we should send a sample of the average culture of our schools and homes and workshops, — a thrifty Yankee youth who has been taught self-respect, faith, and energy under our institutions, and who is ready to honor any position by energy, good sense, and right principle. We hope that the average man among our native people would be found alike in respect to culture, character, and power of independent bearing, unsurpassed by the average standard anywhere in history or among existing nations. We do not claim to have invented any native American species of man, and the red Indian still keeps his exclusive aboriginal specialty. If the Greek philosopher was right when he defined man to be a two-legged animal without feathers, we are of that type, and we have no more feathers than the Greeks, except, perhaps, at balls and on training days. If we take the English chemist's definition, and say that "A man is a little less than fifty pounds of carbon and nitrogen diffused through six pailfuls of water," the definition applies to us as to the John Bull who gives it, although probably we have less brandy and beer in our pails of water than he. No, we do not ask to have any new definition made for us; and in spite of our teeth, which are said to be dropping two of the old-fashioned number, our European brethren must be content to reckon us of their type of humanity, and we are content to read humanity out of the same old Bible, and with the commentary of a genuine manhood such as the old heroes showed. We have brought over from the old homes many seeds of personal and domestic, civil and religious, blessings, and we return the favor when we allow them freer and fairer growth under institutions and circumstances more favorable to individual well-being.

The old doctrine is the best one in spite of the new times, — the best now that Europe is at our doors as well as when it was a far-off and almost inaccessible country. Sterling character, strong by self-reliance ; faith, and industry, guarded by civil order and social economy, — this is the best thing that America has shown to the world, or is likely to show. The greatest thing that England ever did, said Carlyle, was Oliver Cromwell. The greatest thing that America ever did was — we will not say was any one man nor deed, not even the Revolution, not Congress, but the hosts of energetic, honest, faithful men, who have believed in God and their country, and brought up their families in the school and church as citizens of an earthly and of a heavenly kingdom. This simple, earnest humanity we are to keep both at home and abroad against the silken follies that would enslave it to a home luxury and pretension that Europe hardly equals ; against the courtly arrogance that meets it abroad, and insists upon concealing our republican manhood under the tinsel pageantry of superannuated courts. The American will be the best propagandist of liberty and humanity abroad when he dares to be himself before foreign courts and priesthoods, and when the dignity and power of the nation give majesty and force to his simplicity. The great blow will be struck for the New World against the despotisms of the Old World when Americans dare to show a true light in face of foreign oppressions. The worst foes to liberty have always been the traitors within its own camp. Humanity in Europe does not so much ask of us soldiers for Kossuth and Mazzini, as citizens trained in the school of Washington and Franklin.

SLAVERY, IN ITS PRINCIPLES, DEVELOP-
MENT, AND EXPEDIENTS.

WITHIN the memory of men still in the vigor of life, American Slavery was considered by a vast majority of the North, and by a large minority of the South, as an evil which should, at best, be tolerated, and not a good which deserved to be extended and protected. A kind of lazy acquiescence in it as a local matter, to be managed by local legislation, was the feeling of the Free States. In both the Slave and the Free States, the discussion of the essential principles on which Slavery rests was confined to a few disappointed Nullifiers and a few uncompromising Abolitionists; and we can recollect the time when Calhoun and Garrison were both classed by practical statesmen of the South and North in one category of pestilent "abstractionists." Negro Slavery was considered simply as a fact; and general irritation among most politicians of all sections was sure to follow any attempt to explore the principles on which the fact reposed. That these principles had the mischievous vitality which events have proved them to possess, few of our wisest statesmen then dreamed, and we have drifted by degrees into the present war without any clear perception of its animating causes.

The future historian will trace the steps by which the subject of Slavery was forced on the reluctant attention of the citizens of the Free States, so that at last the most cautious conservative could not ignore its intrusive presence, could not banish its reality from his eyes, or its image from his mind. He will show why Slavery, disdaining its old argument from expediency, challenged discussion on its principles. He will explain the process by which it became discontented with toleration within its old limits, and demanded the championship or connivance of the National Government in a plan for its limitless extension. He will indicate the means by which it corrupted the Southern heart and Southern brain, so that at last the elemental principles of morals and religion were boldly denied, and the people came to " believe a lie." He will, not unnaturally, indulge in a little sarcasm, when he comes to consider the occupation of Southern professors of ethics, compelled by their position to scoff at the " rights " of man, and Southern professors of theology, compelled by their position to teach that Christ came into the world, not so much to save sinners, as to enslave negroes. He will be forced to class these among the meanest and most abject slaves that the planters owned. In treating of the subserviency of the North, he will be constrained to write many a page which will flush the cheeks of our descendants with indignation and shame. He will show the method by which Slavery, after vitiating the conscience and intelligence of the

South, contrived to vitiate in part, and for a time, the
conscience and intelligence of the North. It will be
his ungrateful task to point to many instances of
compliance and concession on the part of able Northern statesmen which will deeply affect their fame with
posterity, though he will doubtless refuse to adopt
to the full the contemporary clamor against their
motives. He will understand, better than we, the
amount of patriotism which entered into their "concessions," and the amount of fraternal good-will
which prompted their fatal "compromises." But he
will also declare that the object of the Slave Power
was not attained. Vacillating statesmen and corrupt
politicians it might address, the first through their
fears, the second through their interests ; but the intrepid and incorruptible "people" were but super-
ficially affected. A few elections were gained, but
the victories were barren of results. From political
defeat the free people of the North came forth more
earnest and more united than ever. The insolent
pretensions of the Slavocracy were repudiated ; its
political and ethical maxims were disowned ; and
after having stirred the noblest impulses of the
human heart by the spectacle of its tyranny, its
attempt to extend that tyranny only roused an insurrection of the human understanding against the
impudence of its logic. The historian can then only
say, that the Slave Power "seceded," being determined to form a part of no government which it
could not control. The present war is to decide

whether its real force corresponds to the political force it has exerted heretofore in our affairs.

That this war has been forced upon the Free States by the "aggressions" of the Slave Power is so plain that no argument is necessary to sustain the proposition. It is not so universally understood that the Slave Power is aggressive by the necessities of the wretched system of labor on which its existence is based. By a short exposition of the principles of Slavery, and the expedients it has practised during the last twenty or thirty years, we think that this proposition can be established.

And first it must be always borne in mind that Slavery, as a system, is based on the most audacious, inhuman, and self-evident of lies, — the assertion, namely, that property can be held in men. Property applies to things. There is a metaphysical impossibility implied in the attempt to extend its application to persons. It is possible, we admit, to ordain by local law that four and four make ten; but such an exercise of legislative wisdom could not overcome certain arithmetical prejudices innate in our minds, or dethrone the stubborn eight from its accustomed position in our thoughts. But you might as well ordain that four and four make ten as ordain that a man has no right to himself, but can properly be held as the chattel of another. Yet this arrogant false-hood of property in men has been organized into a colossal institution. The South calls it a "peculiar" institution; and herein perhaps consists its peculiarity, that it is an absurdity which has lied itself into a substantial form, and now argues its right to exist from the fact of its existence. Doubtless the fact that a thing exists proves that it has its roots in human nature ; but before we accept this as decisive of its right to exist, it may be well to explore those qualities in human nature, " peculiar " and perverse as itself, from which it derives its poisonous vitality and strength. It is plain, we think, that an institution embodying an essential falsity, which equally affronts the common sense and the moral sense of mankind, and which, as respects chronology, was as repugnant to the instincts of Homer as it is to the instincts of Whittier, must have sprung from the unblessed union of wilfulness and avarice, — of avarice which knows no conscience, and of wilfulness that tramples on reason ; and the marks of this parentage, the signs of these its boasted roots in human nature, are, we are constrained to concede, visible in every stage of its growth, in every argument for its existence, in every motive for its extension.

It is not, perhaps, surprising that some of the advocates of Slavery do not relish the analysis which reveals the origin of their institution in those dispositions which connect man with the tiger and the wolf. Accordingly they discourage, with true democratic humility, all genealogical inquiries into the ancestry of their system, substitute generalization for analysis, and, twisting the maxims of religion into a philosophy of servitude, bear down all arguments with

the sounding proposition that Slavery is included in
the plan of God's providence, and therefore cannot be
wrong. Certain thinkers of our day have asserted the
universality of the religious element in human nature;
and it must be admitted that men become very pious
when their minds are illuminated by the discernment
of a providential sanction for their darling sins, and
by the discovery that God is on the side of their interests and passions. Napoleon's religious perceptions
were somewhat obtuse, as tried by the standards of
the Church, yet nothing could exceed the depth of
his belief that God " was with the heaviest column ; "
and the most obdurate jobber in human flesh may
well glow with apostolic fervor, as, from the height
of philosophic contemplation to which this principle
lifts him, he discerns the sublime import of his providential mission. It is true, he is now willing to concede that a man's right to himself, being given by
God, can only by God be taken away. " But," he ex-
ultingly exclaims, " it *has* been taken away by God.
The negro, having always been a slave, must have
been so by divine appointment; and I, the mark of
obloquy to a few fanatical enthusiasts, am really an
humble agent in carrying out the designs of a higher
law even than that of the State, of a higher will
even than my own." This mode of baptizing man's
sin and calling it God's providence has not altogether lacked the aid of certain Southern clergymen,
who ostentatiously profess to preach Christ and Him
crucified, and by such arguments, we may fear, cru-

cified *by them.* Here is Slavery's abhorred riot of vices and crimes, from whose soul-sickening details the human imagination shrinks aghast, — and over all, to complete the picture, these theologians bring in the seraphic countenance of the Saviour of mankind, smiling celestial approval of the multitūdinous miseries and infamies it serenely beholds!

It may be presumptuous to proffer counsel to such authorized expositors of religion, but one can hardly help insinuating the humble suggestion that it would be as well, if they must give up the principles of liberty, not to throw Christianity in. We may be permitted to doubt the theory of Providence which teaches that a man never so much serves God as when he serves the Devil. Doubtless Slavery, though opposed to God's laws, is included in the plan of God's providence; but, in the long run, the providence most terribly confirms the laws. The stream of events, having its fountains in iniquity, has its end in retribution. It is because God's laws are immutable that God's providence can be *foreseen* as well as seen. The mere fact that a thing exists, and persists in existing, is of little importance in determining its right to exist, or its eventual destiny. These must be found in an inspection of the principles by which it exists; and from the nature of its principles, we can predict its future history. The confidence of bad men and the despair of good men proceed equally from a too fixed attention to the facts and events before their eyes, to the exclusion of the principles which underlie and animate them; for no insight of principles, and of the moral laws which govern human events, could ever cause tyrants to exult or philanthropists to despond.

If we go farther into this question, we shall commonly find that the facts and events to which we give the name of Providence are the acts of human wills divinely overruled. There is iniquity and wrong in these facts and events, because they are the work of free human wills. But when these free human wills organize falsehood, institute injustice, and establish oppression, they have passed into that mental state where will has been perverted into wilfulness, and self-direction has been exaggerated into self-worship. It is the essence of wilfulness that it exalts the impulses of its pride above the intuitions of conscience and intelligence, and puts force in the place of reason and right. The person has thus emancipated himself from all restraints of a law higher than his personality, and acts *from* self, *for* self, and in sole obedience *to* self. But this is personality in its Satanic form; yet it is just here that some of our theologians have discovered in a person's actions the purposes of Providence, and discerned the Divine intention in the fact of guilt instead of in the certainty of retribution. The tyrant element in man is found in this Satanic form of his individuality. His will, self-released from restraint, preys upon and crushes other wills. He asserts himself by enslaving others, and mimics Divinity on the stilts of diabolism.

Like the barbarian who thought himself enriched by the powers and gifts of the enemy he slew, he aggrandizes his own personality, and heightens his own sense of freedom, through the subjection of feebler natures. Ruthless, rapacious, greedy of power, greedy of gain, it is in Slavery that he wantons in all the luxury of injustice, for it is here that he tastes the exquisite pleasure of depriving others of that which he most values in himself.

Thus, whether we examine this system in the light of conscience and intelligence, or in the light of history and experience, we come to but one result, — that it has its source and sustenance in Satanic energy, in Satanic pride, and in Satanic greed. This is Slavery in itself, detached from the ameliorations it may receive from individual slaveholders. Now a bad system is not continued or extended by the virtues of any individuals who are but partially corrupted by it, but by those who work in the spirit and with the implements of its originators. Every amelioration is a confession of the essential injustice of the thing ameliorated, and a step towards its abolition ; and the humane and Christian slaveholders owe their safety, and the security of what they are pleased to call their property, to the vices of the hard and stern spirits whom they profess to abhor. If they invest in stock of the Devil's corporation, they ought not to be severe on those who look out that they punctually receive their dividends. The true slaveholder feels that he is encamped among his slaves, that he holds them by

the right of conquest, that the relation is one of war,
and that there is no crime he may not be compelled
to commit in self-defence. Disdaining all cant, he
clearly perceives that the system, in its practical
working, must conform to the principles on which
it is based. He accordingly believes in the lash and
the fear of the lash. If he is cruel and brutal, it may
as often be from policy as from disposition, for brutality and cruelty are the means by which weaker
races are best kept " subordinated " to stronger races ;
and the influence of his brutality and cruelty is felt as
restraint and terror on the plantation of his less resolute neighbor. And when we speak of brutality and
cruelty, we do not limit the application of the words
to those who scourge, but extend it to some of those
who preach, — who hold up heaven as the reward of
those slaves who are sufficiently abject on earth, and
threaten damnation in the next world to all who dare
to assert their manhood in this.

If, however, any one still doubts that this system
develops itself logically and naturally, and tramples
down the resistance offered by the better sentiments
of human nature, let him look at the legislation which
defines and protects it, — a legislation which, as ex-
pressing the average sense and purpose of the community, is to be quoted as conclusive against the
testimony of any of its individual members. This
legislation evinces the dominion of a malignant principle. You can hear the crack of the whip and the
clank of the chain in all its enactments. Yet these

laws, which cannot be read in any civilized country
without mingled horror and derision, indicate a mas-
tery of the whole theory and practice of oppression,
are admirably adapted to the end they have in view,
and bear the unmistakable marks of being the work of
practical men, — of men who know their sin, and
"knowing, dare maintain." They do not, it is true,
enrich the science of jurisprudence with any large or
wise additions; but we do not look for such luxuries
as justice, reason, and beneficence in ordinances devised to prop up iniquity, falsehood, and tyranny.
Ghastly caricatures of justice as these offshoots of
Slavery are, they are still dictated by the nature and
necessities of the system. They have the flavor of
the rank soil whence they spring.

If we desire any stronger evidence that slaveholders
constitute a general Slave Power, that this Slave
Power acts as a unit, the unity of a great interest
impelled by powerful passions, and that the virtues
of individual slaveholders have little effect in checking the vices of the system, we can find that evidence
in the zeal and audacity with which this power engaged in extending its dominion. Seemingly aggressive in this, it was really acting on the defensive, —
on the defensive, however, not against the assaults of
men, but against the immutable decrees of God. The
world is so constituted, that wrong and oppression are
not, in a large view, politic. They heavily mortgage
the future, when they glut the avarice of the present.
The avenging Providence, which the slaveholder can-

not find in the New Testament, or in the teachings of conscience, he is at last compelled to find in political economy; and however indifferent to the Gospel according to Saint John, he must give heed to the gospel according to Adam Smith and Malthus. He discovers, no doubt to his surprise, and somewhat to his indignation, that there is an intimate relation between industrial success and justice; and however much, as a practical man, he may despise the abstract principles which declare Slavery a nonsensical enormity, he cannot fail to read its nature, when it slowly but legibly writes itself out in curses on the land. He finds how true is the old proverb, that, "if God moves with leaden feet, He strikes with iron hands." The law of Slavery is, that, to be lucrative, it must have a scanty population diffused over large areas. To limit it is therefore to doom it to come to an end by the laws of population. To limit it is to force the planters, in the end, to free their slaves, from an inability to support them, and to force the slaves into more energy and intelligence in labor, in order that they may subsist as freemen. People prattle about the necessity of compulsory labor; but the true compulsory labor, the labor which has produced the miracles of modern industry, is the labor to which a man is compelled by the necessity of saving himself, and those who are dearer to him than self, from ignominy and want. It was by this policy of territorial limitation, that Henry Clay, before the annexation of Texas, declared that Slavery must eventually expire. The

11

way was gradual, it was prudent, it was safe, it was distant, it was sure, it was according to the nature of things. It would have been accepted, had there been any general truth in the assertion that the slave-holders were honestly desirous of reconverting, at any time, and on any practicable plan, their chattels into men. But true to the malignant principles of their system, they accepted the law of its existence, but determined to evade the law of its extinction. As Slavery required large areas and scanty population, large areas and scanty population it should at all times have. New markets should be opened for the surplus slave-population ; to open new markets was to acquire new territory, and to acquire new territory was to gain additional political strength. The expansive tendencies of freedom would thus be checked by the tendencies no less expansive of bondage. To acquire Texas was not merely to acquire an additional Slave State, but it was to keep up a demand for slaves which would prevent Virginia, North Carolina, Maryland, and Kentucky from becoming Free States. As soon as old soils were worn out, new soils were to be ready to receive the curse ; and where slave-labor ceased to be profitable, slave-breeding was to take its place.

This purpose was so diabolical that, when first announced, it was treated as a caprice of certain hot spirits, irritated by the declamations of the Abolitionists. But it is idle to refer to transient heat thoughts which bear all the signs of cool atrocity ; and needless to seek for the causes of actions in extraneous sources, when they are plainly but steps in the development of principles already known. Slave-breeding and Slavery-extension are necessities of the system. Like Romulus and Remus, " they are both suckled from one wolf."

But it was just here that the question became to the Free States a practical question. There could be no " fanaticism " in meeting it at this stage. What usually goes under the name of fanaticism is the habit of uncompromising assault on a thing because its principles are absurd or wicked; what usually goes under the name of common sense is the disposition to assail it at that point where, in the development of its principles, it has become immediately and pressingly dangerous. Now by no sophistry could we of the Free States evade the responsibility of being the extenders of Slavery, if we allowed Slavery to be extended. If we did not oppose it from a sense of right, we were bound to oppose it from a sense of decency. It may be said that we had nothing to do with Slavery at the South; but we had something to do with rescuing the national character from infamy, and unhappily we could not have anything to do with rescuing the national character from infamy without having something to do with Slavery at the South. The question with us was, whether we would allow the whole force of the National Government to be employed in upholding, extending, and perpetuating this detestable and nonsensical enormity, — especially, whether we would be guilty of that last and foulest atheism to free principles, the deliberate planting of slave institutions on virgin soil? If this question had been put to any despot of Europe, — we had almost said, to any despot of Asia, — his answer would undoubtedly have been an indignant negative. Yet the South confidently expected so to wheedle or bully us into dragging our common sense through the mud and mire of momentary expedients, that we should connive at the commission of this execrable crime!

There can be no doubt that, if the question had been fairly put to the inhabitants of the Free States, their answer would have been at once decisive for freedom. Even the strongest conservatives would have been "Free-Soilers;" not only those who are conservatives in virtue of their prudence, moderation, sagacity, and temper, but prejudiced conservatives, — conservatives who are tolerant of all iniquity which is decorous, inert, long-established, and disposed to die when its time comes, — conservatives as thorough in their hatred of change as Lamennais himself. "What a noise," says Paul Louis Courier, "Lamennais would have made on the day of creation, could he have witnessed it! His first cry to the Divinity would have been to respect that ancient chaos." But even to conservatives of this class, the attempt to extend Slavery, though really in the order of its natural development, must still have appeared a monstrous innovation, and they were bound to oppose the Marats and Robespierres of despotism who were busy in the bad work. Indeed, in our country, conservatism, through the presence of Slavery, has inverted its usual order. In other countries, the radical of one century is the conservative of the next; in ours, the conservative of one generation is the radical of the next. The American conservative of 1790 is the so-called fanatic of 1820; the conservative of 1820 is the fanatic of 1856. The American conservative, indeed, descended the stairs of compromise until his descent into utter abnegation of all that civilized humanity holds dear was arrested by the Rebellion. And the reason of this strange inversion of conservative principles was, that the movement of Slavery is towards barbarism, while the movement of all countries in which labor is not positively chattelized is towards freedom and civilization. True conservatism, it must never be forgotten, is the refusal to give up a positive, though imperfect good, for a possible, but uncertain improvement: in the United States it has been misused to denote the cowardly surrender of a positive good from a fear to resist the innovations of an advancing evil and wrong.

There was, therefore, little danger that Slavery would be extended through the conscious thought and will of the people, but there was danger that its extension might, somehow or other, *occur*. Misconception of the question, devotion to party or the memory of party, prejudice against the men who more immediately represented the Antislavery principle, might make the people unconsciously slide into this crime. And it must be said that for the divisions in the Free

States as to the mode in which the free sentiment of the people should operate, the strictly Antislavery men were to some extent responsible. It is difficult to convince an ardent reformer that the principle for which he contends, being impersonal, should be purified from the passions and whims of his own personality. The more fervid he is, the more he is identified in the public mind with his cause; and, in a large view, he is bound not merely to defend his cause, but to see that the cause, through him, does not become offensive. Men are ever ready to dodge disagreeable duties by converting questions of principles into criticisms on the men who represent principles; and the men who represent principles should therefore look to it that they make no needless enemies and give no needless shock to public opinion for the purpose of pushing pet opinions, wreaking personal grudges, or gratifying individual antipathies. The artillery of the North has heretofore played altogether too much on Northerners.

But to return. The South expected to fool the North into a compliance with its designs, by availing itself of the divisions among its professed opponents, and by dazzling away the attention of the people from the real nature of the wickedness to be perpetrated. Slavery was to be extended, and the North was to be an accomplice in the business; but the Slave Power did not expect that we should be active and enthusiastic in this work of self-degradation. It did not ask us to extend Slavery, but simply to allow its extension to occur; and in this appeal to our moral timidity and moral laziness, it contemptuously tossed us a few fig-leaves of fallacy and false statement to save appearances.

We were informed, for instance, that by the equality of men is meant the equality of those whom Providence has made equal. But this is exactly the sense in which no sane man ever understood the doctrine of equality; for Providence has palpably made men unequal, — white men as well as black.

Then we were told that the white and black races could dwell together only in the relation of masters and slaves, — and, in the same breath, that in this relation the slaves were steadily advancing in civilization and Christianity. But if steadily advancing in civilization and Christianity, the time must inevitably come when they would not submit to be slaves; and then what becomes of the statement that the white and black races cannot dwell together as freemen? Why boast of their improvement, when you are improving them only that you may exterminate them, or they *you*?

Then, with a composure of face which touches the exquisite in effrontery, we were assured that this antithesis of master and slave, of tyrant and abject natures, is really a perfect harmony. Slavery — so said these logicians of liberticide — has solved the great social problem of the working-classes, comfortably for capital, happily for labor; and has effected this by an ingenious expedient which could have occurred only to minds of the greatest depth and comprehension, the expedient, namely, of enslaving labor. Now, doubtless there has always been a struggle between employers and employed, and this struggle will probably continue until the relations between the two are more humane and Christian. But Slavery exhibits this struggle in its earliest and most savage stage, — a stage answering to the rude energies and still ruder conceptions of barbarians. The issue of the struggle, it is plain, will not be that capital will own labor, but that labor will own capital, and no *man* be owned.

Still we were vehemently told that, though the slaves, for their own good, were deprived of their rights as men, they were in a fine state of physical comfort. This was not and could not be true; but even if it were, it only represented the slaveholder as addressing his slave in some such words of derisive scorn as Byron hurls at Duke Alphonso, —

> "Thou! born to eat, and be despised, and die,
> Even as the brutes that perish," —

though we doubt if he could truly add, —

> "save that thou
> Hast a more splendid trough and wider sty."

Then we were solemnly warned of our patriotic duty to "know no North and no South." This was the very impudence of ingratitude; for we had long known no North, and unhappily had known altogether too much South.

Then we were most plaintively adjured to comply

with the demands of the Slave Power, in order to save
the Union. But how save the Union? Why, by violating the principles on which the Union was formed,
and scouting the objects it was intended to serve.

But lastly came the question, on which the South
confidently relied as a decisive argument, "What
could we do with our slaves, provided we emancipated
them?" The peculiarity which distinguished this
question from all other interrogatories ever addressed
to human beings was this, that it was asked for the
purpose of *not* being answered. The moment a reply
was begun, the ground was swiftly shifted, and we
were overwhelmed with a torrent of words about State
Rights and the duty of minding our own business.

But it is needless to continue the examination of
these substitutes and apologies for fact and reason,
especially as their chief characteristic consisted in
their having nothing to do with the practical question
before the people. They were thrown out by the
interested defenders of Slavery, North and South,
to divert attention from the main issue. In the fine
felicity of their inappropriateness to the actual condition of the struggle between the Free and Slave States,
they were almost a match for that renowned sermon,
preached by a metropolitan bishop before an asylum
for the blind, the halt, and the legless, on "The Moral
Dangers of Foreign Travel." But still they were infinitely mischievous, considered as pretences under
which Northern men could skulk from their duties,
and as sophistries to lull into a sleepy acquiescence the

consciences of those political adventurers who are always seeking occasions for being tempted and reasons for being rogues. They were all the more influential from the circumstance that their show of argument was backed by the solid substance of patronage. These false facts and bad reasons were the keys to many fat offices. The South had succeeded in instituting a new political test; namely, that no man is qualified to serve the United States unless he is the champion or the sycophant of the Slave Power. Proscription to the friends of American freedom, honors and emoluments *to the friends of American slavery, — adopt that creed, or you did not belong to any "healthy" political organization! Now we have heard of civil disabilities for opinion's sake before. In some countries no Catholics are allowed to hold office, in others no Protestants, in others no Jews. But it is not, we believe, in Protestant countries that Protestants are proscribed; it is not in Catholic countries that Catholics are incompetent to serve the State. It was left for a free country to establish, practically, civil disabilities against freemen, — for Republican America to proscribe Republicans! Think of it, — that no American, whatever his worth, talents, or patriotism, could two years ago serve his country in any branch of its executive administration, unless he was unfortunate enough to agree with the slaveholders, or base enough to sham an agreement with them! The test, at Washington, of political orthodoxy was modelled on the pattern of the test of religious ortho-

doxy established by Napoleon's minister of police.
" You are not orthodox," he said to a priest. " In
what," inquired the astonished ecclesiastic, " have I
sinned against orthodoxy ? " " You have not pronounced the eulogium of the Emperor, or proved the
righteousness of the conscription."

Now we had been often warned of the danger of
sectional parties, on account of their tendency to break
up the Government. The people gave heed to this
warning; for here was a sectional party in possession
of the Government. We had been often advised not
to form political combinations on one idea. The people gave heed to this advice; for here was a triumphant political combination, formed not only on one
idea, but that the worst idea that ever animated any
political combination. Here was an association of
three hundred and fifty thousand persons, spread over
some nine hundred and fifty thousand square miles of
territory, and wielding its whole political power, engaged in the work of turning the United States into
a sort of slave plantation, of which they were to be
overseers. We opposed them by argument, passion,
and numerical power ; and they read us long homilies
on the beauty of law and order, — order sustained by
Border Ruffians, law which was but the legalizing of
criminal instincts, — law and order which, judged by
the code established for Kansas, seemed based on legislative ideas imported from the Feejee Islands. We
opposed them again, and they talked to us about the
necessity of preserving the Union ; as if, in the Free

States, the love of the Union had not been a principle and a passion, proof against many losses, and insensible to many humiliations; as if, with our teachers, disunion had not been for half a century a stereotyped menace to scare us into compliance with their rascalities; as if it were not known that only so long as they could wield the powers of the National Government to accomplish their designs, were they loyal to the Union! We opposed them again, and they clamored about their Constitutional rights and our Constitutional obligations; but they adopted for themselves a theory of the Constitution which made each State the judge of the Constitution in the last resort, while they held us to that view of it which made the Supreme Court the judge in the last resort. Written constitutions, by a process of interpretation, are always made to follow the drift of great forces; they are twisted and tortured into conformity with the views of the power dominant in the State; and our Constitution, originally a charter of freedom, was converted into an instrument which the slaveholders seemed to possess by right of squatter sovereignty and eminent domain.

Did any one suppose that we could retard the ever onward movement of their unscrupulous force and defiant wills by timely compromises and concessions? Every compromise we made with them only stimulated their rapacity, heightened their arrogance, increased their demands. Every concession we made to their insolent threats was only a step downwards to a deeper abasement; and we parted with our most

cherished convictions of duty to purchase, not their
gratitude, but their contempt. Every concession, too,
weakened us and strengthened them for the inevitable
struggle into which the Free States were eventually
goaded, to preserve what remained of their dignity,
their honor, and their self-respect. In 1850 we conceded the application of the Wilmot Proviso; in 1856
we were compelled to concede the principle of the
Wilmot Proviso. In 1850 we had no fears that slaves
would enter New Mexico; in 1861 we were threatened
with a view of the flag of the rattlesnake floating over
Faneuil Hall. If any principle has been established
by events, with the certainty of mathematical demon-
stration, it is this, that concession to the Slave Power
is the suicide of Freedom. We are purchasing this
fact at the expense of arming five hundred thousand
men and spending a thousand millions of dollars.
More than this, if any concessions were to be made,
they ought, on all principles of concession, to have
been made to the North. Concessions, historically,
are not made by freedom to privilege, but by privilege to freedom. Thus King John conceded Magna
Charta; thus King Charles conceded the Petition of
Right; thus Protestant England conceded Catholic
Emancipation to Ireland; thus aristocratic England
conceded the Reform Bill to the English middle class.
And had not we, the misgoverned many, a right to
demand from the slaveholders, the governing few,
some concessions to our sense of justice and our
prejudices for freedom? Concession indeed! If any

class of men hold in their grasp one of the dear-bought chartered "rights of man," it is infamous to concede it.

> "Make it the darling of your precious eye !
> *To lose or give 't away* were such perdition
> As nothing else could match."

Considerations so obvious as these could not, by any ingenuity of party-contrivance, be prevented from forcing themselves by degrees into the minds of the great body of the voters of the Free States. The common sense, the "large roundabout common sense" of the people, slowly, and somewhat reluctantly, came up to the demands of the occasion. The sophistries and fallacies of the Northern defenders of the pretensions of the slaveholding sectional minority were gradually exposed, and were repudiated in the lump. The conviction was implanted in the minds of the people of the Free States, that the Slave Power, representing only a thirtieth part of the population of the Slave States, and a ninth part of the property of the country, was bent on governing the nation, and on subordinating all principles and all interests to its own. Not being ambitious of having the United States converted into a Western Congo, with the traffic in "niggers" as its fundamental idea, the people elected Abraham Lincoln, in a perfectly Constitutional way, President. As the majority of the House of Representatives, of the Senate, and of the Supreme Court was still left, by this election, on the side of the "rights of the South" (humorously so styled), and as the President could do little to advance Republican principles with all the other branches of the Government opposed to him, the people naturally imagined that the slaveholders would acquiesce in their decision.

But such was not the result. The election was in November. The new President could not assume office until March. The triumphs of the Slave Power had been heretofore owing to its willingness and readiness to peril everything on each question as it arose, and each event as it occurred. South Carolina, perhaps the only one of the Slave States that was thoroughly in earnest, at once " seceded." The " Gulf States " and others followed its example, not so much from any fixed intention of forming a Southern Confederacy as for the purpose of intimidating the Free States into compliance with the extreme demands of the South. The Border Slave States were avowedly neutral between the " belligerents," but indicated their purpose to stand by their " Southern brethren," in case the Government of the United States attempted to carry out the Constitution and the laws in the seceded States by the process of " coercion."

The combination was perfect. The heart of the Rebellion was in South Carolina, a State whose free population was about equal to that of the city of Brooklyn, and whose annual productions were exceeded by those of Essex County, in the State of Massachusetts. Around this centre was congregated as base a set of politicians as ever disgraced human nature. A conspiracy was formed to compel a first-class power, representing thirty millions of people, to submit to the dictation of about three hundred thousand of its citizens. The conspirators did not dream of failure. They were sure, as they thought, of the Gulf States and of the Border States, of the whole Slave Power, in fact. They also felt sure of that large minority in the Free States which had formerly acted with them, and obeyed their most humiliating behests. They therefore entered the Congress of the nation with a confident front, knowing that President Buchanan and the majority of his Cabinet were practically on their side. Before Mr. Lincoln could be inaugurated they imagined they could accomplish all their designs, and make the Government of the United States a Pro-slavery power in the eyes of all the nations of the world. Mr. Calhoun's paradoxes had heretofore been indorsed only by majorities in the national legislature and by the Supreme Court. What a victory it would be, if, by threatening rebellion, they could induce the people of the United States to incorporate those paradoxes into the fundamental law of the nation, dominant over both Congress and the Court! All their previous "compromises" had been merely legislative compromises, which, as their cause advanced, they had themselves annulled. They now seized the occasion, when the "people" had risen against them, to compel the people to sanction their most extreme demands. They determined to convert defeat, sustained at the polls, into a victory which would have far transcended any victory they might have gained by electing their candidate, Breckinridge, as President.

A portion of the Republicans, seeing clearly the force arrayed against them, and disbelieving that the population of the Free States would be willing, *en masse*, to sustain the cause of free labor by force of arms, tried to avert the blow by proposing a new compromise. Mr. Seward, the calmest, most moderate, and most obnoxious statesman of the Republican party, offered to divide the existing territories of the United States by the Missouri line, all south of which should be open to slave labor. As he at the same time stated that by natural laws the South could obtain no material advantage by his seeming concession, the concession only made him enemies among the uncompromising champions of the Wilmot Proviso. The conspirators demanded that the Missouri line should be the boundary, not only between the Territories which the United States then possessed, but between the Territories they might hereafter *acquire*. As the country north of the Missouri line was held by powerful European States which it would be madness to offend, and as the country south of that line was held by feeble States which it would be easy to conquer, no Northern or Western statesman could vote for such a measure without proving himself a rogue or a simpleton. Hence all measures of " compromise " necessarily failed during the last days of the administration of James Buchanan.

12

It is plain, that, when Mr. Lincoln — after having escaped assassination from the " Chivalry " of Maryland, and after having been subjected to a virulence of invective such as no other President had incurred — arrived at Washington, his mind was utterly unaffected by the illusions of passion. His Inaugural Message was eminently moderate. The Slave Power, having failed to delude or bully Congress, or to intimidate the people, — having failed to murder the elected President on his way to the capital, — was at its wits' end. It thought it could still rely on its Northern supporters, as James II. of England thought he could rely on the Church of England. While the nation, therefore, was busy in expedients to call back the seceded States to their allegiance, the latter suddenly bombarded Fort Sumter, trampled on the American flag, threatened to wave the rattlesnake rag over Faneuil Hall, and to make the Yankees " smell Southern powder and feel Southern steel." All this was done with the idea that the Northern " Democracy " would rally to the support of their " Southern brethren." The result proved that the South was, in the words of Mr. Davis's last and most melancholy Message, the victim of " misplaced confidence" in its Northern " associates." The moment a gun was fired, the honest Democratic voters of the North were even more furious than the Republican voters ; the leaders, including those who had been the obedient servants of Slavery, were ravenous for commands in the great army which was to " co-

erce " and " subjugate " the South ; and the whole
organization of the " Democratic party " of the North
melted away at once in the fierce fires of a re-
awakened patriotism. The slaveholders ventured
everything on their last stake, and lost. A North,
for the first time, sprang into being ; and it issued,
like Minerva from the brain of Jove, full-armed. The
much-vaunted engineer, Beauregard, was " hoist with
his own petard."

Now that the slaveholders have been so foolish
as to appeal to physical force, abandoning their
vantage-ground of political influence, they must be
not only politically overthrown, but physically humiliated. Their arrogant sense of superiority must be
beaten out of them by main force. The feeling with
which every Texan and Arkansas bully and assassin
regarded a Northern mechanic — a feeling akin to
that with which the old Norman robber looked on the
sturdy Saxon laborer — must be changed, by showing
the bully that his bowie-knife is dangerous only to
peaceful, and is imbecile before armed citizens. The
Southerner has appealed to force, and force he should
have, until, by the laws of force, he is not only
beaten, but compelled to admit the humiliating fact.
That he is not disposed " to die in the last ditch,"
that he has none of the practical heroism of desperation, is proved by the actual results of battles.
When defeated, and his means of escape are such as
only desperation can surmount, he quickly surrenders, and is even disposed to take the oath of alle-

giance. The martial virtues of the common European
soldier he has displayed in exceedingly scanty measure in the present conflict. He has relied on engi-
neers; and the moment his fortresses are turned or
stormed, he retreats or becomes a prisoner of war.
Let Mr. Davis's Message to the Confederate Congress,
and his order suspending Pillow and Floyd, testify to
this unquestionable statement. Even if we grant
martial intrepidity to the members of the Slavocracy,
the present war proves that the system of Slavery is
not one which develops martial virtues among the
" free whites " it has cajoled or forced into its hateful
service. Indeed, the armies of Jefferson Davis are
weak on the same principle on which the slave-system
is weak. Everything depends on the intelligence and
courage of the commanders, and the moment these
fail the soldiers become a mere mob.

American Slavery, by the laws which control its
existence, first rose from a local power, dominant in
certain States, to a national power, assuming to domi-
nate over the United States. At the first faint fact
which indicated the intention of the Free States to
check its progress and overturn its insolent dominion,
it rebelled. The rebellion now promises to be a failure; but it will cost the Free States the arming of
half a million of men and the spending of a thousand
millions of dollars to make it a failure. Can we afford to trifle with the cause which produced it? We
note that some of the representatives of the loyal
Slave States in Congress are furious to hang individ-

ual Rebels, but at the same time are anxious to surround the system those Rebels represent with new
guaranties. When they speak of Jeff. Davis and his
crew, their feeling is as fierce as that of Tilly and
Pappenheim towards the Protestants of Germany.
They would burn, destroy, confiscate, and kill without any mercy, and without any regard to the laws
of civilized war; but when they come to speak of
Slavery, their whole tone is changed. They wish us
to do everything barbarous and inhuman, provided
we do not go to the last extent of barbarity and in-
humanity, which, according to their notions, is, to
inaugurate a system of freedom, equality, and justice.
Provided the negro is held in bondage and denied the
rights of human nature, they are willing that any
severity should be exercised towards his rebellious
master. Now we have no revengeful feeling towards
the master at all. We think that he is a victim as
well as an oppressor. We wish to emancipate the
master as well as the slave, and we think that thousands of masters are persons who merely submit to
the conditions of labor established in their respective
localities. Our opposition is directed, not against
Jefferson Davis, but against the system whose cumu-
lative corruptions and enormities Jefferson Davis
very fairly represents. As an individual, Jefferson
Davis is not worse than many people whom a general
amnesty would preserve in their persons and property. To hang him, and at the same time guarantee
Slavery, would be like destroying a plant by a vain

attempt to kill its most poisonous blossom. Our opposition is not to the blossom, but to the root.

We admit that to strike at the root is a very difficult operation. In the present condition of the country it may present obstacles which will practically prove insuperable. But it is plain that we can strike lower than the blossom; and it is also plain that we must, as practical men, devise some method by which the existence of the Slavocracy as a political power may be annihilated. The President of the United States has lately recommended that Congress offer the co-operation and financial aid of the whole nation in a peaceful effort to abolish Slavery,— with a significant hint, that, unless the loyal Slave States accept the proposition, the necessities of the war may dictate severer measures. Emancipation is the policy of the Government, and will soon be the determination of the people. Whether it shall be gradual or immediate depends altogether on the slaveholders themselves. The prolongation of the war for a year, and the operation of the internal tax bill, will convert all the voters of the Free States, whether Republicans or Democrats, into practical Emancipationists. The tax bill alone will teach the people important lessons which no politicians can gainsay. Every person who buys a piece of broadcloth or calico,—every person who takes a cup of tea or coffee, — every person who lives from day to day on the energy he thinks he derives from patent medicines, or beer, or whiskey, — every person who signs a note, or draws a bill of

DEVELOPMENT, AND EXPEDIENTS.   183

exchange, or sends a telegraphic despatch, or adver-
tises in a newspaper, or makes a will, or "raises"
anything, or manufactures anything, will naturally
inquire why he or she is compelled to submit to an
irritating as well as an onerous tax. The only answer that can possibly be returned is this, — that all
these vexatious burdens are necessary because a comparatively few persons out of an immense population
have chosen to get up a civil war in order to protect
and foster their slave-property, and the political power
it confers. As this property is but a small fraction
of the whole property of the country, and as its
owners are not a hundredth part of the population
of the country, does any sane man doubt that the
slave-property will be relentlessly confiscated in order
that the Slave Power may be forever crushed?

There are, we know, persons in the Free States
who pretend to believe that the war will leave Slavery
where the war found it, that our half a million of
soldiers have gone South on a sort of military picnic,
and will return in a cordial mood towards their
Southern brethren in arms, and that there is no
real depth and earnestness of purpose in the Free
States. Though one year has done the ordinary
work of a century in effecting or confirming changes
in the ideas and sentiments of the people, these
persons still sagely rely on the party-phrases current
some eighteen months ago to reconstruct the Union
on the old basis of the domination of the Slave
Power, through the combination of a divided North

with a united South. By the theory of these persons, there is something peculiarly sacred in property in men, distinguishing it from the more vulgar form of property in things; and though the cost of putting down the Rebellion will nearly equal the value of the Southern slaves, considered as chattels, they suppose that the owners of property in things will cheerfully submit to be taxed for a thousand millions, — a fourth of the almost fabulous debt of England, — without any irritation against the chivalric owners of property in men, whose pride, caprice, and insubordination have made the taxation necessary. Such may possibly be the fact, but as sane men we cannot but disbelieve it. Our conviction is, that, whether the war is ended in three months or in twelve months, the Slave Power is sure to be undermined or overthrown. The sooner the war is ended, the more favorable will be the terms granted to the Slavocracy; but no terms will be granted which do not look to its extinction. The slaveholders are impelled by their system to complete victory or utter ruin. If they obey the laws of their system, they have, from present appearances, nothing but defeat, beggary, and despair to expect. If they violate the laws of their system, they must take their place in some one of the numerous degrees, orders, and ranks of the Abolitionists. It will be well for them, if the wilfulness developed by their miserable system gives way to the plain reason and logic of facts and events. It will be well for them, if they submit to a necessity, not only inherent in the inevitable operation of divine laws, but propelled by half a million of men in arms. Be it that God is on the side of the heaviest column, — there can be no doubt that the heaviest column is now the column of Freedom.

May, 1862.

THE NEW OPPOSITION PARTY.

In the rapid alternations of opinion produced by the varying incidents of the present war, a few days effect the work of centuries. We may therefore be pardoned for giving an antique coloring to an event of recent occurrence. Accordingly we say, once upon a time (Tuesday, July 1, 1862) a great popular convention of all who loved the Constitution and the Union, and all who hated "niggers," was called in the city of New York. The place of meeting was the Cooper Institute, and among the signers to the call were prominent business and professional men of that great metropolis. At this meeting, that eminently calm and learned jurist, the Honorable W. A. Duer, interrupted the course of an elaborate argument for the constitutional rights of the Southern rebels by a melodramatic exclamation, that, if we hanged the traitors of the country in the order of their guilt, "the next man who marched upon the scaffold after Jefferson Davis would be Charles Sumner."

The professed object of the meeting was to form a party devoted to the support of "the Constitution as it is and the Union as it was." Its practical effect was to give the Confederates and foreign powers a broad hint that the North was no longer a unit. The coincidence of the meeting with the Federal reverses before Richmond made its professed object all the more ridiculous. The babbling and bawling of the speakers about " the rights of the South," and " the infamous Abolitionists who disgraced Congress," were but faint echoes of the Confederate cannon which had just ceased to carry death into the Union ranks. Both the speeches and the cannon spoke hostility to the National Cause. The number of the dead, wounded, " missing," and demoralized members of the great Army of the Potomac exceeded, on that Tuesday evening, any army which the United States had ever, before the present war, arrayed on any battle-field. Jefferson Davis, on that evening, was safer at Richmond than Abraham Lincoln was at Washington. A well-grounded apprehension, not only for the " Union," but for the safety of loyal States, was felt on that evening all over the North and West. It was, in fact, the darkest hour in the whole annals of the Republic. Even the authorities at Washington feared that the Army of the Potomac was destroyed. This was exactly the time for the Honorable Mr. Wickliffe and the Honorable Mr. Brooks, for the Honorable W. A. Duer and the Honorable Fernando Wood, to delight the citizens of New York with their peculiar eloquence. This was the appropriate occasion to stand up for the persecuted and down-trodden South! This was the grand opportunity to assert the noble principle, that, by the Constitution, every traitor had the right to be tried by a jury of traitors! This was the time to dishonor all the New England dead! This was the time to denounce the living worthies of New England! Hang Jeff. Davis? Oh, yes! We all know that he is secure behind his triumphant slayers of the real defenders of the Constitution and the Union. Neither hangman nor Major-General can get near *him*. But Charles Sumner is in our power. We can hang him easily. He has not two or four hundred thousand men at his back. He travels alone and un-attended. Do we want a constitutional principle for combining the two men in one act of treason? Here is a calm jurist, — here, gentlemen of the party of the Constitution and the Laws, is the Honorable W. A. Duer. What does he say? Simply this: "Hang Jeff. Davis and Charles Sumner." Davis we cannot hang, but Sumner we can. Let us take one half of his advice; circumstances prevent us from availing ourselves of the whole. There is, to be sure, no possibility of hanging Charles Sumner under any law known to us, the especial champions of the laws. But what then? Don't you see the Honorable W. A. Duer appeals, in this especial case, to "the higher law" of the mob? Don't you see that he desires to shield Jeff. Davis by weaving around his august person all the fine cobwebs of the Law, while he proposes to have Sumner hanged on "irregular" principles, unknown to the jurisprudence of Marshall and Kent?

But enough for the New York meeting. It was of no importance, except as indicating the existence, and giving a blundering expression to the objects, of one of the most malignant and unpatriotic factions which this country has ever seen. The faction is led by a few cold-blooded politicians universally known as the meanest sycophants of the South and the most impudent bullies of the North; but they have contrived to array on their side a considerable number of honest and well-meaning dupes by a dexterous appeal to conservative prejudice and conservative passion, so that hundreds serve their ends who would feel contaminated by their companionship. Never before has Respectability so blandly consented to become the mere instrument and tool of Rascality. The rogues trust to inaugurate treason and anarchy under the pretence of being the special champions of the Constitution and the Laws. Their real adherents are culled from the most desperate and dishonest portions of our population. They can hardly indite a leading article, or make a stump speech, without showing their proclivities to mob-law. To be sure, if a known traitor is informally arrested, they rave about the violation of the rights of the citizen; but they think Lynch-law is good enough for " Abolitionists." If a General is assailed as being over-prudent and cautious in his operations against the common enemy, they immediately laud him as a Hannibal, a Cæsar, and a Napoleon; they assume to be his special friends and admirers; they adjure him to persevere in what they conceive to be his policy of inaction; and, as he is a great master in strategy, they hint that his best strategic movement would be a movement, à la Cromwell, on the Abolitionized Congress of the United States. Disunion, anarchy, the violation of all law, the appeal to the lowest and fiercest impulses of the most ignorant portions of the Northern people, — these constitute the real stock in trade of "the Hang-Jeff.-Davis-and-Charles-Sumner" party; but the thing is so managed, that, formally, this party appears as the special champion of the Union, the Constitution, and the Laws.

Those politicians who personally dislike the present holders of political power, those politicians who think that the measures of confiscation and emancipation passed by the Congress which has just adjourned are both unjust and impolitic, unconsciously slide into the aiders and abettors of the knaves they individually despise and distrust. The "radicals" must, they say, at all events, be checked; and they lazily follow the lead of the rascals. The rascals intend to ruin the country; but then they propose to do it in a constitutional way. The only thing, it seems, that a lawyer and a jurist can consider is Form. If the country is dismembered, if all its defenders are slain, if the Southern Confederacy is triumphant, not only at Richmond, but at Washington and New York, if eight millions of people beat twenty millions, and the greatest of all democracies ignominiously succumbs to the basest of all aristocracies, the true patriots

will still have the consolation, that the defeat, the
" damned defeat," occurred under the strictest forms
of Law. Better that ten Massachusetts soldiers should
be killed than that one negro should be illegally freed !
Better that Massachusetts should be governed by Jeff.
Davis than that it should be represented by such men
as Charles Sumner and Henry Wilson, notoriously
hostile to the constitutional rights of the South !
Subjection, in itself, is bad ; but the great American
idea of local governments for local purposes, and a
general government for general purposes, still, thank
God ! may survive it. To be sure, we may be beaten
and enslaved. The rascals, renegades, and liberticides may gain their object. This object we shall
ever contemn. But if they gain it fairly, under the
forms of the Constitution, it is the duty of all good
citizens to submit. Our Southern opponents, we
acknowledge, committed some " irregularities ; " but
nobody can assert, that, in dealing with them, we
deviated, by a hair's-breadth, from the powers in-
trusted to the Government by the Fathers of the
Republic. While the country is convulsed by a rebellion unprecedented in the whole history of the
world, we are compelled by our principles to look
upon it as lawyers, and not as statesmen. We apply
to it the same principles which our venerated forefathers applied to Shays's Rebellion in Massachusetts
and the Whiskey Insurrection in Pennsylvania. To
be sure, the " circumstances " are different ; but we
need not remind the philanthropic inhabitants of our

section of the country, that "principles are eternal."
We judge the existing case by these eternal principles. We may fail, and fail ignominiously; but, in
our failure, nobody can say that we violated any
sacred form of the ever-glorious Constitution of the
United States. The Constitution has in it no provisions to secure its own existence by unconstitutional means. It is therefore our duty, as lawyers
as well as legislators, to allow the gentlemen who
have repudiated it, because they were defeated in an
election, to enjoy all its benefits. That they do not
seem to appreciate these benefits, but shoot, in a
shockingly "irregular" manner, all who insist on
imposing on them its blessings, furnishes no reason
why we should partake in their guilt by violating its
provisions. It is true that the Government established by the Constitution may fall by a strict ad-
herence to our notions of the Constitution; but even
in that event we shall have the delicious satisfaction
of contemplating it in memory as a beautiful idea,
after it has ceased to exist as a palpable fact. As
the best constitution ever devised by human wisdom,
we shall always find a more exquisite delight in medi-
tating on the mental image of its perfect features
than in enjoying the practical blessings of any other
Government which may be established after it is
dead and gone; and our feeling regarding it can be
best expressed in the words in which the lyric poet
celebrates his loyalty to the soul of the departed
object of his affection : —

" Though many a gifted mind we meet,
    And fairest forms we see,
To live with them is far less sweet
    Than to remember thee ! "

It is fortunate both for our safety and the safety of
the Constitution, that these politico-sentimental gentlemen represent only a certain theory of the Constitution, and not the Constitution itself. Their leading
defect is an incapacity to adjust their profound legal
intellects to the altered circumstances of the country.
Any child in political knowledge is competent to give
them this important item of political information, —
that by no constitution of government ever devised by
human morality and intelligence were the rights of
rascals so secured as to give them the privilege of
trampling on the rights of honest men. Any child
in political knowledge is competent to inform them
of this fundamental fact, underlying all laws and
constitutions, — that, if a miscreant attempts to cut
your throat, you may resist him by all the means
which your strength and his weakness place in your
power. Any child in political knowledge is further
competent to furnish them with this additional bit of
wisdom, — that every constitution of government pro-
vides, under the war-power it confers, against its own
overthrow by rebels and by enemies. If rebels rise
to the dignity and exert the power of enemies, they
can be proceeded against both as rebels and as enemies. As rebels, the Government is bound to give
them all the securities which the Constitution may

13

guarantee to traitors. As enemies, the Government is restricted only by the vast and vague " rights of war," of which its own military necessities must be the final judge.

" But," say the serene thinkers and scholars whom the rogues use as mouthpieces, " our object is simply to defend the Constitution. We do not believe that the Government has any of the so-called 'rights of war' against the rebels. If Jefferson Davis has committed the crime of treason, he has the same right to be tried by a jury of the district in which his alleged crime was committed that a murderer has to be tried by a similar jury. We know that Mr. Davis, in case the rebellion is crushed, will not only be triumphantly acquitted, but will be sent to Congress as Senator from Mississippi. This is mortifying in itself, but it still is a beautiful illustration of the merits of our admirable system of government. It enables the South to play successfully the transparent game of ' Heads I win, tails you lose,' and so far must be reckoned bad. But this evil is counterbalanced by so many blessings, that nobody but a miserable Abolitionist will think of objecting to the arrangement. We, on the whole, agree with the traitors, whose designs we lazily aid, in thinking that Jeff. Davis and Charles Sumner are equally guilty, in a fair estimate of the causes of our present misfortunes. Hang both, we say ; and we say it with an inward confidence that neither will be hanged, if the true principles of the Constitution be carried out."

The political rogues and the class of honest men
we have referred to are, therefore, practically associated in one party to oppose the present Government.
The rogues lead ; the honest men follow.   If this new
party succeeds, we shall have the worst party in power
that the country has ever known.   Buchanan as President, and Floyd as Secretary of War, were bad enough.
But Buchanan and Floyd had no large army to command, no immense material of war to direct.   As far
as they could, they worked mischief, and mischief
only.   But their means were limited.   The Administration which will succeed that of Abraham Lincoln
will have under its control one of the largest and
ablest armies and navies in the world.   Every general and every admiral will be compelled to obey the
orders of the Administration.   If the Administration
be in the hands of secret traitors, the immense military and naval power of the country will be used for
its own destruction.   A compromise will be patched
up with the Rebel States.   The leaders of the rebellion will be invited back to their old seats of power.
A united South combined with a Pro-slavery faction
in the North will rule the nation.   And all this enormous evil will be caused by the simplicity of honest
men in falling into the trap set for them by traitors
and rogues.

September, 1862.

THE CAUSES OF FOREIGN ENMITY TO THE
UNITED STATES.

THE hostility of foreign governments to the United States is due as much at least to dread of their growing power as dislike of their democracy; and accordingly the theory of the Secessionists as to the character of our Union has been as acceptable to the understandings of our foreign enemies as the acts of the Rebels against its government have been pleasing to their sympathies. They well know that a union of States whose government recognized the right of Secession would be as weak as an ordinary league between independent sovereignties; and as the rapid growth of the States in population, wealth, and power is certain, they naturally desire that, if united, these States shall be an aggregation of forces neutralizing each other, rather than a fusion of forces which, for general purposes, would make them a giant nationality. Accordingly, centralized France reads to us edifying homilies on the advantages of disintegration; and England, rich with the spoils of suppressed insurrections, adjures us most plaintively to respect the sacred rights of rebellion. The simple explanation of this hypocrisy or irony is, that both France and

England are anxious that the strength of the United States shall not correspond to their bulk. The looser the tie of union, the greater the number of confederacies into which the nation should split, the safer they would feel. The doctrine of the inherent and undivided sovereignty of the States will therefore find resolute champions abroad as long as it has the most inconsiderable faction to support it at home.

The European nations are kept in order by what is called the Balance of Power, and this policy they would delight to see established on this continent. Should the different States of the American Union be occupied, like the European States, in checking each other, they could not act as a unit, and their terrific rate of growth in wealth and population, as compared with that of the nations across the Atlantic, would not excite in the latter such irritation and alarm. The magic which has changed English abolitionists into partisans of slaveholders, and French imperialists into champions of insurrection, came from the figures of the Census Reports. It is calculated that the United States, if the rate of growth which obtained between 1850 and 1860 is continued, will have, forty years hence, a hundred millions of inhabitants, and four hundred and twenty thousand millions of dollars of taxable wealth, — over three times the present population, and over ten times the present wealth, of the richest of European nations. It is probable that this concrete fact exerts more influence on the long-headed statesmen of Europe than any abstract dislike of de-

mocracy. The only union which they could bring
against such a power would be a league, a confederacy, a continuous and subsisting treaty, between
sovereign powers. Is it surprising that they should
wish our union to be of the same character? Is it
surprising that the contemplation of a government,
whether despotic or democratic, which could act directly on a hundred millions of people, with the
supreme right of taxing property to the amount of
four hundred and twenty billions of dollars, should
fill them with dismay?

The inherent weakness of a league, even when its
general object is such as to influence the passions of
the nations which compose it, is well known to all
European statesmen. The various alliances against
France show the insuperable difficulties in the way of
giving to confederacies of sovereign States a unity and
efficiency corresponding to their aggregate strength,
and the necessity which the leaders of such alliances
are always under of expending half their skill and
energy in preventing the loosely compacted league
from falling to pieces. The alliance under the lead
of William III. barely sustained itself against Louis
XIV., though William was the ablest statesman in
Europe, and had been trained in the tactics of confederacies from his cradle. The alliance under the lead
of Marlborough owed its measure of success to his
infinite address and miraculous patience as much as
to his consummate military genius; and the ignominious "secession" of England, in the treaty of

Utrecht, ended in making it one of the most conspicuous examples of the weakness of such combinations. When the exceptional military genius, as in the case of Frederick and Napoleon, has been on the side of the single power assailed, the results have been all the more remarkable. The coalition against Frederick, the ruler of five millions of people, was composed of sovereigns who ruled a hundred millions ; and at the end of seven years of war they had not succeeded in wringing permanently from his grasp a square mile of territory. The first coalitions against Napoleon resulted only in making him the master of Europe ; and he was crushed at last merely by the dead weight of the nations which the senselessness of his political passions brought down upon his empire. Indeed, the trouble with all leagues is, that they are commanded, more or less, by debating societies ; and a debating society is weak before a man. The Southern Confederacy is a confederacy only in name : for no despotism in Europe or Asia has more relentless unity of purpose, and in none does debate exercise less control over executive affairs. All the powers of the government are practically absorbed in Jefferson Davis, and a rebellion in the name of State Rights has ended in a military autocracy, in which all rights, personal and State, are suspended.

Now, as it is impossible for European governments to combine efficiently against such a colossal power as the United States promise within a few generations to be, provided the unity of the nation is pre-

served with its growth, they naturally favor every
element of disintegration which will reduce the separate States to the condition of European States. Earl
Russell's famous saying, that "the North is fighting
for power, the South for independence," is to be
interpreted in this sense. What he overlooked was
the striking fact which distinguishes the States of the
American Republic from the States of Europe. The
latter are generally separated by race and nationality,
or, where composed of heterogeneous materials, are
held together by military power. The people of the
United States are homogeneous, and rapidly assimi-
late into American citizens the foreigners they so
cordially welcome. No man has lifted his hand
against the government as an Irishman, a Frenchman, a German, an Italian, a Dane, but only as a
slaveholder, or as a citizen of a State controlled by
slaveholders. The insurrection was started in the
interest of an institution, and not of a race. To
compare such a rebellion with European rebellions is
to confuse things essentially distinct. The American
government is so constituted that nobody has an
interest in overturning it, unless his interest is opposed to that of the mass of the citizens with whom
he is placed on an equality; and hence his treason
is necessarily a revolt against the principle of equal
rights. In Europe, it is needless to say, every rebellion with which an American can sympathize is a
rebellion in favor of the principle against which the
slaveholders' rebellion is an armed protest. An in-

surrection in Russia to restore serfdom, an insurrection in Italy to restore the dethroned despots, an
insurrection in England to restore the Stuart system
of kingly government, an insurrection anywhere to
restore what the progress of civilization had made
contemptible or accursed, would be the only fit parallel to the insurrection of the Southern Confederates.
The North is fighting for power which is its due,
because it is just and right; the South is fighting
for independence, in order to remove all checks on
its purpose to oppress and enslave. The fact that the
power for which the North fights is a very different
thing from the power which a European monarchy
struggles to preserve and extend, the fact that it is
the kind of power which oppressed nationalities seek
in their efforts for independence, only makes our
foreign critics more apprehensive of its effects. It
is a dangerous power to them, because, founded in
the consent of the people, there is no limit to its
possible extension, except in the madness or guilt of
that portion of the people who are restive under the
restraints of justice and impatient under the rule of
freedom.

It would be doing cruel wrong to Earl Russell's
intelligence to suppose that he really believed what
he said, when he drew a parallel between the American Revolution and the Rebellion of the Confederate
States, and asserted that the right of the Southern
States to secede from the American Union was identical with the right of the Colonies to sever their

connection with Great Britain. We believe the Colonies were right in their revolt. But if the circumstances had been different, — if since the reign of William III. they had nominated or controlled almost every Prime Minister, had shaped the policy of the British Empire, had enjoyed not only a representation in Parliament, but in the basis of representation had been favored with a special discrimination in their favor against Kent and Yorkshire, — if both in the House of Lords and the House of Commons they had not only been dominant, but had treated the Bentincks, Cavendishes, and Russells, the Montagus, Walpoles, and Pitts, with overbearing insolence, — and if, after wielding power so long and so arrogantly, they had rebelled at the first turn in political affairs which seemed to indicate that they were to be reduced from a position of superiority to one of equality, — if our forefathers had acted after this wild fashion, we should not only think that the Revolution they achieved was altogether unjustifiable, but we should blush at the thought of being descended from such despot-demagogues. This is a very feeble statement of the case which would connect the Revolt of the American Colonies with the Revolt of the American Liberticides ; and Earl Russell is too well-informed a statesman not to know that his parallel fails in every essential particular. He threw it out, as he threw out his sounding antithesis about " power " and " independence," to catch ears not specially blessed with brains between them.

But European statesmen, in order to promote the causes of American dissensions, are willing not only to hazard fallacies which do not impose on their own understandings, but to give aid and comfort to iniquities which in Europe have long been antiquated. They thus tolerate chattel slavery, not because they sympathize with it, but because it is an element of disturbance in the growth of American power. Though it has for centuries been outgrown by the nations of Western Europe, and is repugnant to all their ideas and sentiments, they are willing to give it their moral support, provided it will break up the union of the people of the States, or remain as a constantly operating cause of enmity between the sections of a reconstructed Union. They would tolerate Mormonism or Atheism or Diabolism, if they thought it would have a similar effect; but at the same time they would not themselves legalize polygamy, or deny the existence of God, or inaugurate the worship of the Devil. Indeed, while giving slavery a politic sanction, they despise in their hearts the people who are so barbarous as to maintain such an institution; and the Southern rebel or Northern demagogue who thinks his championship of slavery really earns him any European respect is under that kind of delusion which it is always for the interest of the plotter to cultivate in the tool. It was common, a few years ago, to represent the Abolitionist as the dupe or agent of the aristocracies of Europe. It certainly might be supposed that persons who

made this foolish charge were competent at least to
see that the present enemy of the unity of the American people is the Pro-slavery fanatic, and that it is
on his knavery or stupidity that the ill-wishers to
American unity now chiefly rely.

For the war has compelled these ill-wishers to
modify their most cherished theory of democracy in
the United States. They thought that the marvellous energy for military combination, developed by a
democracy suddenly emancipated from oppression,
such as was presented by the French people in the
Revolution of 1789, was not the characteristic of a
democracy which had grown up under democratic institutions. The first was anarchy *plus* the dictator;
the second was merely " anarchy *plus* the constable."
They had an obstinate prepossession, that, in a settled democracy like ours, the selfishness of the individual was so stimulated that he became incapable
of self-sacrifice for the public good. The case with
which the government of the United States has raised
men by the million and money by the billion has
overturned this theory, and shown that a republic, of
which individual liberty and general equality form the
animating principles, can still rapidly avail itself of
the property and personal service of all the individuals who compose it, and that self-seeking is not
more characteristic of a democracy in time of peace
than self-sacrifice is characteristic of the same democracy in time of war. The overwhelming and
apparently unlimited power of a government thus *of*

the people and *for* the people is what the war has demonstrated, and it very naturally excites the fear and
jealousy of governments which are based on less firm
foundations in the popular mind and heart and will.

It is doubtless true that many candid foreign
thinkers favor the disintegration of the American
Union because they believe that the consolidation of
its power would make it the meddlesome tyrant of
the world. They admit that the enterprise, skill, and
labor of the people, applied to the unbounded undeveloped resources of the country, will enable them to
create wealth very much faster than other nations,
and that the population, fed by continual streams of
immigration, will also increase with a corresponding
rapidity. They admit that, if kept united, a few generations will be sufficient to make them the richest,
largest, and most powerful nation in the world. But
they also fear that this nation will be an armed and
aggressive democracy, deficient in public reason and
public conscience, disposed to push unjust claims with
insolent pertinacity, and impelled by a spirit of propa-
gandism which will continually disturb the peace of
Europe. It is curious that this impression is derived
from the actions of the government while it was controlled by the traitors now in rebellion against it, and
from the professions of those Northern demagogues
who are most in sympathy with European opinion
concerning the justice and policy of the war. Mr.
Fernando Wood, the most resolute of all the Northern advocates of peace, recommended from his seat

in Congress but a month ago, that a compromise be patched up with the Rebels on the principle of sacrificing the negro, and then that both sections unite to seize Canada, Cuba, and Mexico. The kind of "democracy" which Mr. Jefferson Davis and Mr. Fernando Wood represent is the kind of democracy which has always been the great disturber of our foreign relations, and it is a democracy which will be rendered powerless by the triumph of the national arms. The United States of 1900, with their population of a hundred millions, and their wealth of four hundred and twenty billions, will, we believe, be a power for good, and not for evil. They will be strong enough to make their rights respected everywhere; but they will not force their ideas on other nations at the point of the bayonet; they will not waste their energies in playing the part of the armed propagandist of democratic opinions in Europe; and the contagion of their principles will only be the natural result of the example of peace, prosperity, freedom, and justice, which they will present to the world. In Europe, where power commonly exists only to be abused, this statement would be received with an incredulous smile; but we have no reason to doubt that, among the earnest patriots who are urging on the present war for Liberty and Union to a victorious conclusion, it would be considered the most commonplace of truths.

March, 1865.

RECONSTRUCTION AND NEGRO SUFFRAGE.

THE submission of the Rebel armies and the occupation of the Rebel territory by the forces of the
United States are successes which have been purchased at the cost of the lives of half a million of
loyal men and a debt of nearly three thousand millions of dollars; but, according to theories of State
Rights now springing anew to life, victory has smitten
us with impotence. The war, it seems, was waged for
the purpose of forcing the sword out of the Rebels'
hands, and forcing into them the ballot. At an enormous waste of treasure and blood we have acquired
the territory for which we fought; and lo! it is not
ours, but belongs to the people we have been engaged
in fighting, in virtue of the Constitution we have been
fighting for. The Federal Government is now, it
appears, what Wigfall elegantly styled it four years
ago, — nothing but "the one-horse concern at Washington:" the real power is in the States it has subdued. We are therefore expected to act like the
savage, who, after thrashing his Fetich for disap-
pointing his prayers, falls down again and worships
it. Our Fetich is State Rights, as perversely misun-
derstood. The Rebellion would have been soon put
down, had it been merely an insurrectionary outbreak

of masses of people without any political organization.
Its tremendous force came from its being a revolt of
States, with the capacity to employ those powers of
taxation and conscription which place the persons
and property of all residing in political communities
at the service of their governments. And now that
characteristic which gave strength to the Rebel communities in war is invoked to shield them from
Federal regulation in defeat. We are required to
substitute technicalities for facts; to consider the
Rebellion — what it notoriously was not — a mere
revolt of loose aggregations of men owing allegiance
to the United States; and to hold the States, which
endowed them with such a perfect organization and
poisonous vitality, as innocent of the crime. The
verbal dilemma in which this reasoning places us is
this: that the Rebel States could not do what they did,
and therefore we cannot do what we must. Among
other things which it is said we cannot do, the pre-
scribing of the qualifications of voters in the States
occupies the most important place; and it is necessary
to inquire whether the Rebel communities now held
by our military power are States, in the sense that
word bears in the Federal Constitution. If they are,
we have not only no right to say that negroes shall
enjoy in them the privilege of voting, but no right to
prescribe any qualifications for white voters.

In the American system, the process by which constitutions are made and governments instituted is by
conventions of the people. The State constitutions

were ordained by conventions of the people of the
several States; the Constitution of the United States
was made the supreme law of the land by conventions
of the people of all the States; and the only method
by which a State could be released, with any show of
legality, from its obligations to the United States,
would be the assent of the same power which created
the Federal Constitution,— namely, conventions of
the people of *all* the States. The course adopted by
the so-called "seceding" States was separate State
action by popular conventions in the States seceding.
This was an appeal to the original authority from
which State governments and constitutions derived
their powers, but a violation of solemn faith towards
the Government and Constitution decreed by the people of all the States, and which, by the assent of each
State, formed a vital part of each State constitution.
No State convention could be called for the purpose
of separating from the Union,— of destroying what
the officers calling it had sworn to support,— without
making official perjury the preliminary condition of
State sovereignty. Looked at from the point of view
of the State seceding, the act was an assertion of
State independence; looked at from the point of view
of the Constitution of the United States, it was an act
of State suicide. The State so acting through a convention of its people was no longer a State, in the
meaning that word bears in the Federal Constitution;
for whatever it may have been before it was one of
the United States, it was transformed into a different

14

political society by making the Federal Constitution a part of its own organic law. In cutting that bond, it bled to death as a State, as far as the Federal Constitution knows a State, to rise again as a Rebel community, holding a portion of the Federal territory by force of arms. A State, in the meaning of the Federal Constitution, is a political community forbidden to exercise sovereign powers, and at once a part of the Federal Government and owing allegiance to it. Is South Carolina, which has exercised sovereign powers, which has broken its allegiance to the Federal Government, and which at present is certainly not a part of it, such a political society ?

It is, we know, contended by some reasoners on the subject, that the Rebel States *could not* do what they palpably *did*. This course of argument is sustained only by confounding duties with powers. By the Constitution a State cannot (that is, has no right to) secede, only as, by the moral law, a man cannot (that is, has no right to) commit murder ; nevertheless, States have broken away from their obligations to the Union, as murderers have broken away from their obligations to the moral law. It is folly to claim that criminal acts are impossible because they are unjustifiable. The real question relates to the condition in which the criminal acts of the Rebel States left them as political societies. They cannot claim, as some of their Northern champions do for them, that, being *in* the Union in our view, and *out* of it in their own, the only result of defeating them as Rebels is to restore them as citizens. This would be playing a political game of " Heads I win, tails you lose," which they must know can hardly succeed with a nation which has made such enormous sacrifices of treasure and blood in putting them down. After having, by a solemn act of their own, through conventions of the people, forsworn their duties to the Constitution, they by that act forfeited its privileges. In our view they became Rebel enemies, against whom we had both the rights of sovereignty and the rights of war; in their own view, they became foreigners; and from that moment they had no more "constitutional" control of the area they occupied, were no more "States," than if they had transferred their allegiance to a European power, and the war had been prosecuted to wrest the territory they occupied, and the people they ruled, from the clutch of England or France. Even if we consider the Union a mere partnership of States, the same principle will apply; for partnership implies mutual obligations, and no partner can steal the property of his firm, and abscond with it, and then, after he has been hunted down and arrested, claim the rights in the business he enjoyed before he turned rogue.

But it is sometimes asserted that the small minority of citizens in the Rebel States claiming to be, and to have been, loyal, constitute the States in the constitutional meaning of the term. Now, without insisting on the fact that it is so plainly impossible accurately to distinguish these from the disloyal, that an oath, not required by State constitutions, has, in the recent attempt at reconstruction, been imposed by Federal authority on all voters alike, it is plain that no minority in a political society can claim exemption from political evils it had not power to prevent. Had we gone to war with Great Britain, the property of Cobden and Bright on the high seas would have been as liable to capture as that of Lindsay or Laird. No loyal citizens at the South could have been more bitterly opposed to Secession than some of our Northern Copperheads were to the war for the Union; and yet the persons of the Copperheads were as liable to conscription, and their property to taxation, as those of the most enthusiastic Republicans. There would be an end to political societies, if men should refuse to be held responsible for all public acts except those they personally approved. A member of a community whose people, in a convention, broke faith with the United States, and made war against it, the Southern Unionist was forced into complicity with the crime. By the pressure of a power he could not resist he was compelled to pay Confederate taxes, serve in Confederate armies, and become a portion of the Confederate strength. More than this: the property in human beings, which he held by local law, was confiscated by the Federal Government's edict of emancipation, equally with the same kind of property held by the most disloyal. And now that the war is over, he and those who sympathized with him are not the State, which was extinguished by its own act when it rebelled. He and his friends may be the objects of sympathy, of honor, of reward; but in the work of reconstruction the interest and safety of the great body of loyal citizens of the United States, of the persons who have bought the territory at such a terrible price, are to be primarily consulted. And not simply because such a course is expedient, but because the Southern Unionists can advance no valid claim to be the political societies which were recognized by the Federal Constitution as States before the Rebellion. If they were, they might proceed at once to assume the powers of the States, without any authority from Washington, and without calling any convention to form a *new* constitution. If, on the breaking out of the Rebellion, they had rallied in defence of the old constitutions within State limits, preserved the organization of the States in all departments, raised and equipped armies, and conducted a war against the Confederates as traitors to their respective States as well as to the United States, they might present some claims to be considered the States; but this they did not do, and they were not powerful enough to do it. The large proportion of them were compelled to form a part of the Rebel power.

And this brings us directly to the heart of the matter. It is asserted that the Acts of Secession, being unconstitutional, were inoperative and void. But they were passed by the people of the several States which seceded, and the persons and property of the whole people were indiscriminately employed in making them effective. The States held by Rebel armies were Rebel States. All the population were necessarily, in the view of the Federal Government, Rebel enemies. Consequently the territory of the States was as "void" of citizens of the United States as the Acts of Secession were "void." The only things left, then, were the inoperative ideas of States.

Again, to put the argument in another form, it is asserted that, though the people of a State may commit treason, the State itself remains unaffected by the crime. A distinction is here made between a State and the people who constitute it, — between the State and the persons who create its constitution and organize its government. The State constitution which existed while it was a State, in the Federal meaning of the word, was destroyed in an essential part by the same authority which created it, namely, a convention of the people of the State; and yet it is said that the State remained unaffected by the deed. By this course of reasoning, a State is defined an abstract essence which can comfortably exist in all its rights and privileges, *in potentia*, apart from all visible embodiment; a State which is the possibility of a State and not the actuality of one; a State which can be brought into the line of real vision only by some such contrivance as that employed by the German playwright, who, in a drama on the subject of the Creation, represented Adam crossing the stage *going* to be created.

There is, it is true, one method of getting a kind of body to this abstract State, but it is a method which

may well frighten the hardiest American reasoner.
It was employed by Burke in one of the audacities of
his logic directed against the governments established
after the French Revolution of 1789. He took the
ground that France was not in the French territory
or in the French people, but in the persons who represented its old polity, and who had escaped into England and Germany. These constituted what he called
" Moral France," in distinction from " Geographical
France ; " and Moral France, he said, had emigrated.

But as few or none will be inclined to take the
ground that South Carolina and Georgia exist in the
persons who left their soil on the breaking out of
the Rebellion, we are forced back to the conception
of an invisible spiritual soul and essence of a State sur-
viving its bodily destruction. But even this abstrac-
tion must still, from the point of view of the Federal
Constitution, be conceived of as owing allegiance to
the Federal Government; and it can confessedly get
a new body only by the exercise of Federal authority.
Its leading institution has been destroyed by Federal
power. Its old legislature and governor, who alone,
on State principles, could call a convention of the
people, are spotted all over with treason, and might
be hanged as traitors, by the law of the United States,
while engaged in measures to repair the broken unity
of the State life, — a fact which is of itself sufficient
to show that the old State is dead beyond all bodily
resurrection. The white inhabitants who occupy its
old geographical limits are defeated Rebels, and not

one can exercise the privilege of voting without taking
an oath which no real " State " prescribes. They are
all born again into citizens by a Federal fiat ; they are
" pardoned " into voters ; they derive their rights not
from their old charters, but from an act of amnesty.
Far from any discrimination being made between loyal
and disloyal, the great body of both classes are compelled to submit to Federal terms of citizenship or be
disfranchised ; and they are called upon, not to revive
the old State, but to make a new one, within the old
State lines. And all this would result from the necessity of the case, even if it were not made justifiable by the essential sovereignty of the United States,
of which the war-power is but an incident. But if the
Federal Government can thus give the white inhabitants, or any portion of them, the right of suffrage,
cannot it confer that right upon the black freedmen ?
It will not do, at this stage, to say that the Federal
Government has no right to prescribe the qualifications of voters in the States ; because, in the case of
the whites, it does and must prescribe them ; and
President Johnson has just the same right to say that
negroes shall vote as to say that pardoned Rebels shall
vote. The right of States to decide on the qualifications of its electors applies only to loyal States ; it
cannot apply to political communities which have lost
by Rebellion the Federal character of " States," which
notoriously have no legitimate State authority to decide the question of qualification, and which are now
taking the preparatory steps of forming themselves

into States through the agency of provisional Federal governors, directing voters, constituted such by Federal authority, to elect delegates to a convention of the people. It is a misuse of constitutional language to call North Carolina and Mississippi " States," in the same sense in which we use the term in speaking of Ohio and Massachusetts. When their conventions have framed State constitutions, when their State governments are organized, and when their senators and representatives have been admitted into the Congress of the United States, then, indeed, they will be States, entitled to all the privileges of Ohio and Massachusetts; and woe be to us, if they are reconstructed on wrong principles !

It is often said that, although the Federal Government may have the right and power to decide who shall be considered " the people " of the Rebel States, in so important a matter as the conversion of them into States of the Federal Union, it is still politic and just to make the qualifications of voters as nearly as possible what they were before the Rebellion. Conceding this, we still have to face the fact that a large body of men, held before the war as slaves, have been emancipated, and added to the body of the people. They are now as free as the white men. The old constitutions of the Slave States could have no application to the new condition of affairs. The change in the circumstances, by which four years have done the ordinary work of a century, demands a corresponding change in the application of old rules, even admitting that we should take them as a guide. Having converted the loyal blacks from slaves into the condition of citizens of the United States, there can be no reason or justice or policy in allowing them to be made, in localities recently Rebel, the subjects of whites who have but just purged themselves from the guilt of treason.

The question of negro suffrage being thus reduced to a question of expediency, to be decided on its own merits, the first argument brought against it is based on the proposition that it is inexpedient to give the privilege of voting to the ignorant and unintelligent. This sounds well; but a moment's reflection shows us that the objection is directed simply against deficiencies of education and intelligence which happen to be accompanied with a black skin. Three fifths or three fourths of the poor whites of the South cannot read or write; and they are cruelly belied, if they do not add to their ignorance that more important disqualification for good citizenship, — indisposition or incapacity for work. In general, the American system proceeds on the idea that the best way of qualifying men to vote is voting, as the best way of teaching boys to swim is to let them go into the water. "Our national experience," says Chief-Justice Chase, in a letter to the New Orleans freedmen, " has demonstrated that public order reposes most securely on the broad base of Universal Suffrage. It has proved, also, that universal suffrage is the surest guaranty and most powerful stimulus of individual, social, and political progress." But even if we take the ground that education and suffrage, though not actually, should properly be, indentical, the argument would not apply to the case of the freedmen. What we need primarily at the South is loyal citizens of the United States, and treason there is in inverse proportion to ignorance. If, in reconstructing the Rebel communities, we make suffrage depend on education, we inevitably put the local governments into the hands of a small minority of prominent Confederates whom we have recently defeated; of men physically subdued, but morally rebellious; of men who have used their education simply to destroy the prosperity created by the industry of the ignorant and enslaved, and who, however skilful they may be as "architects of ruin," have shown no capacity for the nobler art which repairs and rebuilds. If, on the other hand, we make suffrage depend on color, we disfranchise the only portion of the population on whose allegiance we can thoroughly rely, and give the States over to white ignorance and idleness led by white intrigue and disloyalty. We are placed by events in that strange condition in which the safety of that "republican form of government" we desire to insure the Southern States has more safeguards in the instincts of the ignorant than in the intelligence of the educated. The right of the freedmen, not merely to the common privileges of citizens, but to *own themselves*, depends on the connection of the States in which they live with the United States being preserved. They must know that Secession and

State Independence mean their re-enslavement. Sauls-
bury of Delaware, and Willey of West Virginia, declared in the Senate, in 1862, that the Rebel States,
when they came back into the Union, would have the
legal power to re-enslave any blacks whom the National Government might emancipate; and it is only
the plighted faith of the United States to the freedmen, which such a proceeding would violate, which can
prevent the crime from being perpetrated. It is as
citizens of the United States, and not as inhabitants
of North Carolina or Mississippi, that their freedom is
secure. Their instincts, their interests, and their position will thus be their teachers in the duties of citizenship. They are as sure to vote in accordance with the
most advanced ideas of the time as most of the embittered aristocracy are to vote for the most retrograde.
They will, though at first ignorant, necessarily be in
political sympathy with the most educated voters of
New York, Ohio, and Massachusetts; if they were as
low in the scale of being as their bitterest revilers assert, they would still be forced by their instincts into
intuitions of their interests; and their interests are
identical with those of civilization and progress. We
suppose that those who think them most degraded
would be willing to concede to them the possession of
a little selfish cunning; and a little selfish cunning is
enough to bring them into harmony with the purposes, if not the spirit, of the largest-minded philanthropy and statesmanship of the North.

It is claimed, we know, by some of the hardiest

dealers in assertion, that the freedmen will vote as their former masters shall direct; but as this argument is generally put forward by those whose sympathies are with the former masters rather than with the emancipated bondmen, one finds it difficult to understand why they should object to a policy which will increase the power of those whom they wish to be dominant. The circumstances, however, under which credulous ignorance becomes the prey of unscrupulous intelligence are familiar to all who have observed our elections. An ignorant Irish Catholic may be the victim of a Pro-slavery demagogue, because the latter flatters his prejudices; but can he be deceived by a bigoted Know-Nothing, who is the object of them? The only demagogue who could control the negro would be an abolition demagogue, and he could control him to his harm only when the negro was deprived of his rights. The slave-masters were wont to pay considerable attention to zoölogy, — not because they were interested in science, but because in that science they thought they could obtain arguments for expelling blacks from the human species. In their zoölogical studies, did they ever learn that mice instinctively seek the protection of the cat, or that the deer speeds to, instead of from, the hunter? The persons whose votes the late masters would be most likely to control would palpably be those whose votes they always have controlled, namely, the poor whites; for in the late Slave States white aristocrat is still bound to white democrat by the strong tie of a common contempt of "the nigger." Meanwhile it is not difficult to believe that, among four millions of black people, there are enough plantation Hampdens and Adamses to give political organization to their brethren, and make their votes efficient for the protection of their interests.

We think, then, it may be taken for granted that, while ignorant, the freedmen will vote right by the force of their instincts, and that the education they require will be the result of their possessing the political power to demand it. Free schools are not the creations of private benevolence, but of public taxation; it is useless to expect a system of universal education in a community which does not rest on universal suffrage; and the children of the poor freeman are educated at the public expense, not so much by the pleading of the children's needs as by the power of the father's ballot. To take the ground that the "superior" race will educate the "inferior" race it has but just held in bondage, that it will humanely set to work to prepare and qualify the "niggers" to be voters, only escapes from being considered the artifice of the knave by charitably referring it to the credulity of the simpleton. We do not send, as Mr. Sumner has happily said, "the child to be nursed by the wolf;" and he might have added, that the only precedent for such a proceeding, the case of Romulus and Remus, has lost all the little force it may once have had by the criticism of Niebuhr.

If the negroes do not get the power of political self-protection in the conventions of the people which are now to be called, it is not reasonable to expect they will ever get it by the consent of the whites. Legal State conventions are called by previous law. There is no previous State law applicable to the Rebel communities, because, revolutionized by rebellion, the very persons who are qualified by the old State laws to call conventions are disqualified by the laws of the United States. The result is, that the people are an unorganized mass, to be reorganized under the lead of the Federal Government; and of this mass of people — literally, in this case " the masses " — the free blacks are as much a part as the free whites. As soon, however, as the machinery of State governments is set in motion by these conventions, — as soon as these governments are recognized by the President and Congress, — no conventions to alter the constitutions agreed upon can be called, except by previous State laws. If negro suffrage is not granted in the election of members to the present conventions, the power will pass permanently into the hands of the whites, and the only opportunity for a peaceful settlement of the question will be lost. At the very time when, abstractly, no party has legal rights, and only one party has claims, we propose deliberately to sacrifice the party that has claims to the party which will soon acquire legal rights to oppress the claimants. For, disguise it as we may, the United States Government really holds and exercises the power which gives vitality to the preliminaries of reconstruction, and it is therefore responsible for all evils in the future which shall spring from its neglect or injustice in the present.

The addition, too, of four millions of persons to the people of the South, without any corresponding addition of voters, will increase the political power of the ruling whites to an alarming extent, while it will remove all checks on its mischievous exercise. The Constitution declares that " representatives and direct taxes shall be apportioned among the several States which may be included in this Union, according to their respective numbers, which shall be determined by adding to the whole number of free persons, including those bound to service for a term of years, and excluding Indians not taxed, three fifths of all other persons." The unanswerable argument presented at the time against the clause relating to the slaves did not prevent its adoption. " If," it was said, " the negroes are property, why is other property not represented? if men, why three fifths?" Still, the South has always enjoyed the double privilege of treating the negro as an article of merchandise and of using three fifths of him as political capital. He has thus added to the power by which he was enslaved, and has been represented in Congress by persons who regarded him either as a beast or as " a descendant of Ham." In 1860, when the ratio of representation was about one hundred and twenty-seven thousand, the South had, by the three-fifths rule, the right to eighteen more representatives in

Congress, and eighteen more electoral votes, than it would have had if only free persons had been counted. The emancipation of the slaves will give it twelve more; for the blacks will now no longer be constitutional fractions, but constitutional units. The three-fifths arrangement was a monstrous anomaly; but the five-fifths will be worse, if negro suffrage be denied. Four millions of free people will, by the mere fact of being inhabitants of Southern territory, confer a political power equal to thirty members of Congress, and yet have no voice in their election. It has been computed by the Honorable Robert Dale Owen, in a paper on the subject, published in the New York "Tribune," that in some States, where the blacks and whites are about equal in number, and where two thirds of the whites shall "qualify" as voters, this new condition of things will give the Southern white voter, in a Presidential or Congressional election, three times as much political influence as a Northern voter. And on whom shall we, in many localities, confer this immense privilege? Here is Mr. Owen's description of a specimen of the class of Southern "poor whites" we propose thus to exalt.

"I have often encountered this class. I saw many of them last year, while visiting, as member of a Government commission, some of the Southern States. Labor degraded before their eyes has extinguished within them all respect for industry, all ambition, all honorable exertion to improve their condition. When

15

last I had the pleasure of seeing you at Nashville, I met there, in the office of a gentleman charged with the duty of issuing transportation and rations to indigent persons, black and white, a notable example of this strange class. He was a Rebel deserter,—a rough, dirty, uncouth specimen of humanity, — tall, stout, and wiry-looking, rude and abrupt in speech and bearing, and clothed in tattered homespun. In no civil tone he demanded rations. When informed that all rations applicable to such a purpose were exhausted, he broke forth, —

"'What am I to do, then? How am I to get home?'

"'You can have no difficulty,' was the reply. 'It is but fifteen or eighteen hours down the river' (the Cumberland) 'by steamboat to where you live. I furnished you transportation; you can work your way.'

"'Work my way!' (with a scowl of angry contempt.) 'I never did a stroke of work since I was born; and I never expect to, till my dying day.'

"The agent replied, quietly, —

"'They will give you all you want to eat on board, if you help them to wood.'

"'Carry wood!' he retorted, with an oath. 'Whenever they ask me to carry wood, I'll tell them they may set me on shore; I'd rather starve for a week than work for an hour; I don't want to live in a world that I can't make a living out of without work.'

"Is it for men like that, ignorant, illiterate, vicious, fit for no decent employment on earth except manual labor, and spurning *all* labor as degradation, — is it in favor of such insolent swaggerers that we are to disfranchise the humble, quiet, hardworking negro? Are the votes of three such men as Stanton or Seward, Sumner or Garrison, Grant or Sherman, to be neutralized by the ballot of one such worthless barbarian?"

But this great power, wielded by a population imperfectly qualified to vote, in the name of a population which do not vote at all, — a power equivalent to thirty members of Congress and thirty electoral votes, — will be directed as much against Northern interests as against negro interests. Added to the power which the South will derive from its voting population, it will enable that section to control one third of all the votes in the House of Representatives; and, says Professor Parsons, "if they stand together, and vote as a unit, they will need only about one sixth more to get and hold control of our national legislation and all our foreign and domestic policy." Our political experience has unfortunately not been such as to justify us in believing it to be impossible for any party, under a resolute Southern lead, to obtain one sixth of the Northern strength in Congress. What would be the result of such a combination? Why, the National government would be substantially in the hands of those who have been engaged in a desperate struggle to overthrow it; and it would be a government converted into a great military and naval power by the war which resulted in their defeat, and fully competent to enforce its decisions at home and abroad by the strong hand. Nothing is purchased at such a frightful price as the indulgence of a preju-dice; the cry against " nigger equality " is a prejudice of the most mischievous kind; and it may be we shall hereafter find cause to deplore that, when we had to choose between " nigger equality " and South-ern predominance, our choice was to keep the " nig-ger " down, even if we failed to keep ourselves up.

One result of Southern predominance everybody can appreciate. The national debt is so interwoven with every form of the business and industry of the loyal States that its repudiation would be the most appalling of evils. A tax to pay it at once would not produce half the financial derangement and moral disorder which repudiation would cause; for repudia-tion, as Mirabeau well observed, is nothing but taxa-tion in its most cruel, unequal, iniquitous, and calamitous form. But what reason have we to think that a reconstructed South, dominant in the Federal Government, would regard the debt with feelings simi-lar to ours? The negroes would associate it with their freedom, of which it was the price; their late masters would view it as the symbol of their humilia-tion, which it was incurred to effect. We must remember that the South loses the whole cost of Rebellion, and is at the same time required to pay its share of the cost of suppressing Rebellion. The cost of Rebellion is, in addition to the devastation of property caused by invasion, the whole Southern debt of some two or three thousand millions of dollars ; and the market value of the slaves, which, estimating the slaves at five hundred dollars each, is two thousand millions of dollars more. The portion of the cost of suppressing Rebellion which the South will have to pay can be approximately reached by taking a recent calculation made in the Census Office of the Department of the Interior.

Estimating the national debt at twenty-five hundred millions of dollars, and apportioning it according to the number of the white male adults over twenty years of age in the different sections of the country, it has been found that the proportion of the New England States is $308,689,352.07 ; of the Middle States, $740,195,342.32 ; of the Western States, $893,288,781.01 ; of the Southern States, $461,929,-846.85 ; and of the Pacific States, $95,896,677.75. This calculation makes the South responsible for over four hundred and sixty millions of the debt. What amount have the Southerners invested in it ? Where both interest and passion furiously impel men to repudiation, can they be trusted with the care of the public credit ? " But," the Northern people may exclaim, " in case of such an execrable violation of justice, we would revolt, —'we would — " Ah ! but in whose hands would then be " the war power " ?

From every point of view, then, in which we can survey the subject, negro suffrage is, unless we are destitute of the commonest practical reason, the logical sequence of negro emancipation. It is not more necessary for the protection of the freedmen than for the safety and honor of the nation. Our interests are inextricably bound up with their rights. The highest requirements of abstract justice coincide with the lowest requirements of political prudence. And the largest justice to the loyal blacks is the real condition of the widest clemency to the Rebel whites. If the Southern communities are to be re-organized into Federal States, it is of the first importance that they should be States whose power rests on the proscription or degradation of no class of their population. It would be a great evil, if they were absolutely governed by a faction, even if that faction were a minority of the "loyal" people, whose loyalty consisted in merely taking an oath which the most unscrupulous would be the readiest to take, because the readiest to break. We are bound either to give them a republican form of government, or to hold them in the grasp of the military power of the nation; and we cannot safely give them anything which approaches a republican form of government, unless we allow the great mass of the free people the right to vote. And least of all should we think of proscribing that particular class of the free people who most thoroughly represent in their localities the interests of the United States, and whose ballots would at once do the work and save the expense of an army of occupation.

August, 1865.

THE JOHNSON PARTY.

The President of the United States has so singular
a combination of defects for the office of a constitutional magistrate, that he could have obtained the
opportunity to misrule the nation only by a visitation
of Providence. Insincere as well as stubborn, cunning as well as unreasonable, vain as well as ill-
tempered, greedy of popularity as well as arbitrary
in disposition, veering in his mind as well as fixed in
his will, he unites in his character the seemingly
opposite qualities of demagogue and autocrat, and
converts the Presidential chair into a stump or a
throne, according as the impulse seizes him to cajole
or to command. Doubtless much of the evil developed in him is due to his misfortune in having been
lifted by events to a position which he lacked the
elevation and breadth of intelligence adequately to
fill. He was cursed with the possession of a power
and authority which no man of narrow mind, bitter
prejudices, and inordinate self-estimation can exercise
without depraving himself as well as injuring the
nation. Egotistic to the point of mental disease, he
resented the direct and manly opposition of statesmen
to his opinions and moods as a personal affront, and

descended to the last degree of littleness in a political leader, — that of betraying his party, in order to gratify his spite. He of course became the prey of intriguers and sycophants, — of persons who understand the art of managing minds which are at once arbitrary and weak, by allowing them to retain unity of will amid the most palpable inconsistencies of opinion, so that inconstancy to principle shall not weaken force of purpose, nor the emphasis be at all abated with which they may bless to-day what yesterday they cursed. Thus the abhorrer of traitors has now become their tool. Thus the denouncer of Copperheads has now sunk into dependence on their support. Thus the imposer of conditions of reconstruction has now become the foremost friend of the unconditioned return of the Rebel States. Thus the furious Union Republican, whose harangues against his political opponents almost scared his political friends by their violence, has now become the shameless betrayer of the people who trusted him. And in all these changes of base he has appeared supremely conscious, in his own mind, of playing an independent, a consistent, and especially a conscientious part.

Indeed, Mr. Johnson's character would be imperfectly described if some attention were not paid to his conscience, the purity of which is a favorite subject of his own discourse, and the perversity of which is the wonder of the rest of mankind. As a public man, his real position is similar to that of a commander of an army, who should pass over to the ranks of the enemy

he was commissioned to fight, and then plead his
individual convictions of duty as a justification of his
treachery. In truth, Mr. Johnson's conscience is, like
his understanding, a mere form or expression of his
will. The will of ordinary men is addressed through
their understanding and conscience. Mr. Johnson's
understanding and conscience can be addressed only
through his will. He puts intellectual principles and
the moral law in the possessive case, thinks he pays
them a compliment and adds to their authority when
he makes them the adjuncts of his petted pronoun
"my;" and things to him are reasonable and right,
not from any quality inherent in themselves, but
because they are made so by his determinations.
Indeed, he sees hardly anything as it is, but almost
everything as colored by his own dominant egotism.
Thus he is never weary of asserting that the people
are on his side; yet his method of learning the wishes
of the people is to scrutinize his own, and, when acting out his own passionate impulses, he ever insists
that he is obeying public sentiment. Of all the wilful
men who, by strange chance, have found themselves
at the head of a constitutional government, he most
resembles the last Stuart king of England, James II.;
and the likeness is increased from the circumstance
that the American James has, in his supple and
plausible Secretary of State, one fully competent to
play the part of Sunderland.

The party which, under the ironical designation of
the National Union Party, now proposes to take the

policy and character of Mr. Johnson under its charge, is composed chiefly of Democrats defeated at the polls and Democrats defeated on the field of battle. The few apostate Republicans, who have joined its ranks while seeming to lead its organization, are of small account. Its great strength is in its Southern supporters, and, if it comes into power, it must obey a Rebel direction. By the treachery of the President, it will have the executive patronage on its side, — for Mr. Johnson's " conscience " is of that peculiar kind which finds satisfaction in arraying the interest of others against their convictions ; and having thus the power to purchase support, it will not fail of those means of dividing the North which come from corrupting it. The party under which the war for the Union was conducted is to be denounced and proscribed as the party of disunion, and we are to be edified by addresses on the indissoluble unity of the nation by Secessionists, who have hardly yet had time to wash from their hands the stains of Union blood. The leading proposition on which this conspiracy against the country is to be conducted is the monstrous absurdity that the Rebel States have an inherent, " continuous," unconditioned, constitutional *right* to form a part of the Federal Government, when they have once acknowledged the fact of the defeat of their inhabitants in an armed attempt to overthrow and subvert it, — a proposition which implies that victory paralyzes the powers of the victors, that ruin begins when success is assured, that the only effect of beating a Southern Rebel in the field is to exalt him into a maker of laws for his antagonist.

In the minority Report of the Congressional Joint Committee on Reconstruction, which is designed to supply the new party with constitutional law, this theory of State Rights is most elaborately presented. The ground is taken, that during the Rebellion the States in which it prevailed were as " completely competent States of the United States as they were before the Rebellion, and were bound by all the obligations which the Constitution imposed, and entitled to all its privileges;" and that the Rebellion consisted merely in a series of "illegal acts of the citizens of such States." On this theory it is difficult to find where the guilt of rebellion lies. The States are innocent because the Rebellion was a rising of individuals; the individuals cannot be very criminal, for it is on their votes that the committee chiefly rely to build up the National Union Party. Again, we are informed that, in respect to the admission of representatives from " such States," Congress has no right or power to ask more than two questions. These are: " Have these States organized governments ? Are these governments republican in form ? " The committee proceed to say : " How they were formed, under what auspices they were formed, are inquiries with which Congress has no concern. The right of the people to form a government for themselves has never been questioned." On this principle, President Johnson's labors in organizing State governments were works of supererogation. At the close of active hostilities the Rebel States had organized, though disloyal, governments as republican in form as they were before the war broke out. The only thing, therefore, they were required to do was to send their Senators and Representatives to Washington. Congress could not have rightfully refused to receive them, because all questions as to their being loyal or disloyal, and as to the changes which the war had wrought in the relations of the States they represented to the Union, were inquiries with which Congress had no concern! And here again we have the ever-recurring difficulty respecting the "individuals" who were alone guilty of the acts of rebellion. "The right of the people," we are assured, "to form a government for themselves, has never been questioned." But it happens that "the people" here indicated are the very individuals who were before pointed out as alone responsible for the Rebellion. In the exercise of their right "to form a government for themselves," they rebelled; and now, it seems, by the exercise of the same right, they can unconditionally return. There is no wrong anywhere: it is all "right." The people are first made criminals, in order to exculpate the States, and then the innocence of the States is used to exculpate the people. When we see such outrages on common sense gravely perpetrated by so eminent a lawyer as the one who drew up the committee's Report, one is almost inclined to define minds as of two kinds, the legal mind and the human mind, and to doubt if there is any possible connection in reason between the two. To the human mind it appears that the Federal Government has spent thirty-five hundred millions of dollars, and sacrificed three hundred thousand lives, in a contest which the legal mind dissolves into a mere mist of unsubstantial phrases ; and by skill in the trick of substituting words for things, and definitions for events, the legal mind proceeds to show that these words and definitions, though scrupulously shielded from any contact with realities, are sufficient to prevent the nation from taking ordinary precautions against the recurrence of calamities fresh in its bitter experience. The phrase "State Rights," translated from legal into human language, is found to mean, the power to commit wrongs on individuals whom States may desire to oppress, or the power to protect the inhabitants of States from the consequences of their own crimes. The minority of the committee, indeed, seem to have forgotten that there has been any real war, and bring to mind the converted Australian savage, whom the missionary could not make penitent for a murder committed the day before, because the trifling occurrence had altogether passed from his recollection.

In fact, all attempts to discriminate between Rebels and Rebel States, to the advantage of the latter, are done in defiance of notorious facts. If the Rebellion had been merely a rising of individual citizens of States, it would have been an insurrection against the States, as well as against the Federal Government, and might have been easily put down. In that case, there would have been no withdrawal of Southern Senators and Representatives from Congress, and therefore no question as to their inherent right to return. In Missouri and Kentucky, for example, there was civil war, waged by inhabitants of those States against their local governments, as well as against the United States ; and nobody contends that the rights and privileges of those States were forfeited by the criminal acts of their citizens. But the real strength of the Rebellion consisted in this, that it was not a rebellion *against* States, but a rebellion *by* States. No loose assemblage of individuals, though numbering hundreds of thousands, could long have resisted the pressure of the Federal power and the power of the State governments. They would have had no ·means of subsistence except those derived from plunder and voluntary contributions, and they would have lacked the military organization by which mobs are transformed into formidable armies. But the Rebellion being one of States, being virtually decreed by the people of States assembled in convention, was sustained by the two tremendous governmental powers of taxation and conscription. The willing and the unwilling were thus equally placed at the disposition of a strong government. The population and wealth of the whole immense region of country in which the Rebellion prevailed were at the service of this government. So completely was it a rebellion of States, that the universal excuse of the minority of original Union men for entering heartily into the contest after it had once begun was, that they thought it their duty to abide by the decision, and share the fortunes, of their respective *States*. Nobody at the South believed at the time the war commenced, or during its progress, that his State possessed any " continuous " right to a participation in the privileges of the Federal Constitution, the obligations of which it had repudiated. When confident of success, the Southerner scornfully scouted the mere suspicion of entertaining such a degrading notion ; when assured of defeat, his only thought was to " get his State back into the Union on the best terms that could be made." The idea of " conditions of readmission " was as firmly fixed in the Southern as in the Northern mind. If the politicians of the South now adopt the principle that the Rebel States have not, as States, ever altered their relations to the Union, they do it from policy, finding that its adoption will give them " better terms " than they ever dreamed of getting before the President of the United States taught them that it would be more politic to bully than to plead.

In the last analysis, indeed, the theory of the minority of the Reconstruction Committee reduces the Rebel States to mere abstractions. It is plain that a State, in the concrete, is constituted by that portion of the inhabitants who form its legal people ; and that, in passing back of its government and constitution, we reach a convention of the legal people as its ultimate expression. By such conventions the acts of secession were passed ; and, as far as the people of the Rebel States could do it, they destroyed their States considered as organized communities forming a part of the United States. The claim of the United States to authority over the territory and inhabitants was of course not affected by these acts; but in what condition did they place the people? Plainly in the condition of rebels engaged in an attempt to overturn the Constitution and government of the United States. As the whole force of the people in each of the Rebel communities was engaged in this work, the whole of the people were rebels and public enemies. Nothing was left, in each case, but an abstract State, without any external body, and as destitute of people having a right to enjoy the privileges of the Constitution as if the territory had been swept clean of population by a pestilence. It is, then, only this abstract State which has a right to representation in Congress. But how can there be a right to representation when there is nobody to be represented? All this may appear puerile; but the puerility is in the premises as well as in the logical deductions, and the premises are laid down as indisputable constitutional principles by the eminent jurists who supply ideas for the National Union Party.

The doctrine of the unconditional right of the Rebel States to representation being thus a demonstrated absurdity, the only question relates to the conditions which Congress proposes to impose. Certainly these conditions, as embodied in the constitutional amendment which has passed both houses by such overwhelming majorities, are the mildest ever exacted of defeated enemies by a victorious nation. There is not a distinctly " radical " idea in the whole amendment, — nothing that President Johnson has not himself, within a comparatively recent period, stamped with his high approbation. Does it ordain universal suffrage ? No. Does it ordain impartial suffrage ? No. Does it proscribe, disfranchise, or ex-patriate the recent armed enemies of the country, or confiscate their property ? No. It simply ordains that the national debt shall be paid and the Rebel debt repudiated ; that the civil rights of all persons shall be maintained ; that Rebels who have added perjury to treason shall be disqualified for office ; and that the Rebel States shall not have their political power in the Union increased by the presence on their soil of persons to whom they deny political rights, but that representation shall be based throughout the Republic on voters, and not on population. The pith of the whole amendment is in the last clause ; and is there anything in that to which reasonable objection can be made ? Would it not be a curious result of the war against Rebellion, that it should end in con-ferring on a Rebel voter in South Carolina a power equal, in national affairs, to that of two loyal voters in New York ? Can any Democrat have the face to assert that the South should have, through its disfranchised negro freemen alone, a power in the Electoral College and in the national House of Representatives equal to that of the States of Ohio and Indiana combined ?

16

Yet these conditions, so conciliatory, moderate, lenient, almost timid, and which, by the omission of impartial suffrage, fall very far below the requirements of the average sentiment of the loyal nation, are still denounced by the new party of "Union" as the work of furious radicals, bent on destroying the rights of the States. Thus Governor James L. Orr, of South Carolina, a leading Rebel pardoned into a Johnsonian Union man, implores the people of that region to send delegates to the Philadelphia Convention, on the ground that its purpose is to organize "conservative" men of all sections and parties, "to drive from power that radical party who are daily trampling under foot the Constitution, and fast converting a constitutional Republic into a consolidated despotism." The terms to which South Carolina is asked to submit, before she can be made the equal of Ohio or New York in the Union, are stated to be "too degrading and humiliating to be entertained by a freeman for a single instant." When we consider that this "radical party" constitutes nearly four fifths of the legal legislature of the nation, that it was the party which saved the country from dismemberment while Mr. Orr and his friends were notoriously engaged in "trampling the Constitution under foot," and that the man who denounces it owes his forfeited life to its clemency, the astounding insolence of the impeachment touches the sublime. Here is confessed treason inveighing against tried loyalty, in the name of the Constitution it has violated and the law it has broken! But why does Mr. Orr think the terms of South Carolina's restored relations to the Union " too degrading and humiliating to be entertained by a freeman for a single instant"? Is it because he wishes to have the Rebel debt paid? Is it because he desires to have the Federal debt repudiated? Is it because he thinks it intolerable that a negro should have civil rights? Is it because he resents the idea that breakers of oaths, like himself, should be disqualified from having another opportunity of forswearing themselves? Is it because he considers that a white Rebel freeman of South Carolina has a natural right to exercise double the political power of a white loyal freeman of Massachusetts? He must return an affirmative answer to all these questions in order to make it out that his State will be degraded and humiliated by ratifying the amendment; and the necessity of the measure is therefore proved by the motives known to prompt the attacks of its vilifiers.

The insolence of Mr. Orr is not merely individual, but representative. It is the result of Mr. Johnson's attempt " to produce harmony between the two sections," by betraying the section to which he owed his election. Had it not been for his treachery, there would have been little difficulty in settling the terms of peace, so as to avoid all causes for future war; but, from the time he quarrelled with Congress, he has been the great stirrer-up of disaffection at the South, and the virtual leader of the Southern reactionary party. Every man at the South who was prominent in the Rebellion, every man at the North who was prominent in aiding the Rebellion, is now openly or covertly his partisan, and by fawning on him earns the right to defame the representatives of the people by whom the Rebellion was put down. Among traitors and Copperheads the fear of punishment has been succeeded by the hope of revenge; elation is on faces which the downfall of Richmond overcast; and a return to the old times, when a united South ruled the country by means of a divided North, is confidently expected by the whole crew of political bullies and political sycophants whose profit is in the abasement of the nation. . It is even said that if the majority of the "Rump" Congress cannot be overcome by fair means, it will be by foul; and there are noisy partisans of the President who assert that he has in him a Cromwellian capacity for dealing with legislative assemblies whose notions of the public good clash with his own. In short, we are promised, on the assembling of the next Congress, a *coup d'état.*

Garret Davis, of Kentucky, was, we believe, the first to announce this executive remedy for the "radical" disease of the State, and it has since been often prescribed by Democratic politicians as a sovereign panacea. General McClernand, indeed, proposed a scheme, simpler even than that of executive recognition, by which the Southern Senators and Representatives might effect a lodgment in Congress. They should, according to him, have gone to Washington,

entered the halls of legislation, and proceeded to occupy their seats, " peaceably if they could, forcibly if
they must;" but the record of General McClernand
as a military man, was not such as to give a high
degree of authority to his advice on a question of
carrying positions by assault, and, there being some
natural hesitation in following his counsel, the golden
opportunity was lost. Mr. Montgomery Blair, who
professes his willingness to act with any men,
" Rebels or any one else," to put down the radicals,
is never weary of talking to conservative conventions
of " two Presidents and two Congresses." There can
be no doubt that the project of a *coup d'état* has
become dangerously familiar to the " conservative "
mind, and that the eminent legal gentlemen of the
North who are publishing opinions affirming the right
of the excluded Southern representatives to their
seats, are playing into the hands of the desperate
gang of unscrupulous politicians who are determined
to have the right established by force. It is computed that the gain, in the approaching elections, of
twenty-five districts now represented by Union Republicans, will give the Johnson party, in the next
Congress, a majority of the House of Representatives,
should the Southern delegations be counted; and it is
proposed that the Johnson members legally entitled
to seats should combine with the Southern pretenders
to seats, organize as the House of Representatives
of the United States, and apply to the President for
recognition. Should the President comply, he would

be impeached by an unrecognized House before an " incomplete " Senate, and, if convicted, would deny the validity of the proceeding. The result would be civil war, in which the name of the Federal Government would be on the side of the revolutionists. Such is the programme which is freely discussed by partisans of the President, considered to be high in his favor; and the scheme, it is contended, is the logical result of the position he has assumed as to the rights of the excluded States to representation. It is certain that the present Congress is as much the Congress of the United States as he is the President of the United States; but it is well known that he considers himself to represent the whole country, while he thinks that Congress only represents a portion of it; and he has in his character just that combination of qualities, and is placed in just those anomalous circumstances, which lead men to the commission of great political crimes. The mere hint of the possibility of his attempting a *coup d'état* is received by some Republicans with a look of incredulous surprise; yet what has his administration been to such persons but a succession of surprises?

But whatever view may be taken of the President's designs, there can be no doubt that the safety, peace, interest, and honor of the country depend on the success of the Union Republicans in the approaching elections. The loyal nation must see to it that the Fortieth Congress shall be as competent to override executive vetoes as the Thirty-Ninth, and be equally removed from the peril of being expelled for one more in harmony with Executive ideas. The same earnestness, energy, patriotism, and intelligence which gave success to the war, must now be exerted to reap its fruits and prevent its recurrence. The only danger is, that in some representative districts the people may be swindled by plausibilities and respectabilities ; for when, in political contests, any great villany is contemplated, there are always found some eminently respectable men, with a fixed capital of certain eminently conservative phrases, innocently ready to furnish the wolves of politics with abundant supplies of sheep's clothing. These dignified dupes are more than usually active at the present time ; and the gravity of their speech is as edifying as its emptiness. Immersed in words, and with no clear perception of things, they mistake conspiracy for conservatism. Their pet horror is the term " radical ; " their ideal of heroic patriotism, the spectacle of a great nation which allows itself to be ruined with decorum, and dies rather than commit the slightest breach of constitutional etiquette. This insensibility to facts and blindness to the tendency of events, they call wisdom and moderation. Behind these political dummies are the real forces of the Johnson party, men of insolent spirit, resolute will, embittered temper, and unscrupulous purpose, who clearly know what they are after, and will hesitate at no " informality " in the attempt to obtain it. To give these persons political power will be to surrender the results of the war, by placing

the government practically in the hands of those
against whom the war was waged. No smooth words
about " the equality of the States," " the necessity of
conciliation," " the wickedness of sectional conflicts,"
will alter the fact, that, in refusing to support Congress, the people would set a reward on treachery
and place a bounty on treason. " The South," says
a Mr. Hill of Georgia, in a letter favoring the Philadelphia Convention, " sought to save the Constitution
out of the Union. She failed. Let her now bring
her diminished and shattered but united and earnest
counsels and energies to save the Constitution in the
Union." The sort of Constitution the South sought
to save by warring against the government is the
Constitution which she now proposes to save by administering it! Is this the tone of pardoned and
penitent treason ? Is this the spirit to build up a
" National Union Party " ? No; but it is the tone
and spirit now fashionable in the defeated Rebel
States, and will not be changed until the autumn
elections shall have proved that they have as little
to expect from the next Congress as from the present,
and that they must give securities for their future
conduct before they can be relieved from the penalties
incurred by their past.

September, 1866.

THE PRESIDENT AND HIS ACCOMPLICES.

ANDREW JOHNSON has dealt the most cruel of all blows to the respectability of the faction which rejoices in his name. Hardly had the political Pecksniffs and Turveydrops contrived so to manage the Johnson Convention at Philadelphia that it violated few of the proprieties of intrigue and none of the decencies of dishonesty, than the commander-in-chief of the combination took the field in person, with the intention of carrying the country by assault. His objective point was the grave of Douglas, which became, by the time he arrived, the grave also of his own reputation and the hopes of his partisans. His speeches on the route were a volcanic outbreak of vulgarity, conceit, bombast, scurrility, ignorance, insolence, brutality, and balderdash. Screams of laughter, cries of disgust, flushings of shame, were the various responses of the nation he disgraced to the harangues of this leader of American "conservatism." Never before did the first office in the gift of the people appear so poor an object of human ambition, as when Andrew Johnson made it an eminence on which to exhibit inability to behave and incapacity to reason. His low cunning conspired with his devouring egotism to make him throw off all the restraints of official decorum, in the expectation that he would find duplicates of himself in the crowds he addressed, and that mob diffused would heartily sympathize with Mob impersonated. Never was blustering demagogue led by a distempered sense of self-importance into a more fatal error. Not only was the great body of the people mortified or indignant, but even his "satraps and dependents," even the shrewd politicians — accidents of an Accident and shadows of a shade — who had labored so hard at Philadelphia to weave a cloak of plausibilities to cover his usurpations, shivered with apprehension or tingled with shame as they read the reports of their master's impolitic and ignominious abandonment of dignity and decency in his addresses to the people he attempted alternately to bully and cajole. That a man thus self-exposed as unworthy of high trust should have had the face to expect that intelligent constituencies would send to Congress men pledged to support *his* policy and *his* measures, appeared for the time to be as pitiable a spectacle of human delusion as it was an exasperating example of human impudence.

Not the least extraordinary peculiarity of these addresses from the stump was the immense protuberance they exhibited of the personal pronoun. In Mr. Johnson's speech, his " I " resembles the geometer's description of infinity, having "its centre everywhere and its circumference nowhere." Among the many kinds of egotism in which his eloquence is prolific, it may be difficult to fasten on the particular one

which is most detestable or most laughable; but it
seems to us that when his arrogance apes humility it
is deserving perhaps of an intenser degree of scorn or
derision than when it riots in bravado. The most
offensive part which he plays in public is that of
" the humble individual," bragging of the lowliness
of his origin, hinting of the great merits which could
alone have lifted him to his present exalted station,
and representing himself as so satiated with the
sweets of unsought power as to be indifferent to its
honors. Ambition is not for him, for ambition as-
pires; and what object has he to aspire to ? From
his contented mediocrity as alderman of a village, the
people have insisted on elevating him from one pin-
nacle of greatness to another, until they have at last
made him President of the United States. He might
have been Dictator had he pleased; but what, to a
man wearied with authority and dignity, would dictatorship be worth ? If he is proud of anything, it
is of the tailor's bench from which he started. He
would have everybody to understand that he is humble, — thoroughly humble. Is this caricature ? No.
It is impossible to caricature Andrew Johnson when
he mounts his high horse of humility and becomes a
sort of cross between Uriah Heep and Josiah Boun-
derby of Coketown. Indeed, it is only by quoting
Dickens's description of the latter personage that wo
have anything which fairly matches the traits suggested by some statements in the President's speeches.
" A big, loud man," says the humorist, " with a stare

and a metallic laugh. A man made out of coarse material, which seemed to have been stretched to make so much of him. A man with a great puffed head and forehead, swelled veins in his temples, and such a strained skin to his face, that it seemed to hold his eyes open and lift his eyebrows up. A man with a pervading appearance on him of being inflated like a balloon, and ready to start. A man who could never sufficiently vaunt himself a self-made man. A man who was continually proclaiming, through that brassy speaking-trumpet of a voice of his, his old ignorance and his old poverty. A man who was the Bully of humility."

If we turn from the moral and personal to the mental characteristics of Mr. Johnson's speeches, we find that his brain is to be classed with notable cases of arrested development. He has strong forces in his nature, but in their outlet through his mind they are dissipated into a confusing clutter of unrelated thoughts and inapplicable phrases. He seems to possess neither the power nor the perception of coherent thinking and logical arrangement. He does not appear to be aware that prepossessions are not proofs, that assertions are not arguments, that the proper method to answer an objection is not to repeat the proposition against which the objection was directed, that the proper method of unfolding a subject is not to make the successive statements a series of contradictions. Indeed, he seems to have a thoroughly animalized intellect, destitute of the notion of relations, with ideas which are but the form of determinations, and which derive their force, not from reason, but from will. With an individuality thus strong even to fierceness, but which has not been developed in the mental region, and which the least gust of passion intellectually upsets, he is incapable of looking at anything out of relations to himself, — of regarding it from that neutral ground which is the condition of intelligent discussion between opposing minds. In truth, he makes a virtue of being insensible to the evidence of facts and the deductions of reason, proclaiming to all the world that he has taken his position, that he will never swerve from it, and that all statements and arguments intended to shake his resolves are impertinences, indicating that their authors are radicals and enemies of the country. He is never weary of vaunting his firmness, and firmness he doubtless has, — the firmness of at least a score of mules ; but events have shown that it is a different kind of firmness from that which keeps a statesman firm to his principles, a political leader to his pledges, a gentleman to his word. Amid all changes of opinion, he has been conscious of unchanged will ; and the intellectual element forms so small a portion of his being, that, when he challenged "the man, woman, or child to come forward" and convict him of inconstancy to his professions, he knew that, however it might be with the rest of mankind, he would himself be unconvinced by any evidence which the said man, woman, or child might adduce. Again, when he was asked

by one of his audiences why he did not hang Jeff.
Davis, he retorted by exclaiming, " Why don't you ask
me why I have not hanged Thad. Stevens and Wendell
Phillips ? They are as much traitors as Davis." And
we are almost charitable enough to suppose that he
saw no difference between the moral or legal treason
of the man who for four years had waged open war
against the Government of the United States, and the
men who for one year had sharply criticised the acts
and utterances of Andrew Johnson. It is not to be
expected that nice distinctions will be made by a magistrate who is in the habit of denying indisputable
facts with the fury of a pugilist who has received a
personal affront, and of announcing demonstrated fallacies with the imperturbable serenity of a philosopher
proclaiming the fundamental laws of human belief.
His brain is entirely ridden by his will, and of all the
public men in the country its official head is the one
whose opinion carries with it the least intellectual
weight. It is to the credit of our institutions and our
statesmen that the man least qualified by largeness of
mind and moderation of temper to exercise uncon-
trolled power should be the man who aspired to usurp
it. The constitutional instinct in the blood, and the
constitutional principle in the brain, of our real statesmen, preserve them from the folly and guilt of setting themselves up as imitative Cæsars and Napoleons the moment they are trusted with a little delegated power.

Still we are told that, with all his defects, Andrew

Johnson is to be honored and supported as a " conservative " President engaged in a contest with a " radical " Congress! It happens, however, that the two persons who specially represent Congress in this struggle are Senators Trumbull and Fessenden. Senator Trumbull is the author of the two important measures which the President vetoed; Senator Fessenden is the chairman and organ of the Committee of fifteen which the President anathematizes. Now, we desire to do justice to the gravity of face which the partisans of Mr. Johnson preserve in announcing their most absurd propositions, and especially do we commend their command of countenance while it is their privilege to contrast the wild notions and violent speech of such lawless radicals as the Senator from Illinois and the Senator from Maine, with the balanced judgment and moderate temper of such a pattern conservative as the President of the United States. The contrast prompts ideas so irresistibly ludicrous, that to keep one's risibilities under austere control while instituting it argues a self-command almost miraculous.

Andrew Johnson, however, such as he is in heart, intellect, will, and speech, is the recognized leader of his party, and demands that the great mass of his partisans shall serve him, not merely by prostration of body, but by prostration of mind. It is the hard duty of his more intimate associates to translate his broken utterances from *Andy-Johnsonese* into constitutional phrase, to give these versions some show of logical arrangement, and to carry out, as best they may, their own objects, while professing boundless devotion to his. By a sophistical process of developing his rude notions, they often lead him to conclusions which he had not foreseen, but which they induce him to make his own, not by a fruitless effort to quicken his mind into following the steps of their reasoning, but by stimulating his passions to the point of adopting its results. They thus become parasites in order that they may become powers, and their interests make them particularly ruthless in their dealings with their master's consistency. Their relation to him, if they would bluntly express it, might be indicated in this brief formula: "We will adore you in order that you may obey us."

The trouble with these politicians is, that they cannot tie the President's tongue as they tied the tongues of the eminent personages they invited from all portions of the country to keep silent at their great Convention at Philadelphia. That Convention was a masterpiece of cunning political management; but its Address and Resolutions were hardly laid at Mr. Johnson's feet, when, in his exultation, he blurted out that unfortunate remark about "a body called, or which assumed to be, the Congress of the United States," which, it appears, "we have seen hanging on the verge of the Government." Now all this was in the Address of the Convention, but it was not so brutally worded, nor so calculated to appall those timid supporters of the Johnson party, who thought, in their innocence, that the object of the Philadelphia meeting was to heal the wounds of civil war, and not to lay down a programme by which it might be reopened. Turning, then, from Mr. Johnson to the manifesto of his political supporters, let us see what additions it makes to political wisdom, and what guaranties it affords for future peace. We shall not discriminate between insurgent States and individual insurgents, because, when individual insurgents are so overwhelmingly strong that they carry their States with them, or when States are so overwhelmingly strong that they force individuals to be insurgents, it appears to be needless. The terms are often used interchangeably in the Address, for the Convention was so largely composed of individual insurgents that it was important to vary a little the charge that they usurped State powers with the qualification that they obeyed the powers they usurped. At the South, individual insurgents constitute the State when they determine to rebel, and obey it when they desire to be pardoned. An identical thing cannot be altered by giving it two names.

The principle which runs through the Philadelphia Address is, that insurgent States recover their former rights under the Constitution by the mere fact of submission. This is equivalent to saying that insurgent States incurred no guilt in rebellion. But States cannot become insurgent unless the authorities of such States commit perjury and treason, and their people become rebels and public enemies; perjury, treason, and rebellion are commonly held to be crimes; and who ever heard, before, that criminals were restored

17

to all the rights of honest citizens by the mere fact of their arrest?

The doctrine, moreover, is a worse heresy than that of Secession; for Secession implies that seceded States, being out of the Union, can plainly only be brought back by conquest, and on such terms as the victors may choose to impose. No candid Southern Rebel, who believes that his State seceded, and that he acted under competent authority when he took up arms against the United States, can have the effrontery to affirm that he had inherent rights of citizenship in " the foreign country " against which he plotted and fought for four years. The so-called " right" of secession was claimed by the South as a constitutional right, to be peaceably exercised, but it passed into the broader and more generally intelligible " right" of revolution when it had to be sustained by war; and the condition of a defeated revolutionist is certainly not that of a qualified voter in the nation against which he revolted. But if insurgent States recover their former rights and privileges when they submit to superior force, there is no reason why armed rebellion should not be as common as local discontent. We have, on this principle, sacrificed thirty-five hundred millions of dollars and three hundred thousand lives, only to bring the insurgent States into just those " practical relations to the Union " which will enable us to sacrifice thirty-five hundred millions of dollars more, and three hundred thousand more lives, when it suits the passions and caprices of these States to rebel again. Whatever they may do in the way of disturbing the peace of the country, they can never, it seems, forfeit their rights and privileges under the Constitution. Even if everybody was positively certain that there would be a new rebellion in ten years, unless conditions of representation were exacted of the South, we still, according to the doctrine of the Johnsonian jurists, would be constitutionally impotent to exact them, because insurgent States recover unconditioned rights to representation by the mere fact of their submitting to the power they can no longer resist. The acceptance of this principle would make insurrection the chronic disease of our political system. War would follow war, until nearly all the wealth of the country was squandered, and nearly all the inhabitants exterminated. Mr. Johnson's prophetic vision of that Paradise of constitutionalism, shadowed forth in his exclamation that he would stand by the Constitution though all around him should perish, would be measurably realized; and among the ruins of the nation a few haggard and ragged pedants would be left to drone out eulogies on "the glorious Constitution" which had survived unharmed the anarchy, poverty, and depopulation it had produced. An interpretation of the Constitution which thus makes it the shield of treason and the destroyer of civilization must be false both to fact and sense. The framers of that instrument were not idiots; yet idiots they would certainly have been, if they had put into it a clause declaring "that no State, or combination of States, which may at any time choose to get up an armed attempt to overthrow the Government established by this Constitution, and be defeated in the attempt, shall forfeit any of the privileges granted by this instrument to loyal States." But an interpretation of the Constitution which can be conceived of as forming a possible part of it only by impeaching the sanity of its framers, cannot be an interpretation which the American people are morally bound to risk ruin to support.

But even if we should be wild enough to admit the Johnsonian principle respecting insurgent States, the question comes up as to the identity of the States now demanding representation with the States whose rights of representation are affirmed to have been only suspended during their rebellion. The fact would seem to be, that these reconstructed States are merely the creations of the executive branch of the Government, with every organic bond hopelessly cut which connected them with the old State governments and constitutions. They have only the names of the States they pretend to *be*. Before the Rebellion, they had a legal people; when Mr. Johnson took hold of them, they had nothing but a disorganized population. Out of this population he by his own will created a people, on the principle, we must suppose, of natural selection. Now, to decide who are the people of a State is to create its very foundations, — to begin anew in the most comprehensive sense of the word ; for the being of a State is more in its people, that is, in the persons selected from its inhabitants to be the depositaries of its political power, than it is in its geographical boundaries and area. Over this people thus constituted by himself, Mr. Johnson set Provisional Governors nominated by himself. These Governors called popular conventions, whose members were elected by the votes of those to whom Mr. Johnson had given the right of suffrage; and these conventions proceeded to do what Mr. Johnson dictated. Everywhere Mr. Johnson; nowhere the assumed rights of the States! North Carolina was one of these creations; and North Carolina, through the lips of its Chief Justice, has already decided that Mr. Johnson was an unauthorized intruder, and his work a nullity, and even Mr. Johnson's " people " of North Carolina have rejected the constitution framed by Mr. Johnson's Convention. Other Rebel communities will doubtless repudiate his work, as soon as they can dispense with his assistance. But whatever may be the condition of these new Johnsonian States, they are certainly not States which can " recover " rights which existed previous to their creation. The date of their birth is to be reckoned, not from any year previous to the Rebellion, but from the year which followed its suppression. It may, in old times, have been a politic trick of shrewd politicians, to involve the foundations of States in the mists of a mythical antiquity; but we happily live in an historical period, and there is something peculiarly stupid or peculiarly impudent in the attempt of the publicists of the Philadelphia Convention to ignore the origins of political societies for which, after they have obtained a certain degree of organization, they claim such eminent traditional rights and privileges. Respectable as these States may be as infant phenomena, it will not do to *Methu-selahize* them too recklessly, or assert their equality in muscle and brawn with giants full grown.

It is evident, from the nature of the case, that Mr. Johnson's labors were purely experimental and provisional, and needed the indorsement of Congress to be of any force. The only department of the Government constitutionally capable to admit new States or rehabilitate insurgent ones is the legislative. When the Executive not only took the initiative in reconstruction, but assumed to have completed it; when he presented *his* States to Congress as the equals of the States represented in that body; when he asserted that the delegates from his States should have the right of sitting and voting in the legislature whose business it was to decide on their right to admission; when, in short, he demanded that criminals at the bar should have a seat on the bench, and an equal voice with the judges, in deciding on their own case, the effrontery of Executive pretension went beyond all bounds of Congressional endurance.

The real difference at first was not on the question of imposing conditions, — for the President had notoriously imposed them himself, — but on the question whether or not additional conditions were necessary to secure the public safety. The President, with that facility "in turning his back on himself" which all other logical gymnasts had pronounced an impossible feat, then boldly took the ground that, being satisfied with the conditions he had himself exacted, the exaction of conditions was unconstitutional. To sustain this curious proposition he adduced no constitutional arguments, but he left various copies of the Constitution in each of the crowds he recently addressed, with the trust, we suppose, that somebody might be fortunate enough to find in that instrument the clause which supported his theory. Mr. Johnson, however, though the most consequential of individuals, is the most inconsequential of reasoners; every proposition which is evident to himself he considers to fulfil the definition of a self-evident proposition; but his supporters at Philadelphia must have known that, in affirming that insurgent States recover their former rights by the fact of submission, they were arraigning the conduct of their leader, who had notoriously violated those "rights." They took up his work at a certain stage, and then, with that as a basis, they affirmed a general proposition about insurgent States, which, had it been complied with by the President, would have left them no foundation at all; for the States about which they so glibly generalized would have had no show of organized governments. The premises of their argument were obtained by the violation of its conclusion; they inferred from what was a negation of their inference, and deduced from what was a death-blow to their deduction.

It is easy enough to understand why the Johnson Convention asserted the equality of the Johnson reconstructions of States with the States now represented in Congress. The object was to give some appearance of legality to a contemplated act of arbitrary power; and the principle that insurgent States recover all their old rights by the fact of submission was invented in order to cover the case. Mr. Johnson now intends, by the admission of his partisans, to attempt a *coup d'état* on the assembling of the Fortieth Congress, in case seventy-one members of the House of Representatives, favorable to his policy, are chosen, in the elections of this autumn, from the twenty-six loyal States. These, with the fifty Southern delegates, would constitute a quorum of the House; and the remaining hundred and nineteen members are in the President's favorite phrase, " to-be kicked out " from that " verge " of the Government on which they now are said to be " hanging." The question, therefore, whether Congress, as it is at present constituted, is a body constitutionally competent to legislate for the whole country, is the most important of all practical questions. Let us see how the case stands.

The Constitution, ratified by the people of all the States, establishes a Government of sovereign powers, supreme over the whole land; and the people of no State can rightly pass from under its authority except by the consent of the people of all the States, with whom it is bound by the most solemn and binding of contracts. The Rebel States broke, *in fact*, the contract they could not break *in right*. Assembled in conventions of their people, they passed ordinances of secession, withdrew their Senators and Representatives from Congress, and began the war by assailing a fort of the United States. The Secessionists had trusted to the silence of the Constitution in relation to the act they performed. A State in the American Union, as distinguished from a Territory, is constitutionally a part of the Government to which it owes allegiance, and the seceded States had refused to be parts of the Government, and had forsworn their allegiance. By the Constitution, the United States, in cases of " domestic violence " in a State, is to interfere, " on application of the Legislature, or of the Executive when the Legislature cannot be convened." But in this case legislatures, executives, conventions of the people, were all violators of the domestic peace, and of course made no application for interference. By the Constitution, Congress is empowered to suppress insurrections; but this might be supposed to mean insurrections like Shays's Rebellion in Massachusetts and the Whiskey Insurrection in Pennsylvania, and not to cover the action of States seceding from the Congress which is thus empowered. The seceders, therefore, felt somewhat as did the absconding James II. when he flung the Great Seal into the Thames, and thought he had stopped the machinery of the English government.

Mr. Buchanan, then President of the United States, admitted at once that the Secessionists had done their work in such a way that, though they had done wrong, the Government was powerless to compel them to do right. And here the matter should have rested, if the Government established by the Constitution was such a government as Mr. Johnson's supporters now declare it to be. If it is impotent to prescribe terms of peace in relation to insurgent States, it is certainly impotent to make war on insurgent States. If insurgent States recover their former constitutional rights in laying down their arms, then there was no criminality in their taking them up; and if there was no criminality in their taking them up, then the United States was criminal in the war by which they were forced to lay them down. On this theory we have a Government incompetent to legislate for insurgent States, because lacking their representatives, waging against them a cruel and unjust war. And this is the real theory of the defeated Rebels and Copperheads who formed the great mass of the delegates to the Johnson Convention. Should they get into power, they would feel themselves logically justified in annulling, not only all the acts of the " Rump Congress " since they submitted, but all the acts of the Rump Congresses during - the time they had a Confederate Congress of their own. They may deny that this is their intention ; but what intention to forego the exercise of an assumed right, held by those who are out of power, can be supposed capable of limiting their action when they are in ?

But if the United States is a Government having

legitimate rights of sovereignty conferred upon it by
the people of all the States, and if, consequently, the
attempted secession of the people of one or more
States only makes them criminals, without impairing
the sovereignty of the United States, then the Government, with all its powers, remains with the representatives of the loyal people. By the very nature of
government as government, the rights and privileges
guaranteed to citizens are guaranteed to loyal citizens ; the rights and privileges guaranteed to States
are guaranteed to loyal States ; and loyal citizens
and loyal States are not such as profess a willingness
to be loyal after having been utterly worsted in an
enterprise of gigantic disloyalty. The organic unity
and continuity of the Government would be broken by
the return of disloyal citizens and Rebel States without their going through the process of being restored
by the action of the Government they had attempted
to subvert ; and the power to restore carries with it
the power to decide on the terms of restoration.
And when we speak of the Government, we are not
courtly enough to mean by the expression simply its
executive branch. The question of admitting and
implicitly of restoring States, and of deciding whether
or not States have a republican form of government,
are matters left by the Constitution to the discretion
of Congress. As to the Rebel States now claiming
representation, they have succumbed, thoroughly exhausted, in one of the costliest and bloodiest wars in
the history of the world, — a war which tasked the

resources of the United States more than they would have been tasked by a war with all the great powers of Europe combined,—a war which, in 1862, had assumed such proportions, that the Supreme Court decided that it gave the United States the same rights and privileges which the Government might exercise in the case of a national and foreign war. The inhabitants of the insurgent States being thus judicially declared public enemies as well as Rebels, there would seem to be no doubt at all that the victorious close of actual hostilities could not deprive the Government of the power of deciding on the terms of peace with public enemies. The Government of the United States found the insurgent States thoroughly revolutionized and disorganized, with no State governments which could be recognized without recognizing the validity of treason, and without the power or right to take even the initial steps for State reorganization. They were practically out of the Union as States ; their State governments had lapsed ; their population was composed of Rebels and public enemies, by the decision of the Supreme Court. Under such circumstances, how the commander-in-chief, under Congress, of the forces of the United States could re-create these defunct States, and make it mandatory on Congress to receive their delegates, has always appeared to us one of those mysteries of unreason which require faculties either above or below humanity to accept. In addition to this fundamental objection, there was the further one, that almost all of the delegates were Rebels presidentially pardoned into "loyal men," were elected with the idea of forcing Congress to repeal the test oath, and were incapacitated to be legislators even if they had been sent from loyal States. The few who were loyal men in the sense that they had not served the Rebel government, were still palpably elected by constituents who had ; and the character of the constituency is as legitimate a subject of Congressional inquiry as the character of the representative.

It not being true, then, that the twenty-two hundred thousand loyal voters who placed Mr. Johnson in office, and whom he betrayed, have no means by their representatives in Congress to exert a controlling power in the reconstruction of the Rebel communities, the question comes up as to the conditions which Congress has imposed. It always appeared to us that the true measure of conciliation, of security, of mercy, of justice, was one which would combine the principle of universal amnesty, or an amnesty nearly universal, with that of universal, or at least of impartial suffrage. In regard to amnesty, the amendment to the Constitution which Congress has passed disqualifies no Rebels from voting, and only disqualifies them from holding office when they have happened to add perjury to treason. In regard to suffrage, it makes it for the political interest of the South to be just to its colored citizens, by basing representation on voters, and not on population, and thus places the indulgence of class prejudices and hatreds under the penalty of a corresponding loss of political power in the Electoral College and the National House of Representatives. If the Rebel States should be restored without this amendment becoming a part of the Constitution, then the recent Slave States will have thirty Presidential Electors and thirty members of the .House of Representatives in virtue of a population they disfranchise, and the vote of a Rebel white in South Carolina will carry with it more than double the power of a loyal white in Massachusetts or Ohio. The only ground on which this disparity can be defended is, that as " one Southerner is more than a match for two Yankees," he has an inherent, continuous, unconditioned right to have this superiority recognized at the ballot-box. Indeed, the injustice of this is so monstrous, that the Johnson orators find it more convenient to decry all conditions of representation than to meet the incontrovertible reasons for exacting the condition which bases representation on voters. Not to make it a part of the Constitution would be, in Mr. Shellabarger's vivid illustration, to allow " that Lee's vote should · have double the elective power of Grant's; Semmes's double that of Farragut's ; *Booth's — did he live — double that of Lincoln's, his victim !*"

It is also to be considered that these thirty votes would, in almost all future sessions of Congress, decide the fate of the most important measures. In 1862 the Republicans, as Congress is now constituted, only had a majority of twenty votes. In alliance with the Northern Democratic party, the South with these thirty votes might repeal the Civil Rights Bill, the principle of which is embodied in the proposed amendment. It might assume the Rebel debt, which is repudiated in that amendment. It might even repudiate the Federal debt, which is affirmed in that amendment. We are so accustomed to look at the Rebel debt as dead beyond all power of resurrection, as to forget that it amounts, with the valuation of the emancipated slaves, to some four thousand millions of dollars. If the South and its Northern Democratic allies should come into power, there is a strong probability that a measure would be brought in to assume at least a portion of this debt, — say two thousand millions. The Southern members would be nearly a unit for assumption, and the Northern Democratic members would certainly be exposed to the most frightful temptation that legislators ever had to resist. Suppose it were necessary to buy fifty members at a million of dollars apiece, that sum would only be two and a half per cent of the whole. Suppose it were necessary to give them ten millions apiece, even that would only be a deduction of twenty-five per cent from a claim worthless without their votes. The bribery might be conducted in such a way as to elude discovery, if not suspicion, and the measure would certainly be trumpeted all over the North as the grandest of all acts of statesmanlike " conciliation," binding the South to the Union in indissoluble bonds of interest. The amendment renders the conversion of the Rebel debt into the most enormous of all corruption funds an impossibility.

But the character and necessity of the amendment are too well understood to need explanation, enforcement, or defence. If it, or some more stringent one, be not adopted, the loyal people will be tricked out of the fruits of the war they have waged at the expense of such unexampled sacrifices of treasure and blood. It never will be adopted unless it be practically made a condition of the restoration of the Rebel States; and for the unconditioned restoration of those States the President, through his most trusted supporters, has indicated his intention to venture a *coup d'état.* This threat has failed doubly of its purpose. The timid, whom it was expected to frighten, it has simply scared into the reception of the idea that the only way to escape civil war is by the election of over a hundred and twenty Republican Representatives to the Fortieth Congress. The courageous, whom it was intended to defy, it has only exasperated into more strenuous efforts against the insolent renegade who had the audacity to make it. Everywhere in the loyal States there is an uprising of the people only paralleled by the grand uprising of 1861. The President's plan of reconstruction having passed from a policy into a conspiracy, his chief supporters are now not so much his partisans as his accomplices; and against him and his accomplices the people will this autumn indignantly record the most overwhelming of verdicts.

November, 1866.

THE CONSPIRACY AT WASHINGTON.

THE people of the United States now have the mortification of standing before the world in the attitude of a swindled democracy. Their collective will is crossed by the will of one individual, whose only title to such autocracy is in the fact that he has cheated and betrayed those who elected him. There might be some little compensation for this outrage, if the man himself possessed any of those commanding qualities of mind and disposition which ordinarily distinguish usurpers; but it is the peculiarity of Mr. Johnson that the indignation excited by his claims is only equalled by the contempt excited by his character. He is despised even by those he benefits, and his nominal supporters feel ashamed of the trickster and apostate, while condescending to reap the advantages of his faithlessness. No party in the South or in the North thinks of selecting him as its candidate; for the vices and weaknesses which make an excellent accomplice and tool are not those which any party would consider desirable in a leader. Whatever office-seekers, partisans, traitors, and public enemies may find in Mr. Johnson, it is certain that they find in him nothing to respect. He is cursed with that form of moral disease which sometimes renders a man ridiculous, sometimes infamous, but which never renders him respectable ; namely, vanity of will. Other men may be vain of their talents and accomplishments, but he is vain of the personal pronoun itself, utterly regardless of what it covers and includes. Reason, conscience, understanding, have no impersonality to him. When he uses the words, he uses them as synonyms of his determinations, or as decorative terms into which it pleases him to translate the rough vernacular of his wilfulness and caprices. The " Constitution," also, a word constantly profaned by his lips, is not so much, as he uses it, the Constitution of the United States as the moral and mental constitution of Andrew Johnson, which, in his view, is the one primary fact to which all other facts must be subordinate. His gross inconsistencies of opinion and policy, his shameless betrayal of his party, his incapacity to hold himself to his word, his hatred of a cause the moment its defenders cease to flatter him, his habit of administering laws he has vetoed, on the principle that they do not mean what he vetoed them for meaning, his delight in little tricks of low cunning, — in short, all the immoral and unreasonable acts of his administration have their central source in a passionate sense of self-importance, inflaming a mind of extremely limited capacity.

Such a person, whose mere presence in the executive chair of a constitutional country is itself " a high crime and misdemeanor," is of course the natural prey of demagogues, and he now appears to be surrounded by demagogues of the most desperate class. His advisers are conspirators, and they have so wrought on his vulgar and malignant nature that the question of his impeachment has now come to be merged in the more momentous question whether he will submit to be impeached. Constitutionally, there is no limit to the power of Congress in this respect but that which Congress may itself impose. The power is plain, and there can be no revision of the judgment of the Senate by any other power in the Government. But Mr. Johnson thinks, or says he thinks, that Congress itself, as at present constituted, is unconstitutional. He believes, or says he believes, that the defeated Rebel States whose representatives Congress now excludes are as much States in the Union, and as much entitled to representation, as New York or Ohio. As he specially represents the defeated Rebel States, it is hardly to be supposed that he will consent to be punished for crimes committed in their behalf by a Congress from which their representatives are excluded; and it is also to be presumed that the measures he is now taking to obstruct the operation of the laws of Congress relating to reconstruction are but preliminary to a design to resist Congress itself.

The madness of such a scheme leads judicious people to disbelieve in its possibility; but in respect to Mr. Johnson it has been found that the only way to prevent the occurrence of mischief is to diffuse extensively among the people the suspicion that it is meditated. Judicious and dispassionate persons are often poor judges of what men of fierce passions and distempered minds will do; for they unconsciously attribute to such men some of their own ideas of honesty, propriety, and regard for the public welfare. The legislators whom Louis Napoleon outwitted were overthrown, because, bad as their opinion of him was, it was not so bad as events proved it ought to have been. In the case of Mr. Johnson, there is not the same excuse for misconception, since his cunning is utterly divorced from sagacity, and he has not the intelligence to conceal what his impulses prompt him to attempt. The kind of man he is would seem to be obvious to the most superficial observer; the natural inference is, therefore, that he will act after his kind; but this is an inference which dispassionate statesmen have hesitated fully to draw. They have been continually surprised at acts which they should have foreseen. They were surprised that, during the months he was left to his own devices and to the counsels of Southern politicians, he matured his policy of reconstruction. They were surprised that he would not abandon his policy rather than break with the Republican party. They were surprised when they learned that he meditated a *coup d'état* on the assembling of the Fortieth Congress. They were surprised when they found that no law could be made which would bind him according to its intent. They were surprised when, as soon as Congress adjourned, he began to take measures which can have no other intelligible purpose than that of making him master of Congress when it reassembles. And to crown all, though it has been apparent since February, 1866, that he was the enemy of the country, they have still had technical reasons for retaining him as the proper executive of its laws.

It would then seem that, in dealing with such a man as Andrew Johnson, it is the part of wisdom to suspect the worst. Without any special knowledge of the treasonable intrigue now going on in Washington, it is still possible to fathom the President's designs, and to understand the resources on which he relics. In the first place, his conceit makes him believe that he is the first man in the nation, and that he is not only adored at the South, but popular at the North. The slightest sign of reaction in Northern and Western elections he considers a testimony to his individual merit, and an indorsement of his policy. In case he refuses to recognize the present Congress, turns its members by military power out of their seats, and appeals for support to the white population of the Rebel as well as Loyal States, he will count on being sustained by the nation. The Democratic party agrees with him as far as regards the constitutionality of the laws which he will, in the name of the Constitution, be compelled to disregard in order to get possession of the military power of the country; and he thinks that party will support him in resuming those functions as commander-in-chief of which he has been deprived by a "usurping" Congress. The army and navy, with all Republican officers removed, including, of course, General Grant and Admiral Farragut, he thinks will obey his orders. The South, he supposes, will rally round him to a man. The thoroughly Rebel military organization in Maryland, controlled by a Governor after his own heart, will interpose obstacles to the passage of troops from the Northern States to Washington. The Democrats in those States will do all they can to prevent troops from being sent. Before there could be any efficient military organization in the Loyal States brought to bear on his dictatorship, he expects to have a Congress of "the whole nation" around him, of which at least a majority will be defeated Rebels and Copperheads. The whole thing is to be done in the name of the Constitution; and the Proclamation he has issued to all officers of the United States, civil and military, telling them to obey the Constitution (that is, Mr. Johnson), may be considered the first step in the development of the scheme.

It is needless to say that such a scheme could only find hospitable reception in the head of a spiteful, inflated, and unprincipled egotist, for such an egotist Mr. Johnson assuredly is. It is needless to say that it would break down through the refusal of General Grant to give up his command, and through the refusal of the great body of the army to obey the Presi-

dent; for the danger is not so much the success of
the attempt as the convulsion which the mere attempt
would occasion. That the danger is a serious one,
provided the October and November elections show
a considerable Republican loss, is evident from a
consideration of the President's position. He has
already gone far enough in his course to exasperate
Congress, and unite its Republican members, conservative and radical, in favor of his impeachment.
Without going over the long list of delinquencies and
usurpations which would justify that measure, it is
sufficient to name the recent Proclamation of Amnesty as an act which promises to secure it. That
Proclamation is a plain violation of the Constitution
as the Constitution is understood by Congress; and
it is upon the Congressional interpretation of the
Constitution that, in the matter of impeachment, the
President must stand or fall. Congress, by giving
the power of granting amnesty to Mr. Lincoln, evidently conceived that it was not a power given to him
by the Constitution; by taking it away from Mr.
Johnson, it as evidently conceived that it could not
be exercised by him except by usurpation. In usurping this power, Mr. Johnson must have known that
his act belonged, in the opinion of Congress, to the
class of "high crimes and misdemeanors," for the
commission of which the Constitution expressly pro-
vides that Presidents may be impeached; and he
must also have known that Congress, in judging of
his infractions of the Constitution, would be bound

neither by his individual opinion of his constitutional powers nor by the opinion of the Supreme Court, but was at perfect liberty to act on its own interpretation of his constitutional duty. It is not therefore to be supposed that he intended to limit his defiance of Congress to the mere issuing of the Amnesty Proclamation, especially as the principle on which that Proclamation was issued would cover his refusal to carry out the whole Congressional plan of reconstruction. His conviction or assertion that Congress has no right to withhold from him the power to pardon defeated rebels and public enemies by the wholesale, is certainly not greater or more emphatic than his conviction or assertion that, in its plan of reconstruction, Congress has granted to subordinates powers which constitutionally belong to him. If he can exalt his will over Congress in the one case, there is no reason why he should not do it in the other.

Indeed, in the Proclamation of Amnesty, Mr. Johnson practically claims that his power to grant pardons extends to a dispensing power over the laws. But it is evident that the Constitution, in giving the President the power to pardon criminals, does not give him the power to dispense with the laws against crime. At one period Mr. Johnson seems to have done this in respect to the crime of counterfeiting, by his repeated pardons extended to convicted counterfeiters. Still, there is a broad line of distinction between the abuse of this power to pardon criminals after conviction, and the assumption of power to restore to whole classes of traitors and public enemies their forfeited rights of citizenship. By the pardon of murderers and counterfeiters, the President cannot much increase the number of his political supporters; by the pardon of traitors and public enemies, he may build up a party to support him in his struggle against the legislative department of the Government. The reasons which have induced Mr. Johnson to dispense with the laws against treason are political reasons, and bear no relation to his prerogative of mercy. Nobody pretends that he pardoned counterfeiters because they were his political partisans; everybody knows he pardons traitors and public enemies in order to gain their influence and votes. A public enemy himself, and leagued with public enemies, he has the impudence to claim that he is constitutionally capable of perverting his power to pardon into a power to gain political support in his schemes against the loyal nation.

But it is not probable that the President will limit his usurpations to a measure whose chief significance consists in its preliminary character. Before Congress meets in November, he will doubtless have followed it up by others which will make his impeachment a matter of certainty. The only method of preventing him from resisting impeachment by force, is an awakening of the people to the fact that the final battle against reviving rebellion is yet to be fought at the polls. Any apathy or divisions among Republicans in the State elections in October and November,

resulting in a decrease of their vote, will embolden
Mr. Johnson to venture his meditated *coup d'état.*
He never will submit to be impeached and removed
from office unless Congress is sustained by a majority
of the people so great as to frighten him into submission. Elated by a little victory, he can only be de-
pressed by a ruinous defeat; and such a defeat it is
the solemn duty of the people to prepare for him.
Even into his conceited brain must be driven the
idea that his contemplated enterprise is hopeless, and
that, in attempting to commit the greatest of political crimes, he would succeed only in committing the
most enormous of political blunders.

Still, it is not to be concealed that there are circumstances in the present political condition of the
country which may give the President just that degree of apparent popular support which is all he
needs to stimulate him into open rebellion against
the laws. It is, of course, his duty to recognize the
people of the United States in their representatives
in the Fortieth Congress; but, on the other hand, it
is the character of his mind to regard the people as
multiplied duplicates of himself, and a mob yelling
for " Andy " under his windows is to him more representative of the people than the delegates of twenty
States. In the autumn elections only two Representatives to Congress will be chosen ; the political strife
will relate generally to local questions and candidates ;
and it is to be feared that the Republicans will not be
sufficiently alive to the fact, that divisions on local

questions and candidates will be considered at Washington as significant of a change in the public mind on the great national question which it is the business of the Fortieth Congress to settle. That Congress needs the moral support of a great Republican vote *now,* and will obtain it provided the people are roused to a conviction of its necessity. But a large and influential portion of the Republican party is composed of business men, whose occupations disconnect them from politics except in important exigencies, and who can with difficulty be made to believe that politics is a part of their business, as long as the safety of their business is not threatened by civil disorders. They think the reconstruction question is practically settled; and when you speak to them of plots such as are now hatching in Washington, and which seem as preposterous as the story of a sensational novel, their incredulity confirms them in the notion that it is safe to allow things to take their course. Their very good sense makes them blind to the designs of such a Bobadil-Cromwell as Andrew Johnson. The great body of the Republican party, indeed, shows at present a little of the exhaustion which is apt to follow a series of victories, and exhibits altogether too much of the confidence which so often attends an incompleted triumph.

The Democratic party, on the contrary, is all alive, and is preparing for one last desperate attempt to recover its old position in the nation. Its leaders fear that, if the Congressional plan of reconstruction

be carried out, it will result in republicanizing the
Southern States. This would be the political extinction of their party. In fighting against that plan,
they are, therefore, fighting for life, and are accordingly more than usually profligate in the character of
the stimulants they address to whatever meanness,
baseness, dishonesty, lawlessness, and ignorance there
may be in the nation. Taxation presses hard on the
people, and they have not hesitated to propose repudiation of the public debt as the means of relief. The
argument is addressed to ignorance and passion; for
Mirabeau hit the reason of the case when he defined
repudiation as taxation in its most cruel and iniquitous form. But the method of repudiation which the
Democratic leaders propose to follow is of all methods
the worst and most calamitous. They would make
the dollar a mere form of expression by the issue of
an additional billion or two of greenbacks, and then
" pay off " the debt in the currency they had done all
they could to render worthless. In other words, they
would not only swindle the public creditor, but wreck
all values. A party which advocates such a scheme
as this, to save it from the death it deserves, would
have no hesitation in risking a civil convulsion for the
same purpose. Indeed, the reopening of the civil war
would not produce half the misery which would be
created by the adoption of their project to dilute the
currency.

Now, if by apathy on the part of Republicans and
audacity on the part of Democrats the autumn elec-

tions result unfavorably, it will then be universally
seen how true was Senator Sumner's remark made in
January last, that "Andrew Johnson, who came to
supreme power by a bloody accident, has become the
successor of Jefferson Davis in the spirit by which he
is governed, and in the mischief he is inflicting on the
country;" that "the President of the Rebellion is
revived in the President of the United States." What
this man now proposes to do has been impressively
stated by Senator Thayer of Nebraska, in a public
address at Cincinnati. "I declare," he said, "upon
my responsibility as a Senator of the United States,
that to-day Andrew Johnson meditates and designs
forcible resistance to the authority of Congress. I
make this statement deliberately, having received it
from an unquestioned and unquestionable authority."
It would seem that this authority could be none other
than the authority of the Acting Secretary of War
and General of the Army of the United States, who,
reticent as he is, does not pretend to withhold his
opinion that the country is in imminent peril, and in
peril from the action of the President. But it is by
some considered a sufficient reply to such statements,
that, if Mr. Johnson should overturn the legislative
department of the Government, there would be an uprising of the people which would soon sweep him and
his supporters from the face of the earth. This may
be very true; but we should prefer a less Mexican
manner of ascertaining public sentiment. Without
leaving their peaceful occupations, the people can do

by their votes all that it is proposed they shall do by their muskets. It is hardly necessary that a million or half a million of men should go to Washington to speak their mind to Mr. Johnson, when a ballot-box close at hand will save them the expense and trouble. It will, indeed, be infinitely disgraceful to the nation if Mr. Johnson dares to put his purpose into act; for his courage to violate his own duty will come from the neglect of the people to perform theirs. Let the great uprising of the citizens of the Republic be at the polls this autumn, and there will be no need of a fight in the winter. The House of Representatives, which has the sole power of impeachment, will in all probability impeach the President. The Senate, which has the sole power to try impeachments, will in all probability find him guilty, by the requisite two thirds of its members, of the charges preferred by the House. And he himself, cowed by the popular verdict against his contemplated crime, and hopeless of escaping from the punishment of past delinquencies by a new act of treason, will submit to be removed from the office he has too long been allowed to dishonor.

November, 1867.

MORAL SIGNIFICANCE OF THE REPUBLICAN TRIUMPH.

THE victory which the Republican party gained in the November election, after the most fiercely contested struggle recorded in our political history, is the crowning victory of the War of the Rebellion, and its real close. A war such as raged in this country between April, 1861, and April, 1865, is ended, not when the defeated party ceases to fight, but when it ceases to hope. The sentiments and principles which led to the Rebellion were overturned, not in 1865, but in 1868. After the exhaustion of physical power, which compelled the Rebels to lay down their arms, came the moral struggle which has resulted in compelling them to surrender their ideas. If these ideas had been on a level with the civilization of the age, or in advance of it; if the "Lost Cause" had been the cause of humanity and freedom, of reason and justice, of good morals and good sense, — such a catastrophe would be viewed by every right-minded man as a great calamity. But the Rebellion was essentially a revolt of tyrants for the privilege to oppress, and of bullies for the right to domineer. Its interpretation of the Constitution was an ingenious reversal of the

purposes for which the Constitution was declared to
be made, and its doctrine of State Rights was a mere
cover for a comprehensive conspiracy against the
rights of man. The success of such a "cause" could
not have benefited even its defenders; for the worst
government for the permanent welfare even of the
governing classes is that in which the intelligent systematically prey upon the ignorant, and the strong
mercilessly trample on the weak. In a large view,
the South is better off to-day for the military defeat
which dissipated its wild dream of insolent domination, and for the political defeat which destroyed the
last hopes of its reviving passions.

Those who are accustomed to recognize a providence in the direction of human affairs may find in
the course and conduct equally of this military and
political struggle the strongest confirmation of their
faith. The great things that have been done appear
to have been done through us, rather than by us.
During the war, it seemed as if no mistakes could
hinder us from gaining victories, no reverses obstruct
our steady advance, no conservative prudence prevent
us from being the audacious champions of radical ideas.
The march of events swept forward Government and
people on its own path, converting the distrusted ab-
straction of yesterday into the "military necessity" of
to-day and the constitutional provision of to-morrow.
President, Congress, parties, all felt the propulsion of
a force more intelligent than individual sagacity, and
mightier than associated opinion. So strong was the

stress on the minds of Republicans, that the charge of inconsistency, made by such politicians as had succeeded in secluding themselves from the heroic impulse of the time, not only fell pointless, but was welcomed as an indication that the men conducting the war were intelligent enough to read aright its grim facts as they successively started into view. The result proved that the very absence of what is called "a leading mind" indicated the presence of a Mind compared with which Cæsars and Napoleons are as little as Soubises and Macks.

What was true of the military is true of the political contest. After the armed Rebellion was crushed by arms, and the meaner rebellion of intrigue, bluster, and miscellaneous assassination began, both parties had reason to be surprised at the issue. The Rebels found that their profoundest calculations, their most unscrupulous plottings, their most vigorous action, only led them to a more ruinous defeat. Their opponents had almost equal reason for wonder; for the plan of reconstruction, which they eventually passed and repeatedly sustained by more than two thirds of both Houses of Congress, would not have commanded a majority in either House at the time the problem of reconstruction was first presented. Whether we refer this unexpected and unpremeditated result to Providence, to the nature of things, or to the logic of events, it still shows that our forecast did little more than "make mouths at the invisible event." The country was not so much ruled as overruled.

19

The form which reconstruction eventually took was, however, the form which from the first reason would have decided to be the best. It offended strong prejudices and roused bitter animosities; but it was necessary to insure the safety and honor of the nation, and it was fitted to the peculiar facts and principles of the case. The question to be decided referred primarily to suffrage. The Republicans were at first inclined to think it should be conferred on the educated alone. How would this principle have applied to the Rebel States? Those who could read and write in those States were the originators of the Rebellion, and remained, after its military overthrow, in a state of sullen discontent with the Government by which they had been subdued. To give them the suffrage, and deny it to the great body of the blacks and the poor whites, would be to put the Rebel States into the hands of the enemies of the United States. This condition of things would be little improved by allowing all whites to vote, and only such blacks as should happen to possess educational qualifications. The class on whose loyalty the Government could depend would be practically sacrificed to the classes whose loyalty the Government had the best reason to distrust. It is true that the blacks were, as a general thing, ignorant; but they at least possessed the instinct of self-preservation, and they were placed in such a position that the instinct of self-preservation would inevitably lead them to take the side of orderly government. Their interests, hopes, and passions, their very right to own themselves, were all bound up in the success of the national cause, to which the interests, hopes, and passions of the so-called educated classes were opposed. Besides, it might be said that education implies the recognition of sentiments of humanity, ideas of freedom, duties of beneficence, which are on a level with the civilization of the age; and the blacks were better educated in this sense than the great majority of their former masters, who had notoriously perverted natural feeling, right reason, and true religion in their vain effort to defend an indefensible institution. Southern education, for many years before the Rebellion broke out, had been an education in self-will, and its most shining results were men distinguished for the vehemence of manner and sharpness of intellect with which they defended paradoxes that affronted common sense, and assailed truths too tediously true to admit of serious debate. They were reasoning beings without being reasonable ones. Now, the blacks could not help being more in sympathy with the sentiments and ideas of the age than such men as these, for their simple, selfish instincts identified them with advanced opinions. And education, if not made the condition of suffrage, would be its result. If made its condition, the negroes would hold no political power, and common schools for all classes are only established by those legislative assemblies in which all classes are represented. At first, therefore, they would vote right, because they would vote as their instincts taught them; and by the time that their in-

stincts might not be the measure of their true interests, they would be educated.

In the first step made towards reconstruction, that
called "the President's Plan," no heed was paid to
these considerations. The negroes were practically
delivered over to the tender mercies of their former
masters, and the political power of the Rebel States
was put into Rebel hands. Profligate as this scheme
really was, it had sufficient plausibility to deceive
many honest minds, and at one period there was imminent danger of its adoption. The reaction consequent on a long conflict, the desire of the people for
a speedy settlement of the questions growing out of
the war, the natural indisposition of the Republican
leaders to quarrel with the President, the fear to face
resolutely the question of negro suffrage, the seeming
apathy or paralysis of the great body of Republican
voters, — all seemed to point to a settlement which
would be a surrender, and by which the supporters of
the war would be swindled out of its fair and legitimate results. Fortunately, however, the great enemy
of the President's plan was the President. His vulgarity undid the work which his cunning had planned.
The force which impelled the Republican party to
overturn Mr. Johnson's policy was derived from Mr.
Johnson himself. It is needless here to recapitulate
the mistakes by which he succeeded in concentrating
Northern opinion, and making his opponents irresisti-
ble. The Republicans owe to him a debt of gratitude
they can never pay ; for the peculiar manner in which

he schemed to split them into factions made them a
unit. The small, intelligent, and unscrupulous clique
of politicians known as "the President's friends" sor-
rowfully admit that Mr. Johnson's policy was a mag-
nificent political game, which must have succeeded
had it not been for the bad playing of Mr. Johnson.
If the executive department of the Government lost
the respect of all parties during his administration, it
was due to the fact that the President confounded the
office with his personality. Nobody could respect the
officer, and yet the officer persistently identified himself with the office.

After Mr. Johnson had broken with Congress, he
became a President in search of a party. He sought
it everywhere, and particularly at the South. At the
North he could get politicians enough, but he could
get no representative politicians, — no politicians who
had "a following." At the South he obtained the
support of the great body of the Rebels, but they were
without any political power. They could speak for
him, mob for him, kill negroes for him, but they could
not vote for him. Believing, however, in the certainty
of his eventual success, they repudiated, with a great
display of indignant eloquence, the first "Congressional Plan" of reconstruction, which merely contemplated the identification of their political interests with
the enfranchisement of the colored race, and denied
them the privilege of counting, in the basis of representation, four millions of people to whom they refused political rights. Certainly no conquerors ever

before proposed such mild terms to the vanquished; and yet the terms were rejected with a fury of contempt such as would have misbecome a triumphant faction, mad with the elation both of military and political success. The ludicrous insolence of this course ruined the last prospect these men had of rebuilding Southern society on its old foundations. The plan of reconstruction which has recently triumphed at the polls was the necessary result of their folly and arrogance. The reorganization of the Southern States on the comprehensive principle of equality of rights became possible only through the madness of its adversaries. Congress and the people repeatedly hesitated; but in every moment of hesitation they were pushed forward by some new instance of Mr. Johnson's brutality of speech, or by some fresh examples of Southern proclivity to murder.

As it regards the right of the Government of the United States to dictate conditions of reconstruction, it must be remembered that the difference between the President's Plan and the Congressional Plan was not, in this respect, a difference in principle; and that the position held by the Democratic party — that the Rebellion was a rebellion of individuals, and not of States — equally condemns both. This position, however, can only be maintained by the denial of the most obvious facts. The enormous sacrifices of blood and treasure in putting down the Rebellion were made necessary by the circumstance that it was a rebellion of States. Had it been merely an insurrection of in-

dividuals, it would have been an insurrection against
State governments as well as against the Government
of the United States. We had, both before the war
and during its continuance, examples of such insurrections. The Whiskey Insurrection in Pennsylvania,
and Shays's Rebellion in Massachusetts, were risings
of individuals against the laws; but nobody believes
that Pennsylvania and Massachusetts lost any State
rights by those disturbances. In Kentucky and Missouri, during the recent war, there was a tenfold more
terrible rebellion of individuals against the United
States Government; but nobody pretends that Missouri
and Kentucky forfeited any State rights by this crime
of their individual citizens. In all these cases, the governments of the States remained in loyal hands. But
the peculiarity of our war against the Confederate States
consisted in the fact that all the State governments were
voted by the people into Rebel hands. The result was,
that the supreme powers of taxation and conscription,
placing every man and every dollar at the service of
the Confederate States, were lodged in a revolutionary
government, and the cost of suppressing the Rebellion
was increased at least fourfold by this fact. After
losing two hundred and fifty thousand men, and two
billions and a half of dollars, — more than would have
been necessary to crush a rebellion of individual insurgents, — we are told that the States never rebelled;
that the loyal but bodiless souls of these communities
still existed, whilst certain Rebel " individuals " exercised their supreme powers ; and that, the moment

these Rebel individuals succumbed, the bodiless souls instantly became embodied and continued loyal in the Rebel individuals aforesaid! Out of Bedlam no such argument was ever propounded before.

In truth, there was no possibility that the Rebel States could " resume their practical relations " with the United States except by the intervention of the United States in their internal affairs. Though the plan of reconstruction eventually adopted is called the " Congressional Plan," it was really the plan of the Government of the country. In our system, a mere majority of Congress is impotent, provided the President, however " accidental " he may be, however mean, base, false, and traitorous he may be, nullifies its legislation by his vetoes; but Congress becomes constitutionally the governing power in the nation, when its policy is supported by two thirds of the Representatives of the people in the House, and two thirds of the Representatives of the States in the Senate. President Johnson has pushed to the extreme the powers granted to the executive by the Constitution; and if he has failed in carrying his policy it has been through no encroachments of the legislature on his constitutional rights. Passed over his vetoes, he was bound to consider the reconstruction laws as the acts of the Government. It is notorious that he has systematically attempted to nullify the operation of the laws which, by the Constitution, it was his simple duty to execute.

It was almost inevitable, however, that, in the

measures by which Congress attempted to make Mr.
Johnson perform his duties, it should commit errors
of that kind which tell against the popularity of a
party, if not against its patriotism and intelligence.
In spite of executive opposition Congress had succeeded in getting new State governments organized
at the South, and the representatives of the legal
people of those States were in the Senate and House
of Representatives. Mr. Johnson and the Democratic
party pronounced these reconstructed State governments to be utterly without validity, though their
Representatives formed part of the Congress of the
United States, and though Congress has by the Constitution the exclusive right of judging of the qualifications of its own members, and, by the decision of
the Supreme Court, has the exclusive right of judging
of the validity of State governments. Whatever popularity, therefore, the Republicans may have lost by
their reconstruction policy, it was more than offset
by the blunder made by their opponents in proposing
the overthrow of that policy by revolutionary measures. Elections are commonly decided by the votes
of a class of independent citizens, who belong strictly
to neither of the two parties ; and the course pursued
by the Democrats pushed this class for the time into
the Republican ranks. The intellect of the Democratic party is concentrated, to a great degree, in its
Copperhead members ; and these had become so embittered and vindictive by the turn events had taken,
that their malignity prevented their ability from hav-

ing fair play. They assailed the Republicans for not giving peace and prosperity to the nation, and then laid down a programme which proposed to reach peace and prosperity through political and financial anarchy. They selected unpopular candidates, and then placed them on a platform of which revolution and repudiation were the chief planks. Perhaps even with these drawbacks they might have cajoled a sufficient number of voters to succeed in the election, had it not been for the frank brutality of their Southern allies. To carry the North, their reliance was on fraud; but the Southern politicians were determined to carry their section by terror and assassination, and no plausible speech could be made by a Northern Democrat the effect of which was not nullified by some Southern burst of eloquence, breathing nothing but proscription and war. The Democratic party was therefore not only defeated, but disgraced. To succeed as it succeeded in New York and New Jersey, in Louisiana and Georgia, did not prevent its fall, but did prevent its falling with honor. To the infamy of bad ends it added the additional infamy of bad means; and it comes out of an overwhelming general reverse with the mortifying consciousness that its few special victories have been purchased at the expense of its public character. The only way it can recover its *prestige* is by discarding, not only its leaders, but the passions and ideas its leaders represent.

The moral significance of the struggle which has just closed is thus found in the fact that the good cause was best served by its bitterest enemies. A bad institution, like slavery, generates a bad type of character in its supporters, and urges them blindly on to the adoption of measures which, intended for its defence, result in its ruin. The immense achievement of emancipating four millions of slaves, and placing them on an equality of civil and political rights with their former masters, is due primarily to such men as Calhoun and McDuffie, Davis and Toombs, Vallandigham, Pendleton, Belmont, Johnson, and Seymour. The prejudice in the United States against the colored race was strong enough to overcome everything but their championship of it. These persons taught the nation that its safety depended on its being just. The most careless glance over the chief incidents in the long contest shows that all the enemies of human freedom needed for success was a little moderation and good sense; but moderation and good sense are fortunately not the characteristics of men engaged in doing the Devil's work for the Devil's pay. "The Lord reigns," — a simple proposition, but one which politicians find it hard to accept, and which they often waste immense energies in the impotent attempt to overturn.

January, 1869.

"LORD" BACON.

SOME attempts have been recently made to extinguish Shakspeare's individuality in Bacon's. Any reader who intimately knows and sincerely loves both authors instinctively feels that the external evidence against Shakspeare's real existence is simply unworthy of critical consideration. Shakspeare's vast mind is in itself a sufficient puzzle for the critic and the metaphysician to explain; to blend it with Bacon's is to double the difficulties of the problem. Shakspeare and Bacon are both high above the ordinary range of even eminent intellects and souls; but to say that Bacon "wrote Shakspeare" is to introduce hopeless confusion into the philosophy of the human mind. Every critic who has the slightest discernment of spirits must know that the mental processes of Shakspeare and Bacon are fundamentally different, —a difference which goes deep down into vital sources of individual genius. Shakspeare individualizes the results of his knowledge; Bacon generalizes the results of his. The mind of Shakspeare *darts* to conclusions; the mind of Bacon *moves* to them with a gravity worthy of a lord chancellor. Both are men of large reason, large understanding, large imagination, large individuality; but they are different not only in degree, but in kind. It would be impossible

for any intelligent critic to reconcile a really characteristic work of Shakspeare with a really characteristic work of Bacon. The mental processes of the
two men are radically dissimilar.

This, however, is a digression. It may be doubted
if such a man as Shakspeare ever lived; it is certain
that no such man as " Lord " Bacon ever existed.

Francis Bacon, Sir Francis Bacon, Baron Verulam,
Viscount St. Albans,—these represent one individuality ; but *Lord* Bacon is demonstrably a fictitious
personage who never had any real existence on our
planet. Lord Verulam, Lord St. Albans is somebody we can recognize ; but Lord Bacon is an individual unknown to the British peerage. Hardwicke,
Brougham, and Macaulay selected their family names
when they were made nobles; but who would speak
of Chesterfield as Lord Stanhope, or Chatham as Lord
Pitt ? Bacon deliberately chose to be Lord Verulam
and Lord St. Albans rather than Lord Bacon. Why
should everybody, including scores of men who know
better, still persist in calling him " Lord " Bacon?
" Posterity," says Macaulay, " has felt that the greatest of English philosophers could derive no accession
of dignity from any title which James could bestow ;
and, in defiance of the royal letters-patent, has obstinately refused to *degrade* Francis Bacon into Viscount St. Albans." But still Macaulay's article in
the " Edinburgh Review," and the reprint of it in his
collected " Essays," supervised by himself, is headed
" Lord " Bacon.

Some ingenious antiquaries may account for this misnomer on the ground that men of science felt a necessity to discriminate between Friar Bacon, one of the first of modern experimental philosophers, and Francis Bacon, his supposed intellectual descendant, by calling the latter "Lord" Bacon, in spite of the inexorable laws of the peerage.

We must confess to a deep distrust of every theory which pretends to account for the fact that Baron Verulam or Viscount St. Albans has been universally converted into "Lord" Bacon. The fact that he is *Lord* Bacon forever, though utterly debarred from the title by his own deliberate choice, remains to be explained. We obstinately put "Lord" before a name in itself ignominious, — a name which suggests the hog, the dirtiest and basest of beasts, — when the owner of it sought to change the name into the more resounding appellation of Verulam and St. Albans.

Still, every essayist, scientist, and philosopher adheres to the family name of "Bacon." The associations connected with the hog do not seem to trouble them at all in celebrating the merits of one of the most humane, most fertile, and most comprehensive of human intellects. But why should they persist in calling him "Lord" Bacon?

We would suggest an explanation, based on the oldest of all old jokes. "Why," said Eve to Adam, when our ancestor was engaged in naming the individuals of the animal kingdom, — "why do you call that beast a lion?" "Because," replied Adam, "he looks like a lion." Well, Bacon is called a Lord because he "looks like" a Lord. King James only ratified a nobility which Nature had anticipated him in conferring. Bacon .was a nobleman from his cradle. He had the autocracy, the largeness, the sobriety of intellect which are generally recognized as the signs of a commanding nature.

Whatever may be our opinion of him as a practical statesman, we all feel, in reading him, that we are in communion with an intellect which is essentially lordly. His "Method of Induction," which some men of science ostentatiously celebrate but practically disregard, is demonstrably inadequate to explain the progress of modern invention and discovery. By his Method he never discovered anything himself; and certainly by his Method nothing has ever been discovered by those who rank themselves among his disciples. Still, he keeps his position as a kind of autocrat by the sheer force of a certain grandeur in his intelligence. It is useless to show that he misconceived the object of science, and was ignorant of its processes; he is still "Lord" Bacon even to such men as Whewell, Herschel, Comte, Mill, Huxley, Lewes, and Herbert Spencer. Every tyro in science can expose the errors of his Method; every eminent scientist persists in calling him "Lord," and persists in calling him Bacon. Verulam is a grander title; but it has never forced itself either into popular or scientific speech.

In his own time Bacon exercised the same power

over intelligent contemporaries that he now exercises over men of science, who more or less despise each other, but who are still faithful to him. "My conceit of his person," says Ben Jonson, the most caustic and irreverent of critics, "was never increased toward him by his place or honors; but I have and do reverence him for *the greatness that was only proper to himself* — in that he seemed to me ever by his work one of the greatest men and most worthy of admiration that had been in many ages. In his adversity I ever prayed that God would give him strength, for greatness he could not want." It is said that no man is a hero to his intimates and domestics. But Bacon's chaplain, Dr. Rawley, quaintly says: "I have been induced to think that if ever there were a beam of knowledge derived from God upon any man in these modern times it was upon him." Ben Jonson's emphatic statement of Bacon's essential "greatness," even in his disgrace and adversity, has been accepted by modern philosophers. They feel a tender respect and veneration for the man whose theories they contemptuously disregard. And they still call him "Lord" Bacon because he "looks like a Lord." In the utter wreck of his system they yet recognize a grand intelligence which in many respects dwarfs their own.

Bacon is by no means the founder of the inductive sciences. It is simply ridiculous to place him above Galileo and Kepler, either in the theories or the discoveries of inductive science. Nobody who has not

patiently read Bacon's "Novum Organum," — which
few modern men of science seem to have done, — can
appreciate the impertinence of such men as Newton
and La Place in violating the directions of their supposed lord and master. Their discoveries have been
made in a very suspicious, a very illegitimate manner, according to the Baconian system. The discovery of the great law of gravitation, which made
astronomy a deductive science, was something of which
Bacon never dreamed. According to his principles of
induction, which contemplated a continual series of
inductive steps, that law should not have been arrived
at for five hundred or a thousand years. Still, we
have not any doubt that Newton, at any period of
his career, would have respectfully referred to Baron
Verulam as "Lord" Bacon. Every admirer, indeed,
"saves his Bacon," but will not give up the "Lord."
All who read him are impressed with a certain dignity, majesty, and grandeur in his intelligence, which
instinctively leads them to endow him with a title
he disowned. In spite of his obvious defects, both as
jurist and scientist, they experience something of the
feeling which led Cowley to select him from mankind
as the one man

> " Whom a wise king and Nature chose
> Lord chancellor of both their laws."

In short, we all feel the essential " greatness " which
Ben Jonson recognized, and call him " Lord " Bacon,
because he " looks like a Lord."

20

LOWELL AS A PROSE WRITER.

THE publication of an additional volume of prose papers by Lowell will be taken, by a considerable portion of the public, as a kind of confirmation of Carlyle's surly dictum, that if a man has anything to say, he had better say it in prose ; while even those who appreciate the subtle melodies of Lowell's verse will be grateful for such a book as " My Study Windows." Lowell is indeed one of the most exquisite prose writers of the century, the master of a style which, while it is flexible to all the demands of statement, description, reflection, epigram, and narrative, is strongly individualized, and suggests no model on which it is formed. It is as much a creation of his own mind and intellectual character as are the thoughts and imaginations it conveys. Many years ago a volume was published under the captivating title of " Prose, by a Poet." We have no recollection whether the matter did or did not answer to the exhilarating announcement; but certainly such a title might, without presumption, be taken as a general one fitly characterizing " My Study Windows," " Among My Books," and " Fireside Travels," the three volumes of Lowell's prose writings. In all three we have learning, wit, humor, thought, sentiment, description, criticism, characterization, in abundance; but the fact that the writer is a poet is too plain to escape the dullest reader. The cheer and charm of a poetic imagination are felt, whether the poet states, reasons, satirizes, denounces, describes, or pokes fun.

The volume not inaptly styled "Fireside Travels" is less known than the other two; but it is one of the most delicious of Lowell's works, for it reproduces as vividly the scenery and character of the backwoods of Maine as it does the scenery, population, and art of Italy. Without stirring from our firesides, we are transported into the places, wild or over-civilized, into which the author has penetrated; and we view them through the eyes of a poetic humorist, who makes us keenly enjoy everything he so clearly represents.

These three volumes are really additions to American and to English *literature*. This cannot be said of thousands of excellent books, published on either side of the Atlantic, which, however valuable they may be for the time, contain nothing, contributed from the minds of their authors, which will survive the occasions which called them forth. The permanent element in Lowell's prose is Lowell's genius, not Lowell's topics; and his genius, like the genius of Addison, or Goldsmith, or Charles Lamb, is sufficiently powerful to give permanence even to trifles. The town-pump of Salem, as we see it through Hawthorne's imagination, will survive Napoleon's campaigns, as told by Sir Archibald Alison; and certainly many an excellent compend of botany and zoölogy will be forgotten when Lowell's "Garden Acquaintance" and "Good Word for Winter" will be read with delight.

But though Lowell can give trifles more importance than the ordinary run of men are able to give to subjects in themselves great, he is, of course, to be judged by his way of dealing with the higher objects of human interest. An earnest student, not only of languages, but of the science of language, his acquirements are on a level with his genius. In the niceties of verbal criticism, as in the application of comprehensive artistic principles, he seems equally at home. The great authors of Greece, Rome, Italy, Spain, Germany, and England he profoundly appreciates and acutely interprets; but at the same time he overwhelms those students of old English literature whom John Russell Smith employed to edit his "Library of Old Authors" with an amount of recondite knowledge of the way forgotten authors employ half-forgotten English words, which must appear to those editors somewhat appalling. They never could have dreamed that the Yankee author of the "Biglow Papers" was competent to overturn their pretensions to Elizabethan scholarship. But Lowell has done it so thoroughly that even the "Saturday Review" would acknowledge the completeness of the demolition. Again, in the article on Chaucer, also included in the collection of papers

called "My Study Windows," there is not only
evinced an open sense to Chaucer's genius, entirely
independent of all controversies regarding his versi-
fication, but a terrible amount of erudition, of which
the pedants of early English literature consider that
they hold the monopoly. Still, all this minute knowledge is so displayed as to entertain as well as to
inform. The antiquary and the philologist never
forgets that he is a poet, whose special function it
is to give artistic pleasure even when he is discuss-
ing topics from the consideration of which ordinary
readers shrink with an instinctive dread of their
dulness.

And this brings us to the peculiar, the almost un-
matched "brilliancy" of Lowell's prose. There is
hardly a sentence — there certainly cannot be a page
— in his three volumes which is not made attractive
through his mode of expression. This attractiveness
comes from the incessant action of his *mind* in composition, — no word, phrase or verbal combination
indicating a resort to those commonplace forms of
utterance such as many original thinkers do not
hesitate to employ. Lowell's thoughts, as Bacon
would say, "are immersed in matter" — allusion,
image, and metaphor, serious or humorous — flowing
from him in an unexhausted and seemingly inexhaust-
ible stream. Take his paper on "Carlyle," or "Thoreau," or "Abraham Lincoln," or "Josiah Quincy,"
or "Emerson the Lecturer," or "Chaucer," or "Pope,"
— all included in his last volume, — and the reader,

whether he agrees or disagrees with the opinions expressed, cannot but be amazed at the endless fertility and constant felicity of the imaginative forms of expression. Lowell thinks in figures, giving us the thought *in* the image, not the thought *and* the image. Let us take some carelessly selected specimens. "The lecturer built up so lofty a pedestal under certain figures as to lift them into a prominence of obscurity, and seemed to mast-head them there." Emerson's "eye for a fine, telling phrase, that will carry true, is like that of a backwoodsman for a rifle; and he will dredge you up a choice word from the mud of Cotton Mather himself." "One may think roses as good in their way as cabbages; though the latter would make a better show in the witness-box, if cross-examined as to their usefulness." If Emerson "were to make an almanac, his direction to farmers would be something like this : October: *Indian Summer;* now is the time to get in your early Vedas." Thoreau "watched Nature like a detective who is to go upon the stand; as we read him, it *seems as if all-out-of-doors had kept a diary and become its own Montaigne.*" "An apostle to the Gentiles might hope for some fruit of his preaching; but of what avail an apostle who shouts his message down the mouth of the pit to poor lost souls, whom he can positively assure only that it is impossible to get out? Mr. Carlyle lights up the lanterns of his Pharos after the ship is already rolling between the tongue of the sea and the grinders of the reef." But it is useless to give such bricks as these

as specimens of Lowell's figurative style. He is so
rich in this respect that one feels, in reading him, as
Voltaire's Candide felt when he lighted on that fabulous country where precious stones were as common
as the unprecious are with us. He cheapens the value
of his brilliants by the profusion with which he scatters
them. Lady Granville, when her husband was the
British minister at the Court of Russia, had her
coronet, the jewels of which were worth scores of
thousands of pounds, broken in one of those fashionable mobs at St. Petersburg, called court balls. She
was, at the time of the accident, making her way
through the crowd to pay her respects to the emperor
and empress; and she looked neither to the right nor
the left, but moved straight on, as the diamonds and
rubies fell on the floor, and were trodden under the
feet of the genteel multitude. In some such way
Lowell marches to his "objective point," careless of
the treasures he drops by the way. He may pride
himself on his sense, his sagacity, his insight, his
power of concentrated thought, his force of character; he never prides himself on his ornaments and
decorations.

In " Among My Books " and " My Study Windows "
there is a large amount of keen literary criticism,
which is hardly suggested by the mere titles of the
essays. In the four articles on Chaucer, Shakspeare,
Dryden, and Pope the whole field of modern European
literature is opened to the reader's view. The scope
of Lowell's scholarship is so extensive that, though

the special representative author he discusses is exhaustively treated, he includes in his criticism scores of other writers who illustrate the age which his principal personage dominates. To thoughtful students of English literature the article on Pope — the most discriminating criticism, on the whole, ever written on that poet — is attractive not only for its analysis of Pope, but for its general estimate of the literature and writers of the reign of Anne and the first two Georges.

It is a good sign for American literature that Lowell is warmly appreciated by all the educated men and women of the country. The wonder is that he is not one of our most popular authors. He is in perfect sympathy with all shrewd and sensible people, whatever may be the degrees of their culture; and certainly none of the American writers of novels for the newspapers which circulate hundreds of thousands of copies weekly can compare with him in his appreciation of " the popular mind " and his command of the raciest English. At any farmer's fireside in the land he would be welcomed as a good " neighborly " man. Why is it that the circulation of his books is not commensurate with the extent of his literary reputation? It is hardly possible to take up a newspaper, whether published in New York or Nebraska, without finding an allusion to Lowell or a quotation from him ; and to all appearance he is as popular as Whittier, or Bret Harte, or Artemus Ward, or Harriet Beecher Stowe. Still, his books are read mainly by what are called "cultivated" people. We are convinced that if the (so-called) "uncultivated" people only knew what delight they might find in Lowell's prose and verse, they would domesticate his books at once in their homes. The only criticism which a "cultivated" man is inclined to make on Lowell is simply this: that he is the most exasperating of literary aristocrats in his dealings with the middle class and lower class of literary people. The middle and lower classes, who live their lives without pretending to versify them, find in him the most sympathizing of brothers and friends; but woe to any one of them who puts his mediocrity into rhyme!

THE reason that everybody likes novels is, that everybody is more or less a novelist. In addition to the practical life that men and women lead, constantly vexed, as it is, by obstructive facts, there is an interior life which they *imagine*, in which facts smoothly give way to sentiments, ideas, and aspirations. In this imagined existence people strengthen themselves with new faculties, exalt themselves with new passions, surround themselves with new companions, devote themselves to new objects. They are richer, handsomer, braver, wittier, nobler, more disinterested, more adventurous, more efficient, than they are in their actual personalities and mode of living. They construct long stories, long as their own lives, of which they are the heroes or heroines; and the novels they best like to read are those whose scenes and characters best fit into the novel they are themselves incessantly weaving. The universality of self-esteem is probably due to the fact that people confuse the possibilities of their existence with its actualities. Each being the hero of "My Novel," gains self-importance in virtue of *that;* and while externally classed with the "nobodies," is internally conscious of ranking with the "somebodies." Burn out of a

man indeed everything else, — sense, sensibility, and
conscience, — you will still find alive in his ashes a
little self-conceit and a little imagination.

" How much do you weigh ? " a man was asked.
" Well," he replied, " ordinarily only a hundred and
twenty pounds; but when I'm mad, I weigh a ton ! "
But the great increase of weight arises when a person is kindled with a conception of what he has a
possibility of becoming.

It is evident that, as these novel-spinning factories
are in full operation in all heads, the only check on
their written production is the necessity for some
talent for narrative and some knack in composition.
Hence, in the first place, a swarm of romancers, who
have properly no place in literature, and who represent every variety of mediocrity, from the fussy and
furious dead-level of sensationalism to the tame and
timid dead-level of conventionality. Some put blood
in their ink, some water ; but it must be said that in
these matters blood is not always thicker than water.
Rise a step above this level, introduce some art in
the plot and some truth in the characterization,
keep as close to actual life as a photographer, be
as diffuse and as dogged in details as is consistent
with preserving a kind of languid interest, econo-
mize material, whether of incident or emotion, realize Carlyle's sarcasm that England contains twenty
millions of people, mostly bores, — and you have
Anthony Trollope, the most unromantic of romancers,
popular in virtue of his skill in reproducing a popula-

tion. Vitalize this dull reality by vivid feeling, put passion into everything, eliminate all that does not stimulate, be as fruitful in incidents as Trollope is in commonplaces, envelop the reader in a whirl of events, drag him violently on through a series of minor unexpected catastrophes to the grand unexpected catastrophe at the end, heap stimulants on him until he feels like a mad Malay running amuck through the streets, — and you have Charles Reade, the great master of melodramatic effect. This social life which Trollope does not penetrate, which Reade exaggerates, — look at it with a curious, sceptical eye, sharpened by a jaded heart; be superior to all the fine illusions of existence, by defect of spiritual insight as well as by subtlety of external observation; lay bare all the hypocrisies and rascalities of "proper" people without losing faith in the possibility of virtue; survey men and women in their play rather than in their real struggle and work; bring all the resources of keen observation, incisive wit, and delicate humor to the task of exhibiting the frailties of humanity without absolutely teaching that it is hopelessly vicious and effete, — be, in short, a sceptical Hume turned novelist, and you have Thackeray, a kindly man of genius, honestly forced by his peculiar intellect and experience to inculcate the dreadful doctrine that life does not pay. Add Thackeray's sharp and bright perception to Trollope's nicety in detail, and supplement both with large scholarship and wide reach of philosophic insight; conceive a person who looks not only *at* life and *into* life, but *through* it, who sympathizes with the gossip of peasants and the principles of advanced thinkers, who is as capable of reproducing Fergus O'Conner as John Stuart Mill, and is as blandly tolerant of Garrison as of Hegel, — and you have the wonderful woman who calls herself George Eliot, probably the largest mind among the romancers of the century, but with an incurable sadness at the depth of her nature which deprives her of the power to cheer the readers she interests and informs.

It may here be said that in a peculiar and restricted domain of imagination the great American novelist, Nathaniel Hawthorne, has fairly outmatched all his English brethren. He is the Jonathan Edwards of the imaginative representation of life, as Thackeray is its Hume. He teaches with vivid distinctness the doctrine of "the exceeding sinfulness of sin." Scott once said that there were depths in human nature which it was unhealthy to attempt to sound; and it is in attempting to sound these that Hawthorne has exhibited his most marvellous gifts of insight and characterization. In the subtlety and accuracy, the penetration and sureness, of his glance into the morbid phenomena of the human soul; in exhibiting the operation of the most delicate laws of attraction and repulsion which human natures can experience; in the capacity to terrify his readers with the consciousness of their latent possibilities for evil, so that they shrink from his pitiless exposures " like guilty things surprised," he makes novelists like Thackeray and Dickens appear relatively superficial; but, as Scott had foretold, the representation is too ghostly and ghastly to give that degree of artistic pleasure which is the condition of a novelist's complete success with the public.

Each of these novelists has a particular class of appreciative readers whose individual experience of life they specially meet. But there are two romancers, Scott and Dickens, who are liked and loved by everybody, because, by the happiness of their natures as well as the force of their genius, they are radiators of *cheer*, and communicate the most delicious imaginative *enjoyment*. Different in many important respects, they agree, in that last and inmost felicity of genius, — of being universally *attractive*. They are the only novelists who have succeeded in domesticating their creations in *all* imaginations as real human beings, whose wit or wisdom, whose joys or sorrows, whose hates or love, we refer to as confidently as Mrs. Gamp did to her dear, ideal Mrs. Harris, — more real to the eye of her mind than the Betsey Prig she daily beheld in superabundant flesh.

To achieve this miracle Dickens must not only have had exceptional powers of observation and imagination, but *extra*ordinary intensity of sympathy with *ordinary* feelings and beliefs. His genius in characterization tends to the grotesque and extravagant; his personages, in their names as in their qualities, produce on us the effect of strangeness; the plots of the novels in which they appear would, with any other·characters, seem grossly improbable; and yet his mind is unmistakably rooted in common sense and common humanity. He thus succeeds in giving his readers all the pleasure which comes from contemplating what is strange, odd, and eccentric, without disquieting them by any paradoxes in morals, or shocking them by any perversions of homely natural sentiment. The " Christmas Carol," for example, is as wild in grotesque fancy as a dream of Hoffmann, yet in feeling as solid and sweet and humane as a sermon of Channing. It impresses us somewhat as we are impressed by the sight of the Bible as illustrated by Gustave Doré. Thus held fast to common, homely truths and feelings by his sentiments, he can safely give reins to his imagination in his creations. The keenest of observers, both of things and persons, all that he observes is still taken up and transformed by his imagination, — becomes *Dickens-ized*, in fact, so that whether he describes a landscape, or a bootjack, or a building, or a man, we see the object, not as it is in itself, but as it is deliciously bewitched by his method of looking at it. Everything is suggested by his outward experience, but modified by his inward experience. The result is that we do not have in him an exact transcript of life, but an individualized ideal of life, from his point of view. He has, in short, discovered and colonized one of

the waste districts of Imagination which we may
call Dickens-land or Dickens-ville; from his own
brain he has peopled it with some fourteen hundred
persons; and it agrees with the settlements made
there by Shakspeare and Scott in being better known
than such geographical countries as Canada and
Australia; and it agrees with them equally in
confirming us in the belief of the *reality* of a population which has no *actual* existence. It is distinguished from all other colonies in Brainland by
the ineffaceable peculiarities of its colonizer; its inhabitants don't die like other people, but alas! they
also now can't increase; but whithersoever any of
them may wander, they are recognized at once, by an
unmistakable birth-mark, as belonging to the race
of Dickens. A man who has done this is not merely
one of a thousand, but one of a thousand millions;
for he has created an ideal population which is more
interesting to human beings than the great body of
their own actual friends and neighbors.

And how shall I describe this population, so numerous and so various?

It must, of course, be divided into classes; and
its most general division is into humane people and
malignant people. The one test of merit in Dickens-
land is goodness of heart; and it contains a considerable number of highly esteemed persons in whom
this quality is connected with confusion of head. No
other novelist ever drew so many fools and half-
witted people, and drew them so humanely. There,

for example, is poor Miss Flite, the crazed suitor
in the Court of Chancery, who has discovered that
the sixth seal mentioned in the Revelation is the
Great Seal of the Lord Chancellor, and who expects
a judgment in her case on the Day of Judgment.
There is Miss Betsey Trotwood's friend, Mr. Dick,
with *his* head hopelessly troubled and intermixed
with that of King Charles the First, and listening
to Dr. Strong's learned dissertations "with his poor
wits wandering, God knows where, on the wings of
hard words." Add a little conscious brain, so that
the heart can stutter into half-intelligent expression,
and you have what Susan Nipper calls "that innocent-
est creeter, Toots." This young gentleman, as the
reader will remember, had been subjected to Dr. Blim-
ber's forcing system in education, but "had stopped off
blowing one day, and remained in the school a mere
stalk;" and who, "when he began to have whiskers,
left off having brains." He is allowed, in his withered condition of mind, to pursue his own course of
study, which chiefly consists in writing "long letters
to himself from persons of distinction, addressed ' P.
Toots, Esq., Brighton, Sussex,' and to preserve them
in his desk with great care." When any sudden and
heavy call is made on his intelligence, such as being
introduced to a new-comer, in the lieu of speech he
blushes, chuckles, and breathes hard. He gratifies
his secret aspirations to be a dandy and a swell, by
"sticking ornamental pins into his shirt, and keeping
a ring in his waistcoat pocket to put on his little

finger by stealth, when the pupils are out walking."
Two instances are given of the dark vices into which
this confiding innocent runs. Once, he is led out
of Mr. Feeder's room into the open in a state of
faintness, consequent on an unsuccessful attempt to
smoke a very blunt cigar, — one of a bundle he had
mysteriously purchased "from a most desperate smug-
gler, who had acknowledged, in confidence, that two
hundred pounds was the price set on his head, dead
or alive, by the Custom House." At another time, in
Mr. Feeder's room, with the doors locked, he and that
profligate tutor "crammed their noses with snuff,
endured surprising torments of sneezing with the
constancy of martyrs, and, drinking table beer at in-
tervals, felt all the glories of dissipation." When he
comes into his property, he hires a set of apartments,
employs a prize-fighter, called the Game Chicken, to
complete his education as a gentleman, and falls in
love with Florence Dombey. The attachment proves
hopeless, and he becomes a prey to Byronic despair.
"The state of my feelings towards Miss Dombey," he
says to Captain Cuttle, "is of that unspeakable description, that my heart is a desert island, and she
lives in it alone. I'm getting more used up every
day, and I'm proud to be so. If you could see my
legs when I take my boots off, you'd form some idea
of what unrequited affection is. I have been prescribed bark, but I don't take it, for I don't wish to
have any tone whatever given to my constitution; I'd
rather not." "The hollow crowd, when they see me

with the Chicken, and characters of distinction like that, suppose me to be happy; but I'm wretched." When he hears of Florence's flight, he tells Captain Cuttle that he has been perfectly frantic. "I have," he exclaims, "been lying on the sofa all night, the Ruin you behold.... I have n't dared to shave, I'm in that rash state. I have n't had my clothes brushed. My hair is matted together. I told the Chicken that if he offered to clean my boots, I'd stretch him a corpse before me!"

Dickens makes Toots indeed as ridiculous a creature as can well be conceived; but then, he makes him as lovable as he is laughable. The readers of "Dombey and Son" feel that he is of infinitely more importance than the haughty Edith, or the keen and cunning Carker of that wonderful novel, for he has a good heart under his stammering brain; and Dickens, in such matters, agrees with his own John Chivery, who says of his foolish son: "My son has a 'art, and my son's 'art is in the right place. Me and his mother knows where to find it, and we find it sitiwated correct."

Next above the half-witted we have the stupid characters of Dickens, — characters in whom stupidity, however, is, as it is in Nature, blended with self-importance. Such are old Joe Willet, Barkis, Jack Bunsby, Mr. F.'s Aunt, and the rest. Intellect just twinkles in them, like a fire-fly in the dark. "That chap, sir," says Mr. Willet, speaking of Hugh, "though he has all his faculties about him, somewheres or another, bottled up and corked down, has no more imagination than Barnaby ĥas. And why hasn't he? Because they was never drawed out of him when he was a boy. That's why. What would any of us have been, if our fathers hadn't drawed our faculties out of us? What would my boy Joe have been if I had n't drawed his faculties out of him?"

Again, the liquor-steeped Durdles, in " Edwin Drood," employs the boy-imp, Deputy, to stone him home, when he is out after ten o'clock at night, and takes great credit on himself for thus giving the boy an object in life. "What was he before?" he says with "the slow gravity of beery soddenness." "A destroyer. What work did he do? Nothing but de-struction. What did he earn by it? Short terms in Cloisterham jail. Not a person, not a piece of prop-erty, not a winder, not a horse, nor a dog, nor a cat, nor a bird, nor a fowl, nor a pig, but what he stoned for want of an enlightened object. I put that en-lightened object before him, and now he can turn his honest halfpenny by the three penn'orth a week." "I wonder he has no competitors," says Mr. Jasper. " He has plenty," answers Mr. Durdles, " but he stones 'em all away."

Then there is that inscrutable old woman, Mr. F.'s Aunt, in " Little Dorrit," who has such a benevolent desire that Arthur Clenman shall be " brought for'ard " in order that she may " chuck him out o' winder ;" who sits down in the pie-shop with the inexorable purpose not to move until the " chucking " process has been accomplished; and who subjects her companion to some embarrassment in consequence of "an idle rumor which circulated among the credulous infants of the neighborhood to the effect that the old lady had sold herself to the pie-shop to be made up, and was then sitting in the pie-shop parlor declining to complete her contract."

Connected with this class of characters is a class in which conceit carries stupidity to an elevation quite ideal. Sim Tappertit, Mr. Kenwigs, Mr. Sapsea, may be cited as its representatives. Where is the person so fortunate as *not* to have met Mr. Sapsea, or somebody who strongly suggested him, — the man who gives a certain grandeur to his fat-wittedness, who is heroically dull and majestically insensible, and whose conceit could hardly be blasted out of him by the heaviest charge of nitro-glycerine? Thinking, in his condescending almightiness, that it is not good for man to be alone, he cast his eye about him for a nuptial partner, whose mind might be absorbed in his own. That eye, thus cast about him, fell on Miss Brobity. " Miss Brobity's being, young man," he says to Mr Jasper, " was deeply imbued with homage to Mind. She revered Mind, when launched, or, as I say, precipitated, on an extensive knowledge of the world. When I made my proposal, she did me the honor to be so overshadowed with a species of Awe, as to be able to articulate only the two words, ' O Thou!' — meaning myself. Her limpid blue eyes were fixed upon me, her semi-transparent hands were clasped together, pallor overspread her aquiline features, and, though encouraged to proceed, she never did proceed a word further. Mrs. Sapsea, thus courted, soon dies of "a feeble action of the liver," and to the very last addressed her august spouse, playing Jove to her Semele, in the same unfinished terms of "O Thou!" And perhaps the most audacious stroke of Dickens's extravagant humor is found in the inscription which Mr. Sapsea places on her monument: —

"ETHELINDA,
Reverential Wife of
MR. THOMAS SAPSEA,
Auctioneer, Valuer, Estate Agent, &c.,
Of this city,
Whose Knowledge of the World,
Though somewhat extensive,
Never brought him acquainted with
A SPIRIT
More capable of
LOOKING UP TO HIM.
STRANGER PAUSE
And ask thyself the question,
CANST THOU DO LIKEWISE.
If Not,
WITH A BLUSH RETIRE."

In these days of Woman's Rights that epitaph cannot but have a healthful influence in keeping woman in her "appropriate sphere."

We do no injustice to that "fool positive," Mr. Sapsea, in saying we make an ascent in the mental scale in proceeding to consider fools after the fashion of Mrs. Nickleby. She is the type of a class, very

numerous in actual life, whose minds are run away
with by the accidental association of ideas, — who
have thoughts, but no power of directing their
thoughts. Flora Casby, in " Little Dorrit," with her
unpunctuated velocity of incoherent talk, belongs to
the same general class. So does Mr. Sparkler, whose
stunted brain stammers under the weight of his admiration for persons who have " no nonsense in
them," — in his case a purely disinterested and pathetic tribute to all human beings who do not share
his special defect. So does the poor little Barnacle
of the Circumlocution Office, who is so shocked by
Arthur Clenman's coming into the office with a demand to " know " something about the matters which
the Department was theoretically instituted to explain. Every one remembers the scene at Pet Mea-
gles's marriage with Henry Gowan, in which this
young Barnacle testifies his horror and indignation
" to two vapid young gentlemen, his relatives," at the
presence of Arthur at the feast. " There was a feller
here, look here, who had come to our Department
without an appointment, and said he wanted to know,
you know; and that, look here, if he was to break
out now, as he might, you know (for you never could
tell what an ungentlemanly Radical of that sort would
be up to next), and was to say, look here, that he
wanted to know this moment, you know, that would be
jolly; would n't it?" So does " the young man by the
name of Guppy," in " Bleak House." He is an attorney's clerk who, in proposing to Esther Summerson,

" files a declaration ; " who represents his mother as
eminently calculated, by her virtues, to be a mother-
in-law; and who, with vast self-esteem, and desire to
strike everybody he meets with an impression of his
superior magnanimity and intelligence, is forced by
his nature to demean himself like the wretched snob
he is, — belonging, as he does, to that family of fools
in which the natural variety of the species blends with
another variety which it would be profanity to name.

It is difficult to say where, in Dickens, the humorist ends and the satirist begins ; but there are in his
works whole classes of character in which the satirist
evidently predominates.   His method of assailing
social and political abuses is to make them ridiculous
or hateful ; and he makes them ridiculous or hateful
by impersonating them in men and women.   We
quote them as we quote a jest or bright saying, — not
as characters, but as epigrams endowed with individuality.   His humorous personages spring from his
sympathies, his satirical ones from his antipathies ;
and antipathy never gives us the whole and inward
truth about anybody, but makes us exaggerate the
trait we dislike until the individual is all merged in
his particular defect.   The popularity of such characters in Dickens is due to the fact that they reflect
popular prejudices, and never go beyond that perception of externals, which is our easy, intolerant way of
judging the people we despise or detest.   The intellectual limitations of Dickens are also revealed in his

satirical sketches. His heart is developed out of all proportion to his brain. The abuses of a system blind his eyes to its merits and its purpose. He is a reformer, but a reformer whose common sense is unaccompanied with comprehensive intelligence, and whose moral sense frequently impels him to be practically unjust. Nobody who is carried away by his delicious satire on the Barnacles and their Circumlocution Office, stops to think that the Circumlocution Office is simply the introduction of *method* into the transaction of public business, — a system which, with all its defects, is the only contrivance ever devised by human wit to check scoundrelism in official place. Nobody who is carried away by his satire on the delays in Chancery stops to think that the Court of Chancery, with all its abuses, means equity jurisprudence; and that equity jurisprudence, in distinction from the common law, is one of the few things in insular England in which the principles of universal reason and universal justice have been fairly applied.

The novel of " Hard Times " is a satire on political economy, of which Dickens knew little, and the little he knew offended his benevolent feelings ; as if the law of gravitation itself did not frequently offend benevolent feeling ! Still, Mr. Gradgrind will for generations prevent a large number of amiable people from admitting the demonstrations of Adam Smith and Ricardo. One sometimes feels, in reflecting on the immense influence exerted by Dickens on matters requiring, for their adequate treatment, wide knowledge and philosophic largeness of mind, that it is a great pity he did not receive in youth a systematic education, which would have given him the austere mental training which, with all his genius, he so evidently lacks. We are occasionally reminded, in reading him, of Tony Weller's reply to Mr. Pickwick's praise of the intelligence of his son Sam. " Werry glad to hear of it, sir," he says. " I took a great deal o' pains in his eddication, sir ; let him run the streets when he wos werry young, sir, and shift for hisself. It 's the only way to make a boy sharp, sir." Undoubtedly, what Dickens picked up in " running the streets " was precious to literature. Undoubtedly he saw much that legislators, statesmen, and thinkers neglect. But it would have been better, when he invaded their province, if he had known more than he did of the subjects that occupied their activity. The fatal defect of his judgment was that he could not fairly represent any system of administration or government, of philanthropy or theology, which worked what he considered injustice or wrong in individual cases. Now, God alone, with an eternity to operate in, can deal with such exceptional cases. Imperfect human beings can, at the best, only frame systems which have a tendency to do the greatest good to the greatest number. As a humorist, Dickens is as tolerant as Nature is ; as a satirist he is, in spirit, almost as intolerant, though in a different way, as Carlyle himself. He has not the Shakspearian toleration, — the toleration which comes from immense force and reach and fairness of mind, as well as from goodness and tenderness of heart.

But, waiving these considerations, and coming down to the real talent of Dickens in looking at these things from his own point of view, we have a crowd of shadowy characters which are indisputably inhabitants of Dickens-land. There is the whole family of the Barnacles, born to receive · salaries and shirk work, preaching and living the gospel of "how not to do it." There is Lord Lancaster Stiltstalking, "who had been maintained by the Circumlocution Office for many years as a representative of the Britannic Majesty abroad." This "noble Refrigerator had iced several European courts in his time, and had done it with such complete success that the very name of Englishman yet struck cold to the stomachs of foreigners who had the distinguished honor of remembering *him*, at the distance of a quarter of a century." At the festive board he "shaded the dinner, cooled the wines, chilled the gravy, and blighted the vegetables."

Then there is the class of professional philanthropists, Mrs. Jellyby, Mrs. Pardiggle, and Messrs. Quale, Gusher, and Honeythunder, caricatures which express one of the most persistent of Dickens's antipathies. Remember poor rueful Mr. Jellyby adjuring his daughter Caddy, when she was to marry young Mr. Turveydrop, not to have a "mission." Unless, he says, you mean with all your heart to strive to make a home for your husband, "you had better murder him than marry him." And then, recurring to the disorders of his own home, owing to Mrs. Jellyby's absorption in Borrioboola-Gha, he calls his neglected children "wild Indians," and declares "that he was sensible the best thing that could happen to them was, their being all tomahawked together."

Then there is the class to which the Rev. Mr. Chadband belongs, — impersonated satires on clerical defects and bigotries, which some clergymen have been so injudicious as to denounce as attacks on religion. Mr. Chadband is "a large yellow man, with a fat smile," a greasy paw, and with "a general appearance of having a good deal of train-oil in his system." His eloquence consists in "piling verbose flights of stairs" one upon another. His sermon on what he calls "Terewth," elicited by the boy Jo on his appearance in Mr. Snagsby's house, is a masterpiece of its kind. "O my juvenile friends," he exclaims, "if the master of this house was to go forth into the city and there see an eel, and was to come back, and was to call untoe him the mistress of this house, and was to say, 'Sarah, rejoice with me, for I have seen an elephant!' would *that* be Terewth? Or put it that the unnatural parents of this slumbering Heathen, — for parents he had, my juvenile friends, without a doubt, — after casting him forth to the wolves and the vultures and the wild dogs and the young gazelles and the serpents, went back to their dwellings and had their pipes, and their pots, and their flutings, and their dancings, and their malt

liquors, and their butcher's meat and poultry,—would
that be Terewth ?"

In the same class of impersonated sarcasms we must
rank his hits, in " Martin Chuzzlewit," on our *Ameri-*
can declaimers, swindlers, and charlatans.   They are
caricatures — but then, what good caricatures!   Not
to speak of Mr. Jefferson Brick, and Colonel Diver,
of the " Rowdy Journal," how delightful is Elijah
Pogram, " honorable " in virtue of his being a member
of Congress!   The Hon. Elijah's eulogy on the rascal
Chollop must remind us of many specimens of Western eloquence.   " Our fellow-countryman is a model of
a man, quite fresh from Natur's mould!" said Pogram,
with enthusiasm.   " He is a true-born child of this free
hemisphere!   Verdant as the mountains of our country ; bright and flowing as our Mineral Licks ; unsp'iled
by withering conventionalities as air our broad and
boundless Perearers!   Rough he may be.   So air our
Barrs.   Wild he may be.   So air our Buffalers.   But
he is a child of Natur's, and a child of Freedom ; and
his boastful answer to the Despot and Tyrant is, that
his bright home is in the settin' sun!"   This is perhaps only a heightened representation of the way in
which some of our politicians make the American
Eagle scream !

Now the difference between characters like these,
and real men and women, is, that they have no *inter-*
nal vitality and individuality.   In short, they have no
souls.   Dickens's force of imagination is such that he
easily succeeds in personifying them ; but he easily

succeeds also in personifying streets, buildings, land-
scapes, furniture, — everything, in short, he touches.
It is so difficult, in this brief survey, to mention even
by name scores of the true characters which enliven
his books, that the deduction we make is comparatively of slight importance.　Among those characters
who have essential individuality, Tony Weller and
Mrs. Gamp stand out as perhaps the best examples of
solid characterization in Dickens's works.　What they
say is deliciously humorous, but what they *are* is more
humorous still.　The same, to a less extent, may be
said of Sam Weller, Squeers, Wilkins Micawber, Es-
quire, Captain Ed'ard Cuttle, Mr. Crummles, Mr. and
Mrs. Boffin ; of the wonderful series of boys, from
Master Wackford Squeers all the way up to the " baby-
devil " Deputy, in " Edwin Drood," and that perfection
of urchin impudence, Bailey, Junior, in " Martin Chuzzlewit ; " of the dilapidated young gentlemen, distinguished for their flow of spirits, animal and alcoholic,
represented by Bob Sawyer, Mr. Chuckster, and Mr.
Richard Swiveller ; and of oddities and " originals " of
all kinds, such as Newman Noggs, Tim Linkinwater,
Mr. Cruncher, Durdles, Mr. Venus, Mr. Wegg, Mr.
Boythorne.　It is useless in such an embarrassment of
riches to attempt specification.　They are all more or
less *overcharged*, as though the author was a little in-
toxicated with his own humorous conceptions, and
could not keep himself within any measure ; but they
are still all *alive*.　Of the novels in which they appear,
" The Pickwick Papers " are the most animated and

joyous, inspired, as they are, by the very genius of
fun ; " David Copperfield " is the most delightful, various, and satisfying of stories; " Dombey and Son " is
the freshest and most vital throughout in style, description, and characterization ; and " The Tale of
Two Cities " is the most intense, passionate, and " en-
training " of narratives.

In all the novels, the characters can hardly be detached from the scenes and incidents in which they
appear, without a loss in ludicrous effect. Still, let
me quote a few sentences in which what they *are*,
flashes through what they *say*. Mr. Sam Weller, on
first encountering the fat boy, accosts him with the
question, " You a'n't got nothing on your mind as
makes you fret yourself, have you ?" " Not as I knows
on," replies the boy. " I should rather ha' thought,"
says Sam, " *to look at you*, that you was a-laborin'
under an unrequited attachment to some young
'ooman."

Mrs. Todgers fears that " that dreadful child," Bailey, Junior, has been so spoilt by the gentlemen of
her boarding-house, " that nothing but hanging will
ever do him any good." Mrs. Gamp gives, as her
opinion, that " there 's nothin' he don't know. All the
wickedness of the world is Print to him." " Reether
so," retorts Bailey, Junior, " adjusting his cravat."
And then he confesses critically to Poll Sweedlepipe,
" There 's the remains of a fine woman about Sairy,
— hey, Poll ! " " Drat the Bragian boldness of that
boy! " cried Mrs. Gamp. " I would n't be that cree-

tur's mother, not for fifty pound!" "Excuge," she
says, in reference to this same Poll Sweedlepipe, the
barber, "excuge the weakness of the man . . . which
not a blessed hour ago he nearly shaved the noge off
from the father of as lovely a family as ever, Mr.
Chuzzlewit, was born three sets of twins; and would
have done it, only he see it a-goin' in the glass and
dodged the rager!"

Mr. Sapsea, in "Edwin Drood," thus discriminates
between equity and legality. "It is not enough," he
says, "that Justice should be morally certain; she
must be *immorally* certain — legally, that is."

Mr. Micawber, who is the prey of pecuniary difficulties, and who is always waiting for something to
"turn up," has a family in every way worthy of him.
"My mamma," said Mrs. Micawber, "departed this life
before Mr. Micawber's difficulties commenced, or at
least before they became pressing. My papa lived
to bail Mr. Micawber several times, and then expired,
regretted by a numerous circle." "My piece of advice
to you, Copperfield," says Mr. Micawber, "you know.
Annual income, twenty pounds; annual expenditure,
nineteen nineteen six; result, happiness. Annual income, twenty pounds; annual expenditure, twenty
pounds aught and six; result, misery. The blossum
is blighted, the leaf is withered, the God of day goes
down on the dreary scene, and — and, in short, you
are forever floored. As I am!"

How many so-called accomplished women of the
world are hit in this picture of Mrs. Merdle! She

"had large, unfeeling, handsome eyes, and dark, unfeeling, handsome hair, and a broad, unfeeling, handsome bosom."

"I am," says Mr. Vincent Crummles, "in the theatrical profession myself; my wife is in the theatrical
profession; I had a dog that lived and died in it from
a puppy; and my chaise-pony goes on, in 'Timour
the Tartar.'"

When Mrs. Crupp, David Copperfield's landlady,
has her house invaded by Miss Betsey Trotwood, she
vehemently expresses her determination to assert her
rights before "a British Judy." Mr. Wegg, when he
charges Mr. Boffin more for reading poetry to him
than for reading prose, justifies the exaction on the
ground that, when "a person comes to grind off poetry
night after night, it is but right he should expect
to be paid for its weakening effect on his mind."
When Mr. Squeers is drunk, he goes to bed not only
with his boots on, but with his umbrella under his
arm. When Arthur Clenuam, ruined by speculation
and utterly crushed in spirit, says to Mr. Rugg, his
attorney, that he cares only for the money left with
him in trust, and not for his own, Mr. Rugg expresses an unmistakable professional surprise at such
extraordinary delicacy of feeling. "I have," he
says "generally found in my experience, that it's
their own money people are most particular about.
I have seen people get rid of a good deal of other
people's money, and bear it very well; very well
indeed."

22

A word may be said here in regard to the *critical*
charge against Dickens, that he preserves the individuality of his characters by the cheap contrivance of
constantly repeating some mere external peculiarity.
Mr. Snagsby always prefaces anything he has to say
with a slight deprecatory cough behind his raised
hand. Uriah Heep is always " 'umble." Mr. Jarn-
dyce's " East Wind " becomes in the end painfully
monotonous. Mr. Tony Weller's fear of the machina-
tions of " widdurs " tires at last on the critical sense
of humor. Mrs. Merdle's " Bosom " is so obtrusively
prominent that it submerges Mrs. Merdle herself in a
physical trait. The objection is just, but still the defect belongs to Dickens's method of characterization.
He repeats these things as the experienced preacher
constantly repeats his text, in order to deepen its
effect on the popular mind. As long as Dickens
makes his characters really *alive,* in internal individuality as well as in external peculiarity, the defect
is but superficial.

The villains in Dickens's novels are not favorable
specimens of the class from which Shakspeare and
Scott drew some of their grandest creations. All his
villains are essentially low villains and utter villains ;
but experience, history, and Shakspeare prove that
villains are commonly the most complicated of all
characters, and require the greatest subtlety and
depth of dramatic insight to be adequately represented
and *explained.* Dickens's villains, Quilp, Carker,
Arthur Gride, Jonas Chuzzlewit, Ralph Nickleby,

Blandois, and the rest, are simply hideous, and belong not to literature, but to the criminal courts. Though he devotes to them much of his strongest, most elaborate, and most ambitious writing, he never succeeds in making them artistically justifiable. Total depravity is not admissible in romance ; and Dickens professes to draw his villains as totally depraved. " What," he says in " Edwin Drood," — the last work he wrote, — " could a virtuous mind know of the criminal intellect, which its own professed students perpetually misread, because they persist in trying to reconcile it with the average intellect of average men, instead of identifying it as a horrible wonder apart ? " And as to the criminal heart under this criminal intellect, he has expressed a sufficiently despairing opinion through the lips of the honest landlady who denounces Blandois, the leading villain of " Little Dorrit." " I know nothing," she says, " of philosophic philanthropy. But this I know, that there are people whom it is necessary to detest without compromise. There are people who must be dealt with as enemies of the human race. There are people (men and women both, unfortunately) who have no good in them—none. There are people who have no human heart, and must be crushed like savage beasts and cleared out of the way."

Individually I may agree with this judgment, and think that the hangman is doing the most useful of all works in launching such existences into nonexistence. Kill them by all means, but don't do what

Dickens does, — don't make them prominent characters in the ideal realm of tragedy and romance. There is a soured and cruelly deceived gentleman in this place, who refused the other day to subscribe to any domestic or foreign missions, because, he said, there were not, in his deliberate opinion, as many persons that went to hell as ought to go there. Whatever we may think of this judgment, there can be no doubt that the people he indicated in his anathema ought not to trouble us in a romance written by a man of genius. Dickens, in his novels, continually thrusts them in our eyes. Consequently, in this department of his art he is manifestly wrong. Shakspeare and Scott bring in their villains artistically, exhibiting the clash and conflict of their consciences with their passions; Dickens sticks to the vulgar, melodramatic villain, without conscience, and satisfies our moral sentiments at the expense of disgusting our sense of artistic propriety.

The pathos of Dickens is no less effective than his humor; perhaps he draws tears even more easily than he provokes laughter. He makes everybody cry, — even his hostile critics; but his critics object that they are made to cry against the rules; that it is sentimentality they cry over, and not true sentiment; that it is exceedingly unnatural thus to have their natures so deeply stirred. Dickens took their tears as the most cogent of all answers to their

maxims, and went on with his work, forcing them
to weep, and disregarding the snarling protest they
made against the magician who extorted from them
such irrepressible drops of uncritical emotion. Still,
the critics were not altogether wrong in saying that
while his humor always cheered, his pathos frequently enfeebled. Vigorous manly and womanly
will to do practical benevolent work is apt to be
dissolved in such tears as Dickens makes us sometimes shed. It is well to sympathize with sorrow;
but to sympathize with it to such an extent as to
make strong-heartedness give way to soft-heartedness
is to deprive us of the power to help the sorrowful.
For example, we all perhaps become somewhat maud-
lin over Little Nell ; but then, Little Nell grown up
in " Little Dorrit ; " grown up in Lucie Manette, of
" The Tale of Two Cities ; " grown up in Esther
Summerson, of the " Bleak House," — is a veritable
character, competent, through pathetic sentiment, to
impress us with the highest obligations of duty.
The affectionateness and self-devotion of these characters are all steeped in an atmosphere of moral
beauty. I think that Esther Summerson is the most
perfect character of its kind in romantic literature,
thoroughly pure, sweet, kindly, maidenly, and humane. Mr. Peggotty again, in " David Copperfield,"
is a wonderful example of the power of goodness to
irradiate the homeliest form, and lift into grandeur
the most uncouth expression. Human nature itself
is indebted to Dickens for such delineations of its

possibilities of purity, tenderness, and humble moral strength.

There is quite a crowd of such characters in Dickens-land, and they thoroughly Christianize it. What a discourse on filial duty is condensed in the advice given by Mr. George, in " Bleak House," to young Woolwich! " The time will come when this hair of your mother's will be gray, and this forehead all crossed and recrossed with wrinkles. Take care, while you are young, that you can think in those days, ' *I* never whitened a hair of her dear head, *I* never marked a sorrowful line in her face!' "

What a living sermon is that preached at the death-bed of little Paul Dombey! How it melts, humanizes, elevates every heart! " Sister and brother wound their arms around each other, and the golden light came streaming in, and fell upon them, locked together. . . . He put his hands together, as he had been used to do at prayers. He did not remove his arms to do it; but they saw him fold them so, behind her neck. ' Mama is like you, Floy. I know her by the face. But tell them that the print upon the stairs at school is not divine enough. The light about the head is shining on me as I go!' The golden ripple on the wall came back again, and nothing else stirred in the room. The old, old fashion! The fashion that came in with our first garments, and will last unchanged until our race has run its course, and the wide firmament is rolled up like a scroll. The old, old fashion — Death. Oh, thank God, all who see it, for that older fashion yet, of Immortality! And look upon us, angels of young children, with regards not quite estranged, when the swift river bears us to the ocean!"

And what a wild, agonized cry is that which bursts from the heart of David Copperfield as he surveys for the last time his friend tranquilly sleeping, and thinks of the inexpiable crime he so soon after committed.

"Never more — Oh, God forgive you, Steerforth! — to touch that passive hand in love and friendship. Never, never more!"

And then there is the death of Davy Copperfield's mother, as told to him by his old nurse, Peggotty. "'Peggotty, my dear,' she said, 'put me nearer to you,' for she was very weak. 'Lay your good arm under my neck,' she said, 'and turn me to you, for your face is going far off, and I want it to be near.' I put it as she asked; and oh, Davy! the time came when my first parting words to you were true — when she was glad to lay her poor head on her stupid cross old Peggotty's arm — and she died like a child that had gone to sleep."

And then there is in "Bleak House" that wonderfully depicted ride which Esther Summerson takes with Mr. Bucket, the detective, to follow and save her mother, Lady Dedlock, who had fled from her haughty husband's house to die at the gate of the paupers' cemetery, where her early love, Esther's wild father, was buried. "She lay there, with one arm creeping

round a bar of the iron gate, and seeming to em-
brace it. She lay there, a distressed, unsheltered,
senseless creature." Esther does not think it is her
mother, but her attendant, Jenny. " I saw," she
says, " but did not comprehend, the solemn and com-
passionate look in Mr. Woodcourt's face. I saw, but
did not comprehend, his touching the other on the
breast, to keep him back. I saw him stand uncov-
ered in the bitter air, with a reverence for something.
But my understanding for all this was gone. I even
heard it said between them, ' Shall she go ? ' ' She had
better go. Her hands should be the first to touch her.
They have a higher right than ours.' I passed on to
the gate, and stooped down. I lifted the heavy head,
put the long dank hair aside, and turned the face.
And it was my mother, cold and dead."

This is essential pathos, going down to the very
roots of the thing in the human heart. And how
numerous the examples are, spread all over Dickens's
works !

And now, in conclusion, let us celebrate, without
any qualification, this humane man of genius, who,
whether he makes us laugh or weep, makes us better ;
who cheers us with a fresh confidence in human nature,
and with an intenser sympathy for the poor, the despised and the wretched ; who has done immense good
while he has seemed only to diffuse vast entertainment ;
who has peopled the imagination with a new company
of ideal beings which the heart clings to and will not

allow to die; who never did or said anything mean or base, or refrained from stigmatizing meanness and baseness when they crossed his path; who was never corrupted by success, but was as kindly and genial in life as in his writings; who tried sincerely to live in accordance with what he honestly believed to be true and right; and who, while he will ever hold a high rank among the great novelists of the world, will also, and *through* his novels, hold a still more precious position among the great benefactors of the human race.

University Press: John Wilson & Son, Cambridge.

www.ingramcontent.com/pod-product-compliance
Lightning Source LLC
Chambersburg PA
CBHW020240290326
41929CB00045B/843